BOUVIER
des Flandres

BOUVIER
des Flandres

The Dogs of Flandres Fields

James R. Engel

Alpine Publications
P.O. Box 7027 • Loveland, CO 80537

ISBN: 0-931866-53-7

Library of Congress Cataloging-in-Publication Data

Engel, James. R., 1943-
    Bouvier des Flandres: The Dogs of Flandres Fields / James R. Engel.
        p.   cm.
    Includes bibliographical references (p.) and index.
    ISBN: 0-931866-53-7
    1. Bouvier des Flandres.   I. Title.
    SF429.B73E53   1991
    636.7'37 — dc20   90-28418
                                                        CIP

Design and Typography:
    Dianne Borneman, Shadow Canyon Graphics, Evergreen, Colorado

Printed in the United States of America

First Edition
    2   3   4   5   6   7   8   9

Dedicated to the memory of my father,
Robert T. Engel

Contents

Foreword

In 1975, during the first tour of the American Bouvier des Flandres Club to Europe, I had the pleasure of introducing Mrs. Claire McLean to Mevrouw Van Gink-Van Es. Each of these ladies had just completed an impressive book about the Bouvier des Flandres. The popularity of these works is apparent from the many subsequently published editions.

Now, fifteen years later, a significant new publication about the Bouvier is long overdue, and I can think of no person more qualified to write such a book than Jim Engel.

For the past ten years, Jim has been in the center of Bouvier and other dog activities in North America. Under the kennel name "Centauri," Jim's wife Kathy Engel and Jim have bred or owned fifteen AKC conformation Champions with Ch. Centauri's Fleur de Lis SchH III, better known as Leah, also placing nine times in the Group. Obtaining eight AKC obedience titles required much time and patience, but the most remarkable feat is that Kathy and Jim together have obtained a total of thirteen Schutzhund titles and five tracking titles on their dogs, as well as three NAWBA Championships. No one has ever come close to these accomplishments, and this record is not likely to be broken in the foreseeable future.

Jim was present at the first North American Working Bouvier Championships in 1980 and is the only person who has attended each subsequent Annual Championship. Since the foundation of the North American Working Bouvier Association in Chicago in 1986, Jim has been an officer and the driving force behind NAWBA and appropriately was elected in 1990 to direct this organization as president. He also has been an officer of the American Bouvier des Flandres Club and is currently secretary of the American Working Dog Federation.

During his many visits to Europe, Jim has become quite familiar with the prominent Belgian and Dutch Bouvier kennels. He has attended most significant dog events, such as the Clubdat (National Specialty) of the Dutch Bouvier Club, the French Ring Sport National Championship, many Belgian and French Ring

sport trials and KNPV (Royal Dutch Police Dog) and German Schutzhund trials. In 1986, he exhibited Ch. Centauri's Hanter at the European Championships in Dortmund in Germany and at the World Show in Vienna, obtaining excellent ratings in both shows.

At the home of Alfons and Annie Verheyen, well-known Belgian judges and breeders, and at the home of Jos and Ria Klep, well-known as the owners of Donar and Bram Pasha, and at the home of Henk Harmers, president of the Dutch Bouvier Club, and his wife Gerda, Jim has been a regular guest. Much of the material in this book was obtained by comparing notes with these and other Bouvier fanciers. Visits to the Dafzicht Kennels of Mr. and Mrs. Krah-Semler and to the Pleinzicht Kennels of Mr. and Mrs. Krist provided a wealth of historical material and photographs of the early days of our breed.

To further research the early days, Jim and I have made many trips to small Belgian and Dutch towns where at one time famous Bouvier kennels had existed. Often, some old folk in the local butcher shop or cafe would tell us that many decades ago a breeder of Bouviers has been well known in the area, usually because his dogs were known as excellent guard dogs.

Jim developed his own computer program but he was not satisfied with just copying the commonly available pedigrees. The Raad van Beheer (Dutch Kennel Club) in Amsterdam allowed Jim to research their archives all the way back to the first Bouvier registered in Holland. Annie Verheyen helped extensively by providing complete Belgian breeding records, and the extensive computerized data of Mrs. Krijnse-Locker (Caya's Home Kennel) were of great help.

Although an electrical engineer by profession, writing about dogs in not new to Jim. For many years as a contributing editor to *Dog Sports Magazine*, Jim's outspoken style has created many fans and admirers but also a few opponents. Let me assure you that his writing is not dull.

If all of this leaves you with the impression that Jim is some kind of a "Superman," think again. Without Kathy and their two daughters looking after the dogs while Jim was roaming through Europe, he probably would not have any dogs left. Also, you should know that Jim cannot dance! He made a complete fool of himself at the lavish twenty-fifth wedding anniversary of Jos and Ria Klep in Holland. But what does that have to do with writing a dog book?

By now I have either bored you with too many details or convinced you that Jim Engel is the most qualified living person to have written this Bouvier book. I am convinced, and after you read and re-read this book, you will be convinced, too.

— *Erik Houttuin*
Flanders Field Kennels

A/C Ch Flanderfield's Bully is shown here going Best of Winners at the 1981 California Club Specialty under judge Carl May. Breeder and owner, Dr. Erik Houttuin, is standing at the right. Bully was whelped in 1978 and was OFA Excellent.

Preface

Over most of the twentieth century, there has been enormous interest among North Americans in the protective-heritage working dogs of central Europe. In the post–World War One era, the Boxer and the German Shepherd became immensely popular. Later came the turn of the Doberman Pincher. Just prior to the Second World War, a handful of pioneers began the painfully slow process of introducing the Bouvier des Flandres.

It is ironic that while breeding stock has come over in quantity, there has been much difficulty making the "working" concept take root. Over the years, our breeding communities have, by and large, failed to really understand why such protective-heritage working breeds came into existence, and how they must be maintained through selection based on the working test as well as on conformation.

The European founders of the breed understood that training and testing are prerequisite to effective breeding-stock selection. Men such as Edmond Moreaux, justly famous through his foundation line "de l'Ile Monsin" in Belgium, and Coen Semler of "van Dafzicht" fame in the Netherlands, were first-rate trainers for many years before they achieved worldwide renown as breeders.

Many breed books have come forth in response to our working-dog interest, but virtually none have been created by those with a real grasp of the European working-dog heritage.

I became involved in Bouvier affairs at a time, in the 1970s, when the clouds of revolution were gathering on the horizon. Even then, a few pioneers were fiercely determined to make the working-dog heritage take root in America, and I gravitated to their cause. My forte turned out to be writing and, almost from the beginning, I was encouraged to create a new kind of Bouvier book, one faithful to the principles and the purposes of the breed founders.

Ten years of assiduous preparation went into this volume. I travelled to Europe to see working trials, including the Ring Sport of Belgium and France and the Police trials in the Netherlands. In attending conformation shows throughout Europe, I had the privilege of seeing Justin Chastel and Annie Verheyen judge the Bouvier des Flandres. I made pilgrimages to the leading kennels on two continents: Thudinie, du Posty Arlequin, Dafzicht, Cerberushof, Buildrager, and du Clos des Cerberes. I cajoled friends and acquaintances into translating manuscripts and old letters from the original French and Dutch. I spent innumerable hours poring over the archives of Miss Edmee Bowles, founder of the breed in America, and over other documents accumulated in my travels.

I gained firsthand knowledge of the working-dog character the old-fashioned way — by training numerous Bouviers in tracking, obedience, and protection. Many times I knew the satisfaction of a good trial placement, as well as the devastation of failure on the sport field. Bouviers with our Centauri Kennel name have received the highest recognition in the conformation ring under Belgian and Dutch judges, as well as in America. I also have experienced profound disappointments.

The objective of our program has been to remain faithful to the original European heritage, which emphasizes the working character of the individual Bouvier above all else. In offering this book to my fellow enthusiasts, I will be content if my contribution to our breed is measured in these terms.

One of the benefits of writing a book is being able to acknowledge those who have made it possible. I wish to credit fellow breeders and trainers who have been infinitely patient in helping my family begin our own Centauri program and gather the material for this book.

We will forever be in the debt of Edmee Bowles, for she is truly the spiritual founder of the breed in America. Her "du Clos des Cerberes" line, begun in Belgium in the 1930s, is the first one reviewed by Justin Chastel in his survey of Bouvier kennels — the only one outside of Europe to be so recognized. Over the years, I had the privilege of visiting Belco Farm on innumerable occasions and spent many hours in conversation with Miss Bowles. I will forever regard myself as having known a founder of the Bouvier breed.

Bruce and Rose Ellen Jacobsohn, partners with Bowles in later years, provided our original breeding stock. They carried on the heritage, breeding Bouviers on the same grounds where Belco is buried and where the other great du Clos des Cerberes Bouviers lived out their lives. Although Centauri's Fleur de Lis, the first Bouvier ever to earn the North American Working Bouvier Association (NAWBA) title "Working Champion," carries our kennel name, she is in fact out of April du Clos des Cerberes, leased to us in whelp by Bruce Jacobsohn.

Over the past twenty years, Erik Houttuin has emerged as the primary force in North American Bouvier affairs. In 1980, he founded the Working Championships, an act of foresight and dedication that would change forever the flow of American Bouvier history. Erik made this book possible by sharing his knowledge and experience and by taking me to a hundred nooks and crannies of Europe where the Bouvier evolved. He was instrumental in our own breeding program and infinitely generous in providing breeding stock, information, counsel, and encouragement.

Since the 1950s, the Madrone Ledge program of Ray and Marion Hubbard has been in the forefront of American conformation competition and breeding excellence. In recent years, the Hubbards have become active in the working movement, taking a leading role in the evolution of the North American Working Bouvier Association. The Hubbards have been helpful in providing information and personal insight into the behind-the-scenes evolution of our breed, both in Europe and America.

Inspiration comes in many forms. For me, a turning point was provided by a special woman and a very special dog, Ria Klep and her male Donar of the Netherlands. When this big, black dog came into my life on an autumn day in 1982, I came to understand fully what the Bouvier was meant to be. There may have been even better working Bouviers, for a couple of German dogs have impressive score books and a number of dogs have demonstrated excellence in the Dutch Police trials and in the Ring of Belgium and France. However, greatness is a matter of fate and timing as well as of individual excellence. Ria and Donar came onto the Bouvier scene at a crucial juncture to remind much of Europe what the Bouvier heritage is all about. The untimely passing of this great dog was an event of immense sadness for me, and in my mind he will always be the standard by which the Bouvier is measured. I will never forget him.

Alfons and Annie Verheyen have become steadfast friends who share a goal of restoring the Bouvier to his rightful place among the true working dogs. They have provided much information, such as breeding records from Belgium and France, important photo-graphs, and the insight gained from two decades of breeding the Bouvier des Flandres.

Kathy Heileman spent long hours translating various letters, as well as the l'Aboi article from which so much of the historical information is drawn.

Over the years, I have spent innumerable hours preparing our Bouviers for working competition. This time has been pleasurable and profitable in large measure because of the support and assistance of my fellow trainers. It seems like only yesterday when Mike Lichtwalt taught me the fundamentals of protection training, skills that I still use today. Among others with whom I have shared so much are Ron Maloney, Betty Sagen, Mike Reppa, and Tom and Holly Rose.

Finally, this enterprise is only possible because of the support of my family. My wife Kathy wrote the grooming section, as well as the breeding chapter, and made major contributions to many others, particularly the "maintenance manual." She supervises our breeding and conformation-show programs and almost always picks our pups. Indeed, the Centauri breeding program has been from the beginning mostly her enterprise, with my role often being to step in at the last moment to take credit! My daughter Sarah has come to know well the bittersweet frustrations of training and competition on the sport field, and over the years both she and Meredith have played essential roles.

The richness of the Bouvier heritage is such that no book can be complete or present the final word. A book is a living thing, and what is rendered in print is but a moment frozen in time. For me, this is a project for a lifetime — something that will never be complete but that perhaps will in some small way contribute to the preservation and advancement of the Bouvier des Flandres.

— *Jim Engel*
Marengo
March 1991

Three generations of Working Champions
From the left: Centauri's Ksar SchH I, Ch and Working Champion Centauri's Fleur de Lis SchH III, and Ch and Working Champion Centauri's Gambit SchH III.

Ria Kelp's Bram Pasja le Jardin du Moulin, 1988 North American Working Champion. Bred and trained by Ria Klep, Ulvenhout, the Netherlands.

CHAPTER ONE

The Nature of the Beast

The lush green fields of Flandres, from the banks of the river Leie to the waters of the North Sea, have for generations been among Europe's most prosperous agricultural areas. In this land that is now northwestern Belgium, a race of rustic, rough-coated, gruff cattle dogs evolved to fulfill the farmer's need for help in cattle herding and guarding.

In the first decades of the twentieth century, the industrial revolution led to the mechanization of the farm and the passing of a way of life. Across Europe, a few farsighted men took notice that regional working farm dogs, developed over generations, were about to vanish. On the plain of Flandres, certain of these men sought out specimens of their native cattle dogs. Combining them with the larger guard dogs of the region, they created the "Bouvier des Roulers," or "cattle dog of Roulers," with the name being derived from the city where the process was centered. Today we know these dogs as the Bouviers des Flandres.

Precisely because of these agrarian roots, there is a unique Bouvier soul that sets our breed apart from all others even more surely than the cobby body, the rough coat, and the beard. To perceive this spirit as forged on Flandres fields and in the farm work of the homelands leads directly to the essence of the dog, rooted in the working partnership with the stockman, the drover, and the farmer.

The progenitors of our Bouviers held their place in the pastoral community by virtue of their diverse utilitarian functions, such as control and defense of the livestock and protection of family and property. In such a setting, each creature, canine and human alike, was blessed with a simpler, more forthright world in which to function. This was certainly a factor in the evolution of the rugged, honest strength of character so much valued today. The herd-guarding function is the key to the Bouvier soul, for in this work he became a partner and came to share the ultimate responsibility for the survival of his human family. The heritage is thus, above all else, that of the working dog, and this is what led to the versatility of our modern Bouvier. Correct specimens serve admirably in multiple working roles, as competitive sport dogs and as faithful and reliable family companions.

According to the European standard, the Bouvier is to be a dog ". . . cobby, short-bodied, and thickset on powerful and muscular limbs, giving the impression of power without clumsiness. The fire in his eyes denotes intelligence, energy, and audacity. He is calm, rational, and prudently bold." The head is to be ". . . massive, made more so in appearance by his beard and mustache; well proportioned to his body and size. To the feel, finely chiselled." Regarding the structure of the neck, it is noted that "the power of attack of the Bouvier lies not only in the spring of his quarters, but in the power of his neck and jaws," leaving very little question as to the original purpose of the breed.

The Bouvier is of medium to large size, the ideal male being twenty-six to twenty-seven inches at the shoulder and perhaps ninety-five pounds. The bitch is to be feminine, perhaps an inch shorter and ten or fifteen pounds lighter. Although much larger specimens are not uncommon, there are sound reasons for the traditional size. Exceeding this size can lead to a lack of the agility so essential to the correct working structure. It also invites physical problems, particularly as the dog grows older. Those seeking a more massive animal should simply select from among the larger breeds.

The color is to be ". . . generally fawn or gray, often brindle or dary gray; the black is also allowed but not to be preferred. . . . Dark brindle is the ideal color." The coat is to be "rough to the touch, harsh and dry — neither too long nor too short (about two and a half inches), slightly tousled without ever being woolly or curly." The tendency toward the longer, softer coat — elaborately groomed for the show ring — is incorrect and undesirable because it is poorly adapted to the working environment.

The Bouvier character is to be ". . . calm, rational,

prudently bold." Such noble words are well and good but are inadequate to convey the essence of the breed character or the range of individual personality. The Bouvier is a subtle blend of sensitivity and courage, tenacity and outright stubbornness, aloof reserve but dedication to his family. Indeed, defining the Bouvier essence is akin to capturing a wisp of smoke!

The ideal is a dog that is calm and rational, and the Bouvier usually is. This, and the fact that shedding is minimal, makes him an excellent in-the-home companion. Although he needs exercise and is willing to work or play to the extent of your energy, he is generally quiet and nondestructive in the house and fits easily into the domestic routine.

Skillful grooming is an important aspect of conformation-show preparation. However, while most owners take pride in the appearance of their Bouviers, coat care need not be a burden. For the home companion or working dog, ten minutes of combing and brushing hair out of the coat once or twice a week are adequate. If this is done without fail, and if the dog is groomed simply with moderate clippering every two or three months, it is easy to maintain a clean, attractive appearance. One of the most desirable Bouvier attributes is minimal shedding, because the loose hair is held in the rough coat. The Bouvier needs the rough outer coat to provide protection from the elements and the undercoat to provide insulation. In our experience, even the most rigorous training, in-

A puppy can always make a smile! *Photo courtesy Ray and Marion Hubbard.*

volving tracking in all sorts of weather and field conditions, is compatible with conformation competition if the coat is correct.

While the Bouvier can be stubborn and even devious in getting his way, he is trainable in many diverse areas by those who understand and respect his background and character. He is a capable tracking and search dog and an effective and responsible personal guard dog and excels in these areas both in the working trial and on the street. The correct Bouvier is neither vicious nor vindictive and applies minimum but adequate force. This stability allows the dog to participate fully in daily life and to be on hand when his services are required.

In harmony with the working heritage, the Bouvier thrives on a close personal relationship. Much of the dog's success depends on a person's willingness to accept and work with the dog as a true partner. *The Bouvier does much better with the person who perceives himself as a leader rather than a master.*

Much of the Bouvier character is also the direct consequence of the herding function, where working without human supervision is often the norm. Consider the herd dog threatened by a marauding man or animal. The correct strategy in most instances is to break off an encounter when the intruder flees. The Bouvier must be shrewd enough not to be drawn away from his charges, leaving them alone and vulnerable. The natural inclination should be to protect rather than to punish. The Bouvier should come to know that his responsibility is the survival of the herd and the family rather than the pursuit and defeat of an individual offender.

Before the creation of barbed wire, it was necessary not only to keep the livestock from wandering off, but also to protect it from predators. Although trucks

Madrone Ledge puppy.

now move livestock to market, cattle once walked, and the drover's dog played an important part in control and protection. Although the need for these services has diminished on the farm due to advances in technology, the modern Bouvier's police work, guard duties, and military applications place a continued premium on the responsible, controlled-protection capability.

Perhaps a personal experience will illustrate this point. I was walking with our first Bouvier, a three-year-old male trained extensively for protection and Schutzhund competition, in our local park where some youngsters of twelve or thirteen years were playing soccer. An inadvertently kicked ball struck the dog in the face, drawing blood but not doing serious damage. Several of the players rushed up after the

Centauri's Gambit, owned by the author, was North American Working Champion in 1987 and 1989 as well as Reserve twice. Gambit is also AKC Champion of Record.

Although the Bouvier must not be obnoxiously aggressive, the stranger approaching home or automobile should be watched and announced, and overt aggression should be met in kind. The balance between aggressive protectiveness and respect for other creatures in the routine social context is the key characteristic of the breed.

ball, intent on the game but surrounding the dog. Time stood still for a moment as I wondered what would happen, for this could easily have been interpreted as an attack. A merely "hard" dog, driven only by fighting instinct, might have been provoked, causing serious injury to an innocent if perhaps slightly careless person. Tory, in fact, recognized that no threat was intended; his reaction was startled but not aggressive or fearful. The incident was immediately and instinctively perceived for what it was — a simple accident.

In the Beginning

Scientific evidence indicates that dogs are for all practical purposes domesticated wolves. Furthermore, the instincts and natural drives that enable the wolf pack to function are the same elements that shape the behavior of the dogs with which we share our lives today. Thus, even though this is a book about the Bouviers des Flandres, it is helpful to know about the primitive canines from which the present-day dog evolved.

The modern view is that the canine species is a continuum that includes the wolf, the jackal, the fox, and the domestic dog.[1] It is believed that differences among individual populations are primarily adaptations in physical structure, feeding strategies, and domestic social order according to local circumstance. The genetic links to the wolf are not entirely ancient, for the Eskimos made a practice of staking out a bitch in heat to be bred by a wolf. Their purpose was to maintain the vigor of their working sled dogs, and there are no doubt similar ties back into the natural gene pool wherever wild canines exist.

This perception of the canine world is useful, for by studying the social structure of the wolf pack and the relationship of the few remaining hunter/gatherer human bands with their dogs, we can gain insight into why our dogs are what they are and why they behave as they do. These insights help the trainer and breeder, and actually anyone who wishes to understand the modern canine.

The fact that the dog is derived from the wolf is significant in that the wolf is a predatory species with a complex social structure. Both man and dog relied on group participation for success in the hunt, for raising the young, and, ultimately, for species survival. Both were able to prey on much larger animals through coordinated group action rather than relying on an individual's size and strength. The typical wolf weighs less than 100 pounds and can not by itself prey effectively on large game. However, the pack is capable of killing moose and other large animals. The hunting and herding functions of today's working dogs are direct outgrowths of this primitive social order.

For uncounted generations, wolves lived by group cooperation and mutual interdependence. Even today, the utility of dogs is a result of the similarities between the social structure of the pack and of the primitive human band — similarities that make it possible for man and dog to work together effectively. By domesticating the wolf to create the dog, man has simply adapted existing social modes and induced (by accident or design) individual wolves to gradually give up their wild existence to join the human band. This became, in effect, a substitute pack. The alliance has proven fruitful.

The working partnership between man and dog is a long and varied story, and the Bouvier as we know him today is a relatively recent chapter. In the beginning, the dog was likely most useful in the hunt and in the common defense against predators. The keen senses of smell and hearing were no doubt among the primary canine attributes that man desired to use. These are discussed in more detail below.

As man began to control and preserve his game, and to domesticate the animals that provided food and clothing, the dog's usefulness was enhanced by his ability to assist in keeping animals larger or more fleet than man. This transition from hunting to husbandry was no doubt gradual, allowing the dog's role to evolve. Different styles and types emerged according to regional circumstance and local agricultural technology, just as the body structure and pigmentation of human beings adapted to climate and to the predominant agricultural methodology. A common thread binding together the alliance was always the protective function, both of the human band itself and then of the livestock on which mutual survival came to depend. So important was the dog to the primitive herdsman that it seems likely, particularly in the northern regions, that man's transition from hunter/gatherer to herdsman would have been difficult or impossible were it not for the previous or simultaneous domestication of wolves.

Man originally made use of dogs because of special canine attributes not possessed by human beings. One of the most essential of these is the sense of smell, which neither man nor his mechanical contrivances can approach in sensitivity or discriminatory power. This olfactory capability enables a dog such as the Bouvier to search for a lost calf or child, to track a criminal, to detect the presence of narcotics, or to find a bomb. He is much better equipped to work in the dark and to detect a person or an animal hidden from view. It is believed that a dog can detect fear and other strong human emotions in large part by means of the person's body odor. This gives the dog the potential to know which individuals are likely to be dangerous in time to give a warning or to take action. Much of the effectiveness of the watch dog lies in the senses of hearing and smell, which make him aware of an intruder and allow him to give a warning or take whatever action is warranted.

Another canine attribute useful to man is the agile

Bouvier with flock, France, Circa 1950. *Photo courtesy Justin Chastel.*

and powerful body that can extend the reach of the team far beyond that of a man. Much of the working dog's utility is due to his speed, mobility, and agility. He is able to head off sheep or cattle in flight or to run down a deer, a wolf, or a man. Some dogs, such as the sight hounds, are capable of covering tremendous distances and running down game and vermin by sheer speed alone. The Bouvier is not of this mold, for nature has equipped him for short spurts of speed and quick changes in direction, but not for long-distance pursuit. He is powerful, agile, and quick but not fleet, and he does not possess great relative endurance.

The dog's powerful jaws and strong teeth make him a formidable adversary. While essential for the hunt, these attributes proved useful in defending against other predators and in maintaining the pack's territory. Most wild animals, including wolves, prefer

to avoid conflicts with other animals simply because such confrontations are, in general, "no-win" situations. Predators forage for food and are aggressive against others of their own species when maintaining their territory or breeding precedence but are not generally "bloodthirsty" in the sense of possessing an inherent desire to kill. Man has always made use of this defensive capability by enlisting the dog to defend domestic stock and by taking advantage of the dog's natural inclination to drive off potential predators.

For countless generations, and over much of the world, the farmer and stockman have lived and worked with their dogs. Structure and function have varied considerably, and the working breeds in the modern, formal sense are a construct of the last hundred years or so. The German Shepherd was created toward the end of the nineteenth century from dogs with diverse physical form. The Rottweiler's

Job de la Thudinie.
Primary stud dog for Justin Chastel in the early sixties, sire of Marc de la Thudinie. Later imported by Mr. & Mrs. Walsh at Deewal. Note the barges on the river Sambre in the background, which flows through the village of Thuin, location of so many important Bouvier kennels such a de Gratte-Saule, du Ble d'Or and du Posty-Arlequin in addition to Thudinie.

Cendrillo de l'Ile Monsin LOSH.165684
Hion de la Thudinie Ch; LOSH.184492 '58
Demoiselle de la Thudinie ALSH.2837
B/A Ch Job de la Thudinie LOSH.194620 '60
Bonzo l'Ideal de Charleroi
Hulotte de la Thudinie LOSH.182357 '58
Flambee de la Thudinie ALSH.3610 '56

claimed antiquity is mostly a matter of myth, for there is no clear, direct link between today's breeding stock and the similar dogs of the Roman era. The style is ancient, but the modern breed is relatively recent. Man has for uncounted generations been able to create certain types, allow them to disappear back into the genetic morass, then recreate them centuries later when a need or desire again arises.

The natural capacity for rapid evolution among all canines is certainly their most remarkable attribute. It dous pliability of the stock is apparent when one considers that the four-pound Poodle is simply the result of selectively breeding domesticated wolves.

From the Fields of Flandres

The key to understanding today's Bouviers des Flandres is to be found in the role of his progenitors

A SNAPSHOT FROM OUT OF THE PAST — This photo, taken in 1945 or possibly early in 1946, is of Belco (on the left) and son Marius du Clos des Cerberes. Belco was of course the male Miss Edmee Bowles slipped out of Europe literally under the Nazi gun, having lost most of the remainder of her dogs in the brutal German occupation of Belgium.

Although at first glance these dogs seem vastly different from the Bouviers of today, much of the difference is in length and texture of coat. The dogs of this era tended to be less angulated, with a muzzle a little longer relative to the skull. These dogs were of virtually pure Dutch breeding, and it was not until some ten years later that the Belgian lines began to predominate in America.

is the key to man's ability to mold his dogs according to his needs and to create the physically diverse types of the various breeds. The artificial evolution that we practice is more rapid than natural evolution. This is because consistent selection according to desired characteristics is much more efficient than the natural process, where a trait may have only marginal advantage in the beginning. This means that many animals lacking the desired property would continue to breed, albeit at a slightly reduced relative rate. The tremen-

as working cattle and farm dogs on the lush, broad Flemish plain. The herding and farming needs of this society required that each dog have one-on-one interaction with his people. In contrast, many of the hunting breeds were and still are essentially pack oriented, working as a group rather than as individuals. Generations could be useful (and thus kept and bred) without individual human contact. The historical trends persist in that the protective-heritage working breeds of today are derived primarily from the herding dogs that served the complex and demanding husbandry role rather than those used mainly as pack hunters.

Many herding breeds, including the Bouvier, did not work primarily at the direction of the shepherd or cattleman, but rather took on much individual responsibility. If a young animal strayed, it was returned to the safety of the herd. Even when it wandered out of sight, the dog's olfactory capability made it possible for him to find and return it. If a predator threatened, it was driven off; however, the dog was not drawn into a cross-country chase that would leave the herd without protection.

Herding dogs serve two broad functions. One is control, keeping the flock or herd together and directing its movements. The other is protection from predators such as the wolf and other human beings. Some breeds perform one function or the other almost exclusively, while others are more diverse.

Typical of the herd-protection dogs are the relatively large central and eastern European sheep dogs, such as the Komondor, which are essentially surrogate herd members. These dogs are by their very nature adapted to living with the sheep as virtual members of one extended family. Because of these loyalties, they drive off any predator — human as well as animal — that poses a threat. They do not control or direct the herd. Even their typical white coloration aids their ability to blend into the herd as members. Such dogs do not typically have a close relationship with the shepherds and are not especially personable or trainable, nor are they particularly protective of human beings.

Other herding breeds, such as the Border Collie, exert strong control over the sheep. They keep the herd together and move them into pens or for other purposes at the direction of the shepherd. The motions and methods are strikingly similar to those employed in the hunt. Indeed, there is a very thin line between herding and hunting. Because they evolved having a close relationship with the shepherd, such dogs work well with their human partners. Their "extended family" consists of the people who watch over the herd rather than the sheep themselves. Such animals do well in obedience competition but are not necessarily inherently protective of either the animals or the people. They evolved to meet a set of specific needs — controlling the herd and assisting the shepherd in moving and directing the sheep. Protection from predators is not an important function, because predators have not been a serious problem in the British Isles for several centuries.

Neither of these molds is an exact fit for the Bouvier, which, as evidenced by his structure and tradition, is fundamentally a cattle dog. However, photos in older European books often depict him with sheep rather than with cattle. Indeed, the official printed version of the Franco-Belgian standard includes as its only herding photo one of a Bouvier guarding sheep. My impression is that the French much more often used the Bouvier with sheep than either the Belgians, who had many native shepherd breeds, or the Dutch. This is consistent with the historical French preference for a much smaller Bouvier than that favored by the Flemish or the Dutch.

The underlying determinant of the Bouvier's diversity is the nature of agriculture and life in his Flemish homeland. In contrast to eastern Europe, with its large, mobile sheep herds, Flemish farms tended to be smaller, less specialized economic units. It is natural that such farmers, who raised and kept diverse livestock, developed dogs that were generalists also, capable of many functions. They served both as herding dogs and as protectors. On the whole, they were general-purpose farm dogs that assisted their people in whatever was to be done. They were dogs that could guard and herd both sheep and cattle and that could protect the farmer and his family.

Other elements were significant in the Bouvier's genesis. As will be documented in the chapters on breed history, more massive dogs of the type "matin" were introduced early in this century as the Bouvier left the farms to become one of many police-style breeds evolving in that era. The choice was to adapt or to disappear, for the age-old way of life on the farm was being transformed. Nowhere in the world does the Bouvier serve in the herding role that was the wellspring of so many of his progenitors. The introduction of guard-dog stock is a key difference between the Bouvier and the shepherds' dogs such as the Tervuren, Malinois, or Laeken.

The Protective Heritage

The modern police-style working dogs possess complex control and search capabilities. They are not derived from the estate-style guard dogs of an earlier era, such as the Mastiff, which were bred for power and simple aggressiveness. Nor do they descend from the powerful and fierce breeds, such as the Akita, developed for hunting large animals. On the contrary, modern police breeds evolved in a relatively small region of central Europe, encompassing Germany, Belgium, the Netherlands, and northern France. Other regions have produced estate-style guard dogs and independent livestock guardians. However, the Bouvier des Flandres, the Malinois, the Rottweiler, the German Shepherd, and others are different from breeds anywhere else in the world. Because of their high level of trainability, responsibility, and discriminatory ability, they are the only breeds truly suited to the modern police-style working function. The British Isles, the other region with diverse, sophisticated breeds, produced nothing even remotely comparable.

The breeds serving police and other protective roles are useful because they are willing and able to take aggressive action against a human being. However, it is not sufficiently appreciated that the animals excelling in these roles are not the largest of dogs nor the most ferocious fighters. Bouviers and even the Rottweiler are by no means small; however, there are any number of substantially larger and more powerful breeds. The correct Bouvier is large and strong enough

Ch & Working Ch Centauri's Fleur de Lis
SchH III, CD, TD

to deal with the most determined man, yet compact and agile enough to ride comfortably in a vehicle. The medium to large size is compatible with agility, reasonable speed, and endurance, which a significantly larger animal is likely to lack. When put together properly, a ninety-five-pound male is large enough to deal effectively with a man yet can be reasonably compact and agile.

A somewhat suspicious nature is an integral element of the Bouvier essence, for suspicion was essential in

his work as guardian of the stock. When my children were young, they invited some people into the house who had come to see a pup, even though we were not home. Our Bouvier, Tory, responded by holding the visitors in the front hall, giving them a good scare in the process. He perceived that they should not have been allowed in, but he also understood that this situation did not call for direct aggressive action. This is typical Bouvier behavior. The factor that brings all of these character traits together is the Bouvier's ability to discriminate — to use his instinctive ability to sense the intent of a potential adversary and then respond accordingly. The essence of the excellent Bouvier is this capacity to react according to the situation.

Life in America

Although much has been made of the Bouvier as a working dog, the fact remains that the majority of Bouviers, in Europe as well as in America, do not work on a full-time basis. Most never go on patrol with a police officer, herd cattle, or enter a Schutzhund trial or dog show. The typical Bouvier serves as a canine companion, playing with the children and going for long walks in the woods.

Are these two roles compatible? Why should the person seeking a canine companion be interested in the working character of the Bouvier? You may be concerned about the consequences of taking a powerful dog into your home and may wonder if he is going to be dangerous to family or guests. The answer is, quite simply, that the same qualities of stability, courage, and trainability that equate to excellence in work are also the characteristics of outstanding companion dogs. The Bouvier is well suited to the needs and desires of many — but not all — who want a dog simply to live with.

Although relatively few Americans have imported trained Bouviers, many of us have purchased Schutzhund-titled German Shepherds over the years and have had no particular difficulty in integrating them into family life. Many have no real idea what their dogs are trained to do, and a few would no doubt be shocked to see their family companion in action. Most Schutzhund dogs, in fact, spend the week as suburban house dogs, and many police dogs serve as the officer's family companion when off duty.

The Bouvier is not — and should not be — a dog for every family. As with other strongly protective breeds, such as the Rottweiler and German Shepherd, he should go to a home where he will be taken seriously. Such dogs require extra commitment, a willingness to work with and train the dog, and the assertive-

Tory over the jump.

ness and confidence necessary to gain and maintain the animal's respect. Certainly not everyone need spend the hours in training that the dog-sport enthusiast does. For most people, a simple obedience class will suffice. Letting the dog know who is boss has little to do with size or strength, for diminutive women can handle a large and powerful dog. It really is a matter of attitude and character rather than of physical strength.

Why should a person living in a peaceful suburban or city neighborhood have a dog from a breed such as the Bouvier? One important consideration is that a good Bouvier can provide a real element of protection. While few of us are subject to a yearly home invasion or an assault on the street, crime is still prevalent in America, and most of us feel the need to take precautions. Many of my clients require a reliable dog, one that will be accepting of family and guests but that will also give a potential troublemaker something to think about. No Bouvier can render his family impervious to harm in every situation, but a good one can be the extra edge that makes the difference.

Beyond the protection element, most people obtain a dog to provide companionship, because they expect living with a dog to be fun. The working dog is by his very nature energetic and active, always ready for

work or play. There is a great deal of play involved in effective training, and it is not far off the mark to note that in order to work well, a dog must naturally have an intense fondness for play.

Though certainly not a dog for everyone, a good Bouvier can make an excellent companion. Unlike some breeds specifically created to attack with a hair-trigger reaction, the Bouvier is relatively slow to anger and is confident enough to give warning before taking more serious action. This allows an adversary time to reconsider and back down, which is certainly the most desirable outcome in a confrontation. The fact that the Bouvier tends to warn before taking action also provides his owner time to respond and to verbally restrain the dog if necessary.

The properly bred and raised Bouvier can be a fearless protector, a competitive sport dog, a guardian of the livestock, and, perhaps most important, a faithful companion.

References

[1]Fiennes, Richard and Alice. *The Natural History of Dogs*. New York: Bonanza Books, 1968.

Ch Delys Calm Winchester has been one of the top Specialty winners of the eighties, owner handled by Cheryl Calm. This photo is an excellent example of the correct parallel head planes.

CHAPTER TWO

Structure and Stride

Although the Flemish farm dogs varied greatly in appearance, adaptation to climate, to terrain, and especially to work imposed common elements of physical structure. Because of their demanding and dangerous work, the cattle dogs were under special pressure to become quick, strong, and agile; that is, able to do their work and yet avoid injury from a flying hoof. Much of the difference in appearance was simply due to variation in coat texture, length, pattern, and color.

In creating the breed, the founders consolidated and made more uniform the type produced by natural selection, artificially completing nature's design process. In selecting breeding stock, there was certainly much from which to choose. The differentiation between cattle dogs and sheep dogs was vague and ill defined, with much of the working farm-dog population being capable of serving either function more or less effectively. From among those dogs with diverse physical attributes, they simply made choices and bred the dogs that fit the picture, precluding animals that did not appear to contribute to their idealized concept of type.

The purpose of this chapter is to describe how the Bouvier founders envisioned the ideal structure, based on their knowledge of the factors that suited the dog to his work. This information will allow Bouvier enthusiasts to carry on the preservation of the breed.

One might ask that if being a cattle dog makes a Bouvier what he is, why is it that he doesn't look like a Rottweiler, a breed that is also considered a native cattle dog? This is an important question, and a theory incapable of dealing with it would certainly lack credibility. Part of the answer is that the Rottweiler is more of a drover's dog — a dog used to take animals to market rather than standing watch over them in the field. In the pasture, dogs who serve year round are almost without exception rough coated. The rough Collie derived from the field dogs, while the smooth Collie was the drover's dog. Even the German Shepherd develops a heavy coat in cold weather, and in spite of ninety years of effort to breed it out, many "long-coated" shepherds are still produced.

Also note that a Rottweiler should be reasonably short-coupled and certainly powerful, so that a specimen that is not overly large and in good condition would be in the 100- to 110-pound range or even lighter. Thus, the Bouvier and Rottweiler, particularly the primitive types, share important attributes and are not so different as one might at first think.

The founders could easily have produced a breed with a different appearance had they chosen to do so. Overall, it was very much a matter of breeding for consistent coat texture, color, and length that created the external impression of uniformity with relatively minor modification of the actual physiques present in the primitive stock.

The men who consolidated the Belgian shepherd's dogs into breeds in the modern sense did, in fact, create four of them — the Malinois, the Tervuren, the Groenendael, and the Laeken — all of which are strikingly different in external appearance but remarkably similar in structure underneath the coat.

What are the physical attributes of the cattle dog? Certainly he must be relatively large and powerful in order to be taken seriously by his charges. But he also must be quick and agile, for a well-placed hoof carries death or disability. The flock of sheep is not a lethal threat, but a cow or a bull can inflict a severe injury as a consequence of the smallest mistake — even the most momentary failure of agility.

The shepherd's dogs of central Europe, such as the Malinois and the German Shepherd, would bite as an aid in controlling the flock, as long as relatively few sheep were harmed. Those of us from urban backgrounds think of a sunny field with the shepherd and his dog walking among the lambs. In reality, sheep can be headstrong and aggressive; it is said that the shepherd dog that kills one sheep a year is not out of line but rather is simply aggressive enough to maintain the respect of the flock.

The cattle and horses were much larger and more difficult. The dog grabbing a cow or bull by the leg would risk serious injury. Also, the economic value of the hide is reduced greatly if scarred. This need to control large and powerful animals without biting led to a reliance on agility of mind and body, and on a relatively large size. Even Bouviers never exposed to cattle or horses are apt to react to a sudden motion by dropping to the "down" position, ready to spring to either side. This is an instinctive reflex designed by nature to avoid a blow by a hoof. The Bouvier is

European saying is that "viewed from the side the correct Bouvier must stand in a square.") Sloping toplines, extreme angulation, or excessive length, while appropriate to a more fleet shepherd's dog, are serious deviations from correct Bouvier type. In order to be quick and agile, a large, powerful dog must be short coupled with moderate angulation and a level topline.

Viewed from the side, the Bouvier gait must be

Ch Nack du Clos des Cytises OFA

Brd: Simone Jousse, Villiers-sur-Marne, France
Sire: Viscot de la Thudinie F Ch
Dam: Lisbeth du Clos des Cytises LOF.17353
Imported by Marion Hubbard & Judy Higgins in
   1982, Nack became a very influential stud.

Ch Nack du Clos des Cytises OFA

inclined to move in, jab with a foot or strike a blow with the shoulder, and then retreat out of harm's way, prepared for whatever further action proves necessary. The bite is not the instinctive first reaction. In modern vernacular, the Bouvier is "laid back."

Developing an agile and quick, yet massive physique was a difficult design challenge. Nature's solution was a compact, short-coupled structure with relatively moderate angulation. This was not compatible with an extremely long and efficient stride; therefore, the Bouvier does not exhibit the effortless, graceful, flying trot that characterizes a good German Shepherd. The Bouvier is also well-muscled and strong, with a square outline and a level topline. (A

strong, reaching, and efficient, with no wasted motion. He should have adequate reach and drive without hackneyed motion or excessively short strides, which would render him incapable of standing up to the strain of his work. While his reach is not as extreme as is typical of the shepherd's breeds, this is a matter of degree. A smooth, powerful stride is just as essential in the Bouvier as in any other herdsman's breed.

While the short back necessary for agility and quickness is a required Bouvier attribute, it means nothing if achieved with choppy or hackneyed movement. We have seen an overemphasis on extreme angulation and the floating trot in the German Shepherd lead to a grievous lack of balance in the American show ring. In a similar way, an overemphasis on the short back and high tail carriage, as ends in and of themselves, can lead to fundamentally incorrect structure in the Bouvier. (This comment is often confirmed by European judges who see large numbers of American dogs.)

The parallel between the Flemish cattle dog and the horse that evolved in the American West for work-

get him from *behind*! The Bouvier can run rings around the typical shepherd dog in close quarters but is not able to cover distances as easily or as effortlessly. The work of the shepherd's dog demands a smooth, efficient stride for covering distances day after day, but the Bouvier design sacrifices some of this in order to gain the required substance and agility.

Although the Bouvier should be a relatively massive dog, this must be kept in perspective. The ideal Ger-

French import Ch Lutteur du Val de Rol illustrates correct side movement with moderate reach, drive and extension.

ing cattle on the open range is striking and instructive. The Quarter Horse is powerfully built, heavily muscled, short coupled, agile, and quick for a few hundred yards but not especially competitive when raced at a distance. The function of each animal required him to stand duty hour after hour, day after day, always ready for an intensive burst of activity.

Because of his structure, the Bouvier accelerates more quickly and is in general much more maneuverable than the German Shepherd or the Tervuren. In the Schutzhund courage test, the agitator who signals to send the dog and relies on a sense of timing for turning and facing a German Shepherd is apt to turn and face an *airborne* Bouvier; that is, if the dog doesn't

man Shepherd male weighs about eighty-five pounds; the Tervuren and Groenendael a little less. The Bouvier should be somewhat larger — eighty-five to ninety-five pounds in the male. If he exceeds this weight, he tends to become gross with a corresponding loss of agility and stamina.

To create the Bouvier physique for day-in-and-day-out work, every means that could help conserve energy for the occasional burst of effort was incorporated into the design of his structure and motion. These adaptations are evident in the natural gaits, for although the trot is characteristic, the Bouvier will also pace (move both feet on the same side in unison). A tired dog or one on bad footing will often pace, while a fresh or excited dog will be likely to trot. The pace is thus a natural distance-covering, energy-conserving gait, while the trot is the movement of a Bouvier prepared for action. Conformation judges require that the dog be shown at a trot, because it is the best gait at which to evaluate agility, reach, and general movement. This leads some to believe that the pace is an indication of faulty structure. This is certainly not true in the Bouvier, for the pace is a natural and useful gait.

Although reference has been made to the Bouvier as a draught or cart dog, a moment's reflection will indicate that this runs counter to common sense. The physical structure that suits the herding dog to his work is in almost all details contrary to what would suit a dog to pulling heavy loads and transporting over long distances. The very attributes that make a good general-purpose herding and stock dog — speed, agility, quickness, aggressiveness — would be of no use and often a hindrance for a serious draught application. As may be seen in various old European photos, the dogs used for cart pulling — particularly in Belgium — were typically the smooth-coated and big-headed type commonly referred to as the "Matin." While Bouvier-style dogs are common in old photos of police and border-patrol dogs, such dogs are virtually never seen in harness. Indeed, a draught dog would be relatively bulky, straight of limb, and docile, and probably would have a short, easily maintained coat. This is certainly not the description of a good Bouvier! While there are certainly Matin-type ancestors in a nook or cranny of the Bouvier family tree (and Bouvier-type dogs no doubt were pressed into occasional carting service), the Bouvier as a serious draught dog is mostly a matter of myth.

The Bouvier is rough coated because the farmer and his dog were required to stand watch over their stock throughout the year. There was no such thing as an afternoon's sport and then retirement to the hearth in inclement weather. These were men and dogs for all seasons, able to work in wide-ranging temperatures and damp weather and able to stand up to the elements of the homeland year-round. The rough Bouvier coat therefore enabled him to function in extremes of temperature and precipitation. The coat is reasonably well adapted to both warm and cold weather, as evidenced by a number of Bouviers functioning on various Southern California police forces. A protective breed not drawn from the herding heritage, such as the Doberman, tends to suffer in versatility from its lesser ability to stand up as well to either warm or cold weather.

Although as cattle dogs the Bouviers were less reliant on the bite for herd or flock control, guarding and defending against predators required a powerful dog capable to winning against a wolf or a man. The specific introduction of guard stock in the early years of this century further emphasized these requirements.

The quick, agile, powerful body that evolved for herding was also ideal for the attack. In order to deliver a strong, authoritative bite, there was emphasis on a broad muzzle, on large, properly aligned teeth, and on a strong jaw. Strong muscles for an effective bite must be well anchored, which is the functional reason for the massive skull. The neck is broad, powerful, and compact rather than long and elegant. Indeed, there is no more use for the word "elegant" in describing the Bouvier than there is for describing a bricklayer or any other honest-working craftsman.

The foreshortened appearance of the face must be due to the massive skull, to the lack of stop, to the set of the ears, and to the beard and mustache rather than to a reduction in the breadth and musculature of the muzzle. If the beard is held back, the powerful and well-developed muzzle and jaw should be found, rather than the artificial foreshortening of the Boxer.

Viewed from the side, the plane of the skull and the top of the muzzle must be parallel. There should be very little apparent stop. In this same view, the ratio of the length of the skull to the length of the muzzle should approach three to two.

What all of this means in practical terms is that just as the farmers and stockmen selected their dogs for structure and character according to their functional needs, the modern breeder must persistently seek to understand and select for the traditional physical attributes as passed on by oral tradition and embodied in the formal, written standard. The characteristic Bouvier features, such as the short coupling, the massive skull, the powerful jaws, the double coat, and the rest, are not arbitrary whims of some committee. Rather, they are fundamental and necessary attributes precisely because they are what suited the animal to his work.

Puppy Selection

Puppies are usually evaluated and distributed at seven to twelve weeks of age. In the beginning, the breeder typically is willing to part with those that he considers lesser specimens, delaying final decisions on the breeding candidates. The best way to select pups is to monitor their development during these critical weeks.

When buying a pup, we are not so presumptuous as to begin by "evaluating the litter." Rather, we tend to wait for the breeder's suggestions as to which puppies are most suitable for our needs. In Europe, especially, the social protocol is important; conversation

Dayan Claudia van Hagenbeek, second only to his sire, Hoscy Dukke, among Dutch stud dogs in the 80s. He is Champion of Holland as well as the Dutch Specialty winner in 1984. He is sire of two specialty winners: Dutch Ch Tino Faisca van de Vanenblikhoeve, and Dutch Ch Darwin Grenda v h Grendar-cohof, as well as two world show winners. Bred in Holland by D. Postma, he was imported into the U.S. by Dr. Erik Houttuin, where he became a key stud dog in this county.

Sire: D Ch Hoscy Dukke Bianca fan it Hanenhiem
Dam: Claudia van de Macecliers
Brd: D.H. Postma, Zwaagwesteinde

Ch Centauri's Hanter, co-owned by Sarah Dowling. Shown with judge Tom Gaitley and handler Penny Duffee.

Sire: Ch Abbas v d Boevers Garden OFA/Good
Dam: Fancy du Clos des Cerberes OFA/Good

about lines and combinations occurs over coffee before the pups are even seen. When all is said and done, we normally go home with the pup that the breeder had in mind for us. Of course, we are now working with people whom we have known for many years; nevertheless, the novice's approach should be similar. Because of the breeder's knowledge of his or her lines and because the breeder watches the pups develop, the experienced breeder is the best person to evaluate a litter.

never be purchased as breeding stock. They are severely flawed and tend to reproduce the fault.

High priority must go to selecting for a short back and a level topline. Lift up the tail and make sure that it is an extension of the backbone, with no dip in front of the tail. The topline should be level, with no dip or roach. Feel the loin area (the top of the back between the end of the rib cage and the beginning of the pelvis). A pup can be short backed but long in the loin because the rib cage is too small. You want

Ch Lutteur de Val De Rol OFA

Sire: Ch Vulcain du Clos des Cytises
Dam: Tamise du Val de Rol LOF.13986
Brd: Marie-Claude Niquet, Le Vaudreuil, France
Born: 1975
Owned: Miss Bowles & Bruce Jacobsohn

Typical "de Overstort" puppy at 8 weeks.

It is not unusual for the choice of best male or female to change perhaps a couple of times between seven and twelve weeks of age. The biggest variations are in proportions, that is, the ratio of back length to height at the withers, and in the slope of the croup.

A pup that is going to have a good harsh coat as an adult will tend to have harsh- or crisp-feeling hair on the top of his front paws. Skin color should have a definite blue cast with strong pigmentation around the eyes, nose, lips, and gums. Reject a pup with a pink nose; only black is acceptable here. Coat color should not be lighter than a medium gray. Fawn is the most unstable color and may turn from a bright rich red-gold with a black mask to gray, cream, or white. Pups with pale and washed-out colors should

a short-coupled pup that is also short in back. Examine the coupling by laying your fingers side by side, nails pointed toward the floor and placed between the end of the rib cage and the pelvis. You will gradually calibrate your hand and think in terms of "three fingers;" this will give you an idea of how a particular pup compares.

Have someone call the pup and watch the pup move. The topline should not bounce or hinge as though joined in the middle. Back feet should not interfere with the front during movement. A pup can be too short backed, which will cause him to trip over his own feet. For an athletic puppy suitable for work, look for legs, from the bottom of the paw to the elbow, that are slightly more than half the overall height of the pup from the floor to the withers. Both front and rear legs should be parallel to each other. Lift and then gently lower either end to observe the most natural stance.

In examining the head, seek a wide, square, scissor bite. The muzzle should be shorter than the skull in the proportion of three to two. When viewed from the side, the top of the muzzle and the top of the skull should form parallel planes. There should be very little stop (the area between the eyes where the muzzle and skull join). Both the skull and muzzle should be wide and strong. A weak muzzle is a serious flaw. The head should have good fill-in with very little or no prominence to the occiput (the protruding bump that you can sometimes feel at the back of the skull). The length of the neck should be moderate, with good shoulder lay-back and balanced rear angulation.

In evaluating temperament, look for an outgoing, confident pup that runs to you. Test sound sensitivity by dropping a metal pan or dish or hitting it with a spoon ten feet away from the pup. The more interest he shows, the better. If he hides, consider him unacceptable. If much of the litter shows fear or cannot be approached, do not buy any pup, even one that seems normal. (Most serious breeders will cull a pup with significant physical or character faults.)

When you first enter the room with the litter, the pups should jump all over you and strongly compete for attention, although a few Bouviers seem to be "watchers" that hang back and observe what is going on. If you like such a dog, remove the other pups and sit on the floor. If he immediately comes forward and shows interest, he may make a fine companion dog. Most trainers, however, would select another pup. Pups that reject human contact or show unusual fear should be put down.

If you have your eye on a particular pup, separate him from the others and see how he reacts to a tennis ball. Bounce the ball several times to get his attention, then slowly roll the ball. A desirable reaction is for the pup to pick it up and prance with it. If he comes running back to you to roll it again, or to get you to play tug-of-war or keep-away, so much the better.

To gauge the "prey drive" that is so valued in the working candidate, tie a rag to ten feet of cord and drag it past the pup, like you would play with a cat and a ball of yarn. The most desirable reaction, for a working prospect, is for the pup to pounce on it and shake it, like a terrier would kill a rat.

Those looking for a companion dog should look toward the more middle-of-the-road pups, while those looking for working prospects should pick among the most outgoing and aggressive. This applies to those intending to do only obedience as well as those interested in the protection sports.

Remember that the character and structure of the parents and grandparents are as important as what you see in the litter box. Most litters have cute and appealing individuals, but adults with good type and fine working characters come for the most part from lines that have a strong record of producing such dogs.

I will now reveal a little secret. Many of our best-known working and show dogs went on to fame because nobody wanted to buy them or because a dissatisfied owner returned them to the breeder. Knowledge of lines, of structure, and of the developmental process greatly increases your chances, but in the end, you need to be lucky too!

Official AKC Standard for the Bouvier des Flandres

The Bouvier des Flandres is a powerfully built, compact, short-coupled, rough-coated dog of notably rugged appearance. He gives the impression of great strength without any sign of heaviness or clumsiness in his overall makeup. He is agile, spirited and bold, yet his serene, well-behaved disposition denotes his steady, resolute and fearless character. His gaze is alert and brilliant, depicting his intelligence, vigor and daring. By nature he is an equable dog.

His origin is that of a cattle herder and general farmer's helper, including cart pulling. He is an ideal farm dog. His harsh coat protects him in all weather, enabling him to perform the most arduous tasks. The coat may be trimmed slightly only to accent the body line. Overtrimming which alters the natural rugged appearance is to be avoided.

He has been used as an ambulance and messenger dog. Modern times find him as a watch and guard dog as well as a family friend, guardian and protector. His physical and mental characteristics and deportment, coupled with his olfactory abilities, his intelligence and initiative enable him to also perform as a tracking dog and a guide dog for the blind.

Head
The head is impressive in scale, accentuated by beard and mustache. It is in proportion to body and build.

Skull
Well developed and flat, slightly less wide than long. When viewed from the side, the top lines of the skull and the muzzle are parallel. It is wide between the ears, with the frontal groove barely marked. The stop is more apparent than real, due to upstanding eyebrows. The proportions of length of skull to length of muzzle are 3 to 2.

Eyes

The expression is bold and alert. They neither protrude nor are sunken in the sockets. Their shape is oval with the axis on a horizontal plane, when viewed from the front. Their color is a dark nut brown. The eye rims are black without lack of pigment and the

Muzzle

Broad, strong, well filled out, tapering gradually toward the nose without ever becoming snipy or pointed. The cheeks are flat and lean, with the lips being dry and tight fitting. A narrow, snipy muzzle is faulty.

Miss Bowles' sketch of the ideal Bouvier des Flandres.

haw is barely visible. Yellow or light eyes are to be strongly penalized, along with a walleyed or staring expression.

Ears

Placed high and alert. They are rough-coated. If cropped, they are to be a triangular contour and in proportion to the size of the head. The inner corner of the ear should be in line with the outer corner of the eye. Ears that are too low or too closely set are serious faults.

Nose

Large, black, well developed, round at the edges, with flared nostrils. A brown, pink or spotted nose is a serious fault.

Jaws and Teeth

The jaws are powerful and of equal length. The teeth are strong, white and healthy, with the incisors meeting in a scissors bite. Overshot or undershot bites are to be severely penalized.

Neck

The neck is strong and muscular, widening gradually into the shoulders. When viewed from the side, it is gracefully arched with upright carriage. A short, squatty neck is faulty. No dewlap.

Body or Trunk

Powerful, broad and short. The length from the point of the shoulder to the tip of the buttocks is equal to the height from the ground to the highest point of the withers. The chest is broad, with the brisket extending to the elbow in depth. A long-lined, rangy dog should be faulted.

Ribs

The ribs are deep and well sprung. The first ribs are slightly curved, the others well sprung and very sloped nearing the rear, giving proper depth to the chest. Flat ribs or slabsidedness is to be strongly penalized.

Back

Short, broad, well muscled with firm level topline. It is supple and flexible with no sign of weakness.

Flanks and Loins

Short, wide and well muscled, without weakness. The abdomen is only slightly tucked up.

Croup or Rump

The horizontal line of the back should mold unnoticeably into the curve of the rump, which is characteristically wide. A sunken or slanted croup is a serious fault.

Tail

Is to be docked, leaving 2 or 3 vertebrae. It must be set high and align normally with the spinal column. Preferably carried upright in motion. Dogs born tailless should not be penalized.

Forequarters

Strong boned, well muscled and straight.

Shoulders and Upper Arms

The shoulders are relatively long, muscular but not loaded, with good layback. The shoulder blade and humerus are approximately the same length, forming an angle slightly greater than 90 degrees when standing. Straight shoulders are faulty.

Elbows

Close to the body and parallel. Elbows which are too far out or in are faults.

Forearms

Viewed either in profile or from the front are perfectly straight, parallel to each other and perpendicular to the ground. They are well muscled and strong boned.

Wrists

Exactly in line with the forearms. Strong boned.

Pasterns

Quite short, slightly sloped forward. Dewclaws may be removed.

Feet

Both forefeet and hind feet are rounded and compact turning neither in nor out; the toes close and well arched; strong black nails; thick tough pads.

Hindquarters

Firm, well muscled with large, powerful hams. They should be parallel with the front legs when viewed from either front or rear.

Thighs

Wide and muscular. The upper thigh must be neither too straight nor too sloping. There is moderate angulation at the stifle.

Legs

Moderately long, well muscled, neither too straight nor too inclined.

Hocks

Strong, rather close to the ground. When standing and seen from the rear, they will be straight and perfectly parallel to each other and perpendicular to the ground. In motion, they must turn neither in nor out. There is a slight angulation at the hock joint. Sickle or cowhocks are serious faults.

Metatarsi

Hardy and lean, rather cylindrical and perpendicular to the ground when standing. If born with dewclaws, they are to be removed.

Coat

A tousled, double coat capable of withstanding the hardest work in the most inclement weather. The outer hairs are rough and harsh, with the undercoat being fine, soft and dense.

Topcoat

Must be harsh to the touch, dry, trimmed, if necessary, to a length of approximately 2½ inches. A coat too long or too short is a fault, as is a silky or woolly

Ch. Rombo High Mighty and Proud
Shown winning the 1985 American Club Specialty
From the left: Dr. Erik Houttuin, American Club President, Judge Wenzel Dvornik and Breeder/handler Rick Gschwender.

Leon Spinks v d Overstort
Dutch Champion
NHSB.1550360

Sire: D Ch Spinks Centy v d Overstort
Dam: Tamara Elza v d Bramma Stuwa
Brd: Joop Pater
Born: 1987

---

coat. It is tousled without being curly. On the skull, it is short, and on the upper part of the back, it is particularly close and harsh always, however, remaining rough.

Undercoat

A dense mass of fine, close hair, thicker in winter. Together with the topcoat, it will form a water-resistant covering. A flat coat, denoting lack of undercoat is a serious fault.

Mustache and Beard

Very thick, with the hair being shorter and rougher on the upper side of the muzzle. The upper lip, with its heavy mustache and the chin with its heavy and rough beard gives that gruff expression so characteristic of the breed.

Eyebrows

Erect hairs accentuating the shape of the eyes without ever veiling them.

Color

From fawn to black, passing through salt and pepper, gray and brindle. A small white star on the chest is allowed. Other than chocolate brown, white, or parti-color, which are to be severely penalized, no one color is to be favored.

Height

The height as measured at the withers: Dogs, from 24½ to 27½ inches; bitches, from 23½ to 26½ inches. In each sex, the ideal height is the median of the two limits, i.e., 26 inches for a dog and 25 inches for a bitch. Any dog or bitch deviating from the minimum or maximum limits mentioned shall be severely penalized.

Gait

The whole of the Bouvier des Flandres must be harmoniously proportioned to allow for a free, bold and proud gait. The reach of the forequarters must compensate for and be in balance with the driving power of the hindquarters. The back, while moving in a trot, will remain firm and flat. In general, the gait is the logical demonstration of the structure and build of the dog. It is to be noted that while moving at a fast trot, the properly built Bouvier will tend to single-track.

Temperament

As mentioned under general description and characteristics, the Bouvier is an equable dog, steady, resolute and fearless. Viciousness or shyness is undesirable.

Faults

The foregoing description is that of the ideal Bouvier des Flandres. Any deviation from this is to be penalized to the extent of the deviation

Approved June 10, 1975

Spencer Jordina v d Boevers Garden IPO III
Dutch & International Champion

Sire: D Ch Hoscy Dukke Bianca fan it Hanenhiem
Dam: Jordina Bretta v d Boevers Garden
Breeder & owner: Theo de Wagenaar

Theo de Wagenaar has set the standard in Holland, breeding and training two male Bouviers, Spencer and Halvar, who became not only spectacular conformation winners, but also held the most advanced Schutzhund or IPO degrees.

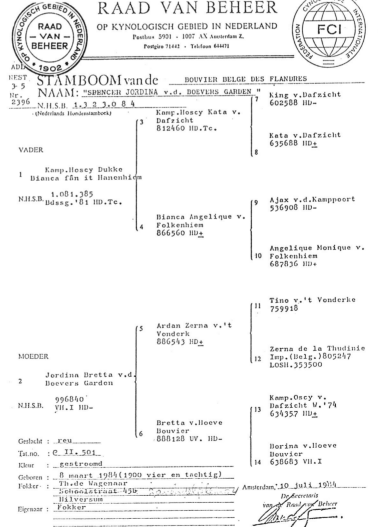

Pretty picture of a "van Dafzicht" Bouvier.

CHAPTER THREE

In Search of the Bouvier

Dogs are acquired and kept for diverse reasons. Unfortunately, many people fail to take dog ownership seriously, and they acquire and dispose of dogs casually according to transient wants and desires. The consequences of this for the individual dog can be cruel, for he may be abandoned or taken to a "shelter" where he is more likely than not "put to sleep."

Thus, the preliminary step for a person contemplating dog ownership should be to examine his or her motivations and be certain that he or she is prepared to make the commitment in terms of time, inconvenience, and disruption of life-style to care properly for a dog. The Bouvier is large, demanding, and assertive and thus poses a greater commitment than other breeds. The purpose here is to assist a person seeking a dog in determining whether a Bouvier is likely to provide for his or her needs and desires.

It goes without saying that not everyone with the cash should own a Bouvier, for the price should also include a commitment to the dog and to his development and training. There is certainly nothing wrong with doing your research and concluding that you would rather own a Rottweiler, a Labrador Retriever, a Standard Poodle, or a cat.

Nothing on earth can compare to the joy of a puppy, the vision of future success on the sport field or in the show ring, and, most of all, the simple innocent joy of the creature itself. Each pup is unique, a new venture, something that has never been before and can never be again. Pups in the natural order of things grow into dogs, and to regret the rapidity of the process is natural but futile. Much of the charm of puppyhood is in its brevity, as with the spring flowers of the fields.

Some pups grow up to fulfill the hopes of their beginning, and others in some way fall short as they mature. Most of us have watched a pup grow and have wondered if the bite would hold, if the animal would be too large or too small, if he would track, or if he would have courage and character. Perfection

is not of this world, for each pup in some ways — hopefully minor — falls short. How can a person acquire a pup with the greatest likelihood of satisfaction with the dog that he is to become?

The key, simple as it may sound, is in knowing what it is that you want, for vague or unrealistic expectations can only lead to disappointment. People who want a guard dog but want to be sure that he won't bite anybody or disturb the neighbors by barking have serious problems to resolve before buying a pup. Once you nail down a general idea of what you want in a dog, you need to know as much as possible about the breeds that you find attractive and make an informed choice. You can then begin the process of selecting a breeder and an individual pup.

When all of these hurdles have been cleared, it comes down to what you put into the dog in terms of care, understanding, and training. Each pup's owner plays a vital role in the pup's development and growth and must bear much of the responsibility for the ultimate product. Although much is predestined by the genetic background, it is easy but unfair and unrealistic to blame all shortcomings on the pup's breeding. While this is true with all dogs, it is especially important that a person who lives with a serious working breed understand all that must be done in order for the pup to realize his potential.

Much of the character of the adult Bouvier is the consequence of his environment, that is, how he is raised, trained, and disciplined. Character is a function of upbringing as well as of inherited genetic potential, and those unwilling to put in time and effort should not select a utility-breed dog. Assertive, strong dogs — like fast and powerful automobiles — are among life's greatest pleasures but are potentially dangerous when treated as casual diversions. The Bouvier is not, and should not be, a dog for everyone, but rather a special dog preserved for those able to appreciate the heritage and willing to take on the responsibility.

The Right Stuff

The Bouvier des Flandres has a strong protective character, comparable in some ways with that of a good German Shepherd or Rottweiler. Proper specimens of these utility breeds are protective by their very nature, and if the individual does not possess the innate instinct to defend home and family, then he is not a true specimen of the breed. The Bouvier protectiveness and the potential for aggression are essential attributes, and the specimen lacking these qualities is fundamentally flawed. Thus, those who desire a Bouvier because of the historical working functionality, whether for utilitarian or aesthetic reasons, must select a breeder and an individual dog carefully in order to avoid a dud — an empty shell that looks like a Bouvier but that lacks the soul.

None of this is meant to imply that the Bouvier (or the Doberman or the German Shepherd) is to be a savage dog that only a big, strong man with a whip and a chair should own. It is not necessary to physically dominate a dog; in fact, the dog that requires such treatment to maintain control is a bad individual, regardless of breed. Many police and sport dogs are also family dogs, and many are trained successfully by women of moderate physical stature. Thus, demanding that the Bouvier be protective and aggressive does not imply that he should be some sort of attack machine. On the contrary, it implies a willingness to take as his own the interests of his people. An affinity for casual aggression for its own sake renders a dog useless and dangerous.

It may seem contradictory to describe the Bouvier as being a powerful and effective protector, yet at the same time being somewhat inhibited in biting a human being. The essence of real protectiveness — as opposed to the macho strutting and pretense — is in the measured response. The Bouvier will typically bark a warning and follow up with a jab of the foot or a block of the shoulder, and only then will he escalate the level of aggression.

While a really good Bouvier is strong and protective, his equitable nature and inherent stability render him eminently suitable for participation in the typical American household. The Bouvier can be an excellent family member for those willing to put out a moderate amount of effort in training and understanding. He is also an exciting working partner for those who have the need and desire for an effective working dog.

Many breeders tout show-ring success, as evidenced by resident champions and this or that "win." Such goals are certainly relevant but are not definitive indicators of quality. The AKC championship is a "beauty contest;" there is no working or character test or even the most elementary medical screening. Champions

may be token — kept on hand but not essential to the breeding program — and perhaps are not even related to the pups being offered for sale. The professional handler can be hired to put the mantle on relatively nondescript animals. Dog shows should be a means to the end of better dogs, but, unfortunately, for many people the dogs are but a means to the end of fulfilling vanity, with the show win becoming an end in and of itself.

At the other extreme are those who would have you believe that, because their dogs are so ugly and/or oversized that they would surely lose to a pig in a beauty contest, they must by definition be superior working dogs. This is, of course, nonsense, for ugly does not equate to good at work anymore than size is a measure of the proper protective potential. The 130-pound dog could perhaps be powerful and properly aggressive, but he may also be a fat, lazy brute. Working temperament is proven on the sport field, and those who would deny this, or who would whine about the "right" form of competition not being available, usually know in their hearts that their dogs would be apt to fail a truly valid test.

Working potential is, in fact, infinitely more than the willingness to lunge and snarl on the end of a lead, to take a close-in bite of the sleeve, or to bark when safely behind a fence. It is a multifaceted combination of physical and mental attributes, including good hips, correct size, a correctly aligned and powerful bite, courage, stamina, responsibility, and endurance. Above all, the great dog has the almost undefinable quality of heart — the ability to come back one more time — which elevates a dog (or a man) above his peers.

There are significant and fundamental variations in the quality of Bouviers offered for sale, which makes the task of choosing a pup difficult and complex. Those seeking a serious working or sport dog face special difficulties, because very few North American breeders have the experience to breed and select such dogs. Persons seeking a Bouvier because of the historical working character, and who are attracted to the breed because of the strong working tradition, should be wary of breeders whose only standard of excellence is conformation-show success. They should seek out breeders who train their breeding stock and who compete with them on the sport field.

Although I dislike the term "pet," it is nevertheless true that most dogs serve as family companions. In my opinion, the companion dog should be selected according to the same general guidelines as for the breeding-potential, working/show dog. Presumably, the character and physical attributes that attract you to the breed are important to you, or you would not have read this far. When selecting from our own litters, we make a real effort to place the high-energy, active pups with people who will most appreciate them and work with them. We find that the slightly less energetic, more laid-back dogs do very well in the typical family situation.

Selecting a Breeder

The traditional advice to the person seeking a pup is to "go to an established breeder with a proven record and a good reputation." However, the trouble with this is that a "proven record" is often understood to mean success in the show ring, and a "good reputation" means that the customers are satisfied with

even approaches the true Bouvier essence. Ugly, dull, and timid "Bouviers" are offered for sale. To avoid becoming the owner of such a dog, you must be able to tell the difference, because ugly, dull, and/or timid parents are likely to produce get with these same undesirable attributes. As ye sow, so shall ye reap!

People who are simply looking for a Bouvier as a family companion should seek out a breeder with happy, confident, healthy-appearing dogs. The pups should come with tails done, ears cropped, and a health guarantee. Those interested in a working or show dog should look to breeders who have been successful in these arenas. This seems almost too obvious, but time after time, people pay big money for a "show-quality" or "working-potential" pup from

Public Relations Duty: Pete Rademacher of Rodsden Kennels with Dux v.d.Blume and Kathy Engel with Centauri's Gambit after a Schutzhund protection demonstration at the Chicago Internationl AKC show in 1987. Both dogs are Schutzhund III as well as AKC conformation Champions. *Photo Steve Monyko.*

the dogs that they have purchased. If you want and need such a dog, well and good. But such things are essentially irrelevant to the person seeking a working dog.

In America, people involved with the working breeds are deeply divided. There are breeders who value true functionality, and breeders who would have you believe that "things are different over here" in America and that working dogs do not have to be able to work. Breeders who rely solely on show results to guide their program are much less likely to produce effective working dogs, and the deeper the pedigree is in "only for show" animals, the less the likelihood of a decent character. Not every dog with "Bouvier des Flandres" on his registration form lives up to or

a breeder who has never finished a Champion or put a Schutzhund title on a dog.

The key element for the novice is to select a good breeder, and in this context, "good" means honest, knowledgeable, and dedicated. Such a person is reasonably certain to provide a good companion Bouvier or make the situation right if unforeseen problems should develop. Many refer to the various national canine magazines, which, in fact, provide a convenient guide to some of the more active and larger breeders. But there is no reason to be overly impressed with such an ad, for anybody with the cash can run one.

Seek out and select from among breeders whose real interests and ideals correspond to your own.

Many have "show dogs" — some better, some worse. A lesser number also breed the Bouvier as a functional working dog. If you are seeking a Bouvier for work or competition, look for litters with parents and grandparents that have working titles as proof of correct character.

In the past few years, many Americans have purchased European Rottweilers or German Shepherds with Schutzhund titles and have gone into the business of selling working dogs. The problem with this is that while on paper many litters are impressive, the results often are not. Unfortunately, many of those doing the breeding are not knowledgeable of lines, do not know

"It's great down here in Florida, and Dad says it's where all the bitches are!" (Gambit's retirement portrait.)

how to select the best pups, and do not provide the early environment that is so important to the young working dog. A variation on the theme is the imported stud dog that is bred to every bitch in the city, most of modest quality. When looking for a pup, experienced breeders and trainers look first at the quality of the bitch, because she influences the pups in the whelping box when the stud is long out of the picture.

Many Bouvier enthusiasts were attracted to the breed by the vision of the strong, honest, trustworthy dogs of the stockman. To find such a dog, you must

patronize a breeder who shares it, who trains his dogs, who competes with them in a credible arena, and finally, who breeds dogs that have stood up to the test and proven fidelity to the heritage, and thus that have earned the right to carry it on. Many pay lip service to temperament and character, but talk is cheap. The buyer must beware and believe 10 percent of what he or she is told and only half of what is seen.

At the most primitive level, a breeder is simply someone who puts a dog and a bitch together at the right time and lets nature take its course. Dogs are bred and shown to fulfill many needs. The soul of any breed, the heart of the gene pool, has always been in the hands of a few iron-willed, long-term breeders, rarely numbering as many as fifty worldwide. If you are serious about the Bouvier and have thoughts of more than companion ownership in the back of your mind, then you must determine for yourself who these people are and act accordingly.

Screening Out Hereditary Problems

Hip dysplasia is an abnormality of the hip joints that occurs in virtually all large canine breeds. Elbow dysplasia is a similar but usually less common and serious affliction. External manifestations range from the literally crippled dog, one that cannot stand up by himself or go up a set of stairs, to virtually no visible impairment. There is no question that the tendency to develop dysplasia is an inherited defect that is much more likely to occur in a dog whose ancestors suffered from the affliction. Thus, the solution to the problem is, as much as possible, to use dysplasia-free dogs in breeding programs.

Environment also plays an important role in the development of dysplasia. Oversupplementation of the young dog, encouraging unnaturally rapid growth, can greatly increase the incidence and severity of the affliction.

One of the frustrations is that dogs evaluated through radiography as severely dysplastic can sometimes exhibit no or only slightly discernible external manifestations. I know of a number of successful sport dogs, active at four years of age or more, that, in fact, had very poorly conformed hips. Other dogs with similar defects are functionally crippled.

There are those who claim that, because some dogs function well in spite of poorly rated hips, the hip dysplasia problem is being inflated. Nothing could be further from the truth, because these dogs are likely to produce offspring with greater-than-normal propensity for the defect. The seven- or eight-month-old pup, the new friend of a child and a loved family

The charm of puppyhood!

member, having to be put down because he simply cannot walk or stand normally is sad indeed.

Bouviers, especially big strong males, can have incredible pain tolerance and go about their business when any vet would immediately hospitalize them. We once took a young male to the vet for a routine examination, intending to mention that he seemed to be "not quite right" and was somewhat reluctant in his road work. Before we could get down to details, the vet put a stethoscope to the dog's chest, turned white, and asked, "How often does he fall down?" The animal turned out to have a serious heart defect, and although he survived corrective experimental surgery, he was eliminated from the breeding program. Although the indomitable character of the Bouvier is one of his most prized attributes, because of it, you must be watchful for the least sign of trouble.

Some breeders say that the Bouvier, or at least *their* Bouviers, never have dysplastic hips. I recall a young lady who had a bitch from a well-known breeder. She approached us about a stud service for this bitch. When we mentioned that we would have to see the X-rays, she said that there was nothing to worry about — that these lines were free of dysplasia and that the breeder had already provided a stud service for a previous litter. We insisted, and a day or two later we received a tearful phone call; it seems that the bitch was severely dysplastic. Nobody has lines "free of dysplasia," but by proper selection, many breeders have been able to reduce the incidence.

Several generations of dogs certified by the Orthopedic Foundation for Animals (OFA) as free of dysplastic changes enhance the likelihood of produc-

ing dysplasia-free pups. The OFA is an organization based at the University of Missouri that is helping breeders to control dysplasia. X-rays of the hips are sent in and evaluated. Owners with dogs found free of dysplasia are issued a certificate with a rating of excellent, good, or fair hip conformation.

There is a natural and desirable tendency for evaluation agencies, such as the OFA, to gradually tighten up their standards. The key word here is "gradual," for if the process is moved too fast, the breeding community cannot keep up and maintain type and character. We must have balance, that is, put a gradually rising floor under acceptable hip configuration while at the same time making corresponding progress in refining type and strengthening character.

Our practice is to do a preliminary X-ray at about one year, even though it is not possible to get a certificate until the dog is two years old. We find that there is rarely a major change between one and two years. Local veterinarians vary widely in their ability to evaluate hips. Do not ever put down or otherwise eliminate a young dog with no clinical symptoms without getting a second or even a third expert opinion!

If you are a potential Bouvier owner, take this problem seriously. Inquire about the OFA status of the parents and the grandparents, and about what guarantee there will be on the pup; in other words, what will the breeder do if the pup becomes afflicted?

The other major Bouvier problem that I believe has a strong genetic predisposition is gastric torsion (bloat), which is the turning of the stomach or intestines within the body cavity, quickly producing an unpleasant death. Although in recent years surgical correction has in many instances been successful, the problem is serious and should be a breeding consideration.

Laryngeal paralysis, a throat defect that interferes exists. There are problems with uterine inertia and pyrometria but no clear indication that these occur with frequency or with genetic predisposition among the Bouvier. Thyroid-level problems seem to crop up in certain lines, but again, hard evidence for incidence

A Madrone Ledge puppy in a basket!

with swallowing and barking, was a serious problem in certain Dutch lines a few years ago but was caught early and seems to have been pretty much eliminated. There have been sporadic reports of subaortic stenosis, a heart-valve defect, but no clear pattern levels or genetic relationships are hard to determine. On the whole, I think that the Bouvier is not especially plagued by genetic problems and that the more responsible breeders have done well in dealing with those about which we know.

Making the Purchase

Once the breed has been determined and a pup selected, the question of price arises. Price is a matter of agreement, for ultimately a dog is worth what someone is willing to pay. As in all matters of commerce, breeders will ask what they think they can get. The purchaser who is knowledgeable of the market and the breed will best be able to realistically evaluate quality and thus get the most for his or her money.

A written guarantee or contract is a good idea, not so much so that you will be able to enforce it in a court of law, but rather so that you will understand exactly what you can expect the breeder to do if defects show up as the pup grows. It is not a bad idea to do a little "comparison shopping" before you get emotionally attracted to a particular pup. Most breeders will replace a pup that turns out to be dysplastic, but some make no guarantee at all. If you are asked to pay more than half of the going price for a pup without a guarantee, you ought to give the proposition the most critical thought before going ahead.

Most breeders make a distinction between show- and/or work-quality and companion-potential pups. These breeders tend toward replacing a dog with a serious defect or in some instances refunding part of the purchase price. A really detailed written contract is especially desirable from the buyer's point of view, because a lot more money is at stake.

Do not be in a hurry to buy, and do not be lured into taking home a cute pup before your research is complete. The better breeder will welcome your diligence and will be confident that the more knowledgeable you become, the more likely you are to become his client. High-pressure salesmanship is likely to come from one who knows that his or her product and/or price cannot stand up under knowledgeable scrutiny; if you cannot be pushed into taking the pup home, you are unlikely to be back.

By long-standing custom, the Bouvier is delivered with the tail docked and ears cropped, both of which are the responsibility of the conscientious breeder. The breeder who offers ear cropping only as an optional, extra-cost item should in general be avoided. The tail is done a few days after birth and will be all set when you get your pup, but the ears may have been done wtihin a week or so of delivery and may thus require some care to ensure correct, upright carriage. The rear dewclaws (if present) should also have been removed. The front ones are optional, and we normally leave them in the belief that they aid in manipulating objects.

We have on one or two occasions sold an uncropped pup to someone who was adamantly opposed to the practice, although there was no reduction in price.

Also, we often will send a pup home with a local client at about eight weeks and then have him returned in two or three weeks for the ear cropping. We generally like to keep the pup for at least forty-eight

San Bernardino Deputy Sheriff David Barron with police canine "Rouska".

hours after cropping to make sure that there are no complications from the anesthetic.

Once the pup and price are established, you must attend to a number of business matters before you can take him home. You should receive the proper "papers," that is, the American Kennel Club (AKC) (or CKC) registration form. You will send this in with the chosen name and the other necessary information for official registration so that you can exhibit the dog in a conformation show or compete in a working trial. Registration is, of course, essential should you ever breed your Bouvier.

Canadian procedures are similar to the American, and a dog can be registered in several countries. Note carefully that registration has nothing to do with ownership; no kennel club can settle disputes about who actually owns a dog. Being the registered owner of a dog does not necessarily mean that your legal right to him will be recognized in a court of law. Thus, while you do not ordinarily receive a bill of sale with a pup, it is not a bad idea to ask for one.

Both the Canadian and American kennel clubs now issue registration certificates that do not allow the offspring of the animal to be registered. These are appropriate where specific defects or overall quality render the dog unsuitable for reproduction.

Finally, although there is a natural tendency to prefer a pup, so as to share the joy of watching him grow into a fine young Bouvier, do not automatically preclude the acquisition of an older dog. You will have a much more accurate idea of what you are getting, and this can be crucial if you are seeking breeding stock or a sport-competition candidate.

The Name

When filling in the registration papers, use great care in selecting and entering the name, for once the form is in the mail, it can never be changed. While the registered name is in many instances long and formidable, the "call" name need not necessarily be part of it. The call name should be short and easy to project out-of-doors and should not sound like any of the commonly used obedience commands. Avoid "cute" names, and select a name appropriate to the adult Bouvier.

By custom, the breeder's kennel name is incorporated into the formal name; the breeder is proud of his or her program and wants others to know where

Ch Centauri's Griffe des Cerberes, primary stud at Belco Farm in the mid-eighties. Bred by Dr. Erik Houttuin. Sired by Dutch Work.Ch. Donar SchH III, FH x Ch & Work.Ch Centauri's Fleur de Lis SchH III. Owned by Jim Engel & Bruce Jacobsohn. Shown with Mr. Jacobsohn.

the dog came from. Many also follow the Belgian convention of using a first letter in the other part of the name to indicate the year of birth. As an example, Rico de la Thudinie is a prominent stud of Justin Chastel, one of the Bouvier breed founders in Belgium. The "R" in Rico indicates that the dog was born in 1968, and Thudinie is Mr. Chastel's kennel name. It is taken from the name of the village on the river Sambre, "Thuin," near Charleroi in Belgium, where Chastel has been a pillar of the breed for more than half a century.

As further examples, Cayce du Clos des Cerberes whelped in 1978, and Centauri's Gambit was born in 1982. Other breeders use letters sequentially for litters rather than according to the year of birth. The Dutch typically use the dam's name as a second name.

The mother of Halvar Bretta van de Boevers Garden, for example, is Bretta van Hoeve Bouvier. The Dutch convention is a matter of custom that is followed only part of the time, while the Belgian system is imposed by the kennel club.

Indeed, the only exception that I can find in the Belgian registry from 1944 until the present is the bitch Wandru des Coudreaux, who whelped in France in 1948 and was imported by Emee Bowles in the early 1950s. She subsequently went on to play a pivotal role in Bowles's "du Clos des Cerberes" breeding program at Belco Farm. Because at that time the AKC would not recognize the French registration, the bitch was registered in Belgium by Verbanck, something that to my knowledge has never been done before nor since. Such was the stature of Bowles in the

Ch Dejoy Totem Bear At Wahkenna CD, TDX
First TDX (Tracking Dog Excellent) Bouvier, owned & trained by Helen Wilson, Bred by Denny Criss.

Tory, Ch. Vacher's Alpha Centauri, about to make contact with agitator David Dodd. (This dog was the first Champion/ Schutzhund III Bouvier in America, as well as the first to hold the coveted "FH", the advanced Schutzhund tracking title.)

eyes of the Europeans!

One of my primary sources of names comes from a collection of pedigrees and various European registration books — there is a certain satisfaction and a sense of the Bouvier heritage in knowing that the name of your dog is taken from a progenitor who played a prominent role in the evolution of the breed.

In addition to the registration forms, you should receive a pedigree, which is the family tree with the name of the sire and dam and the other direct ancestors, back four or perhaps five generations. Not only will it be interesting to know about your dog's roots, but this information is vital should you ever contemplate breeding.

The Prospective Bouvier Owner's Checklist

The Breeders
1. Are they patient and willing to answer your questions? Can they provide credible answers to your questions?
2. Have others with this breeder's dogs been satisfied? Everybody breeding dogs eventually has some unhappy clients, so do not take one bad report as definitive, but rather as an indication that more research is in order.

3. What happens when things don't go well — when a pup turns out to be dysplastic or has other serious congenital defects? Are such dogs replaced? Is the replacement truly of comparable quality? Will you get anything in writing?

4. Does the breeder train; does the breeder have dogs that can demonstrate proficiency in the work of the breed? Does the breeder have knowledge of protection and tracking? Do his or her dogs hold relevant working titles?

5. Do all of the dogs appear reasonably clean and well cared for?

6. If multiple litters are on the premises, are the separated or clearly marked so that you can be sure of an accurate pedigree?

7. Are you certain that you will receive proper registration papers?

8. Are the ears to be cropped and the tail docked when the pup is delivered?

9. If the dam is not on the premises, who actually whelped and raised the pups?

10. Is the breeder willing and able to provide follow-up assistance with grooming, handling, and training?

11. Will the breeder recommend other kennels to visit?

12. Exactly what does the breeder guarantee?

13. Do you trust the breeder?

The Sire and the Dam

1. What is the state of the hips of the parents? Are the parents free from hip dysplasia? Have they been X-rayed? Are they OFA certified? What about the grandparents and the previous pups?

2. Are the teeth correctly aligned, large, white, and strong? Is the bite correct, neither over nor undershot?

3. How do the sire and dam compare structurally to the ideal as described in the standard?

4. Are both parents confident and approachable? You should be able to thoroughly examine each one, put your hands all over, and feel the substance and coat texture. This is particularly true of protection-trained dogs, whose stability should be above reproach. If you cannot approach the dog, not only is the structure unknown, but the temperament must be seriously questioned.

5. Ask to have both parents gaited. Is the stride smooth, powerful, and reaching? When brought to a halt, does the dog naturally stand square, upright, and confident, and is he broad both front and rear?

6. Do the sire and/or dam hold relevant working titles, such as the Schutzhund degree, as proof of working potential?

7. Will the breeder allow you to gun-test the parents? If so, are they alert, seeking out the source of the noise, or do they show fear?

8. Is the color correct? White, cream, or any other washed-out colors are serious defects.

9. Is the topline straight, with the tail set correctly as an extension of the backbone? There should be no dip before the tail.

10. Overall, are the sire and dam confident, approachable, good-looking, and moving — the kind of Bouviers with which you want to share your home?

The Puppy

1. Does he appear to be in general good health?

2. Is he up-to-date on his inoculations?

3. Are the ears cropped? Do they appear to have healed properly? Do they match?

4. Does he appear to be lively and energetic?

5. Does the pup seem interested in people? Is he curious and approachable? The independent pup is apt to grow into the aloof adult, which is all right up to a point.

6. Is the pup large or small compared to the littermates?

7. Is the color correct?

8. Is the bite correct?

9. If a male, are both testicles descended?

10. Does the entire litter seem to be of good, consistent quality?

Ch Nack du Clos des Cytises, OFA. Imported by Marion Hubbard and Judy Higgins in 1982, Nack became a very influential stud.

Henk Harmers' Gillroy is an outstanding example of his Cerberushof line.

Gillroy Kelly v d Cerberushof
Champion of Holland & Dutch Specialty Winner.
NHSB.1104738A
Sire: D Ch Picard Generique v h Lampegat
Dam: Kelly Dusty v d Cerberushof
Born: 1980

Caring For Your Bouvier

The New Puppy

The Trip Home

Bringing the new Bouvier pup into your home should be a joyful occasion. The reaction of the pup will depend on the individual, on his background, and on his age. Some are a little fearful in the beginning, but others acclimate quickly. We had an eight-week-old female that marched out of her traveling basket straight up to the two resident adults and barked (her meaning being clear): "I'm here suckers; you two can compete for second place!"

The trip home may be traumatic, because the pup has probably never been away from his littermates except to have his tail and ears cropped. He may be frightened and may need your reassurance, particularly if he has been shipped by air.

Make the pup's transition as smooth and pleasant as possible. Provide a comfortable, reassuring environment the first days and weeks, and you will be rewarded by a rapid acclimation into your home and family life. Participating in the pup's maturing into a handsome, confident young Bouvier can and should be a special joy.

When You Arrive Home

When you arrive home, take the pup to a quiet, confined, warm place and offer him water and a chance to relieve himself in a place that will always be appropriate. Stay with him until he begins to relax, and keep the kids and other dogs at bay for the moment. This is not some sort of new toy; the pup's needs must come first. Allow him to sleep in a secure place that has been prepared ahead of time. After a couple of hours, offer him food, but do not be concerned if he is not interested.

It is important to get off to a good start and to understand that you are establishing lifelong behavior patterns. The pup immediately starts to sort out what is permissible and desirable and what is not allowed.

He does this according to your reactions; therefore, encourage correct behavior from the beginning and gently show him what is not allowed.

When the pup leaves the place where he was born and spent the first few weeks of life, he is subjected to many radical changes. It is wise not to alter his diet at the same time. The breeder should provide a small bag of the pup's food to tide you over until you can obtain some of the same variety, if you have not already done so. Be certain that you understand the feeding instructions and schedule so that his routine will be normal. You should also receive a record of the medical history so that your vet will know about the pup's inoculations, worming, and any other medical details.

Visiting the Vet

Visit your veterinarian's office as soon as possible (on the way home if practical), and have the vet examine the pup. The conscientious breeder will make every effort to provide an animal in good condition, and in most instances, the vet will be able to assure you of the pup's good health. On occasion, the vet may find something that only his or her special skills can detect. A reputable breeder will of course accept the return of a pup that fails a physical examination within twenty-four hours of delivery. If a problem occurs, it is best to find it immediately so that the pup can be returned and the breeder can deal with it as soon as possible. Also, because of his or her knowledge of special problems in your region, the vet may have particular instructions for the care of your pup. Ask the vet about the local incidence of heartworms.

If you have no resident dogs, you may not have a vet, in which case you should talk with one or several ahead of time. A good relationship with a medical practitioner in whom you can develop real confidence is vital. How well you relate to the person is as important as the vet's technical skills, and if you are not comfortable with one individual, try another.

Ch Cynosure Kingpin from Cynosure Kennels.
Photo courtesy Russell and Vicki Jacobs.

Avoiding Danger

For the puppy, many dangers lurk in every home: electrical cords to chew, people to step on him, and stairs to fall down. The house and its contents may also be in danger from the marauding pup. If you fall asleep while he is loose, you may awake to find that your shoes have been chewed and the curtains have been pulled down. A pup going through the teething process has a strong urge to chew. As much as possible, provide safe outlets for puppy energy. A fenced backyard or a puppy-proof room are useful. Also, provide items that he is allowed to chew, such as bones and rawhide chew bones. Your personal attention, however will be his favorite diversion.

Crating Your Pup

There will be times, of course, when the pup must be confined. One good way is to use a crate. Crates are available commercially, and those used for air shipment are perfectly acceptable. The crate is a good, safe place for the pup to spend the night or an hour or two during the day when he cannot be supervised. It should be big enough to allow an adult dog to turn around easily. While routine crating of the adult is unusual, on occasion it is convenient to do so. Many dogs prefer to sleep in a crate with an open door.

Follow these guidelines for safe and effective use of the crate:

1. The pup should always be put out immediately to relieve himself when he is released from the crate.

2. The crate must never be left in direct sunlight; the dark coat makes this particularly important for the Bouvier.
3. Remove the collar before crating a dog.
4. Don't put anything in or on the crate that the dog should not chew.
5. A child or other dog must never be allowed to tease a crated dog.

Crates are also useful in a vehicle, to keep the dog from doing damage and from interfering with the driver. But do not expose the dog to direct sunlight in warm weather. Never leave a dog in a parked car in warm weather, because the rapidly accumulating heat can cause a *very* unpleasant death in only a few minutes.

If you work and the pup is crated during the day, you may want to confine him at night by attaching him to your bed by a short lead and buckle collar. Make sure that there is nothing within reach that he can chew. An old rug can save your carpet in case of an accident. Do not leave a tied pup, because he can chew through the lead and can possibly choke himself.

Do not overuse the crate. If you continually crate the pup because it is inconvenient to have him loose, then perhaps you should not have acquired the pup in the first place. When properly managed, the pup will not resent the crate but will come to regard it as his retreat. He will typically go into it to sleep on his own accord.

If You Work

Today, many dogs are owned by single people or by working couples. In this situation, the dog must be able to do without attention for perhaps sixteen hours a day, when his owners are asleep or at work. "Quality time" is an expression that has been worked to death, but the basic concept is still valid. If you give the dog attention in the morning and really devote an hour to him most evenings (by taking a long walk, for instance), he will be content. To make this work, he needs extra attention on the weekends so that he can feel as if he is a regular part of your life. Training him for obedience or working competition is, of course, ideal.

If you work, you either need to arrange for the pup to be taken out once during the day or leave him someplace where he can relieve himself. Ten hours is just too long to tightly confine a dog in a crate. Most adult dogs can be left loose in the house all of the time.

Housebreaking

Teaching the pup where he can relieve himself requires good planning, perseverance, and family cooperation. Some pups are easy and are, in fact, virtually housebroken from the beginning. Others present more of a problem. If bad habits are allowed to take root, they are likely to persist. It is most desirable to start your training program immediately when the pup arrives.

If you think that the pup may have to go, select an acceptable outdoor area and take him out on a leash if the area is not fenced. Later, when the dog is obedience trained, he will be able to go out off lead.

Take the pup out when you let him out of his crate, after each meal, before retiring for the evening, and whenever he seems restless or goes to the door. As he grows older, his control will improve, but you still will need to watch him carefully.

When he produces something, even the slightest amount, praise him. Tell him to "hurry up" when he produces; then you can use those words when traveling or are otherwise in a hurry. Do not confuse going out to relieve himself with play periods; otherwise, he will wake you up in the middle of the night to go out and play!

Even if your yard is enclosed, take the pup out on lead some of the time. On occasion, such as when you are traveling, you have to keep him on leash. Some dogs get the idea that being taken off lead is the signal to go and refuse to produce otherwise.

When an accident occurs and the pup is caught in the act, take him by the ruff and show him what he did, telling him that he is bad. Don't spank him or put his nose in it — such punishment is not necessary. If you don't see him do it, there is not much point in punishing him, because the puppy's attention span is short. Clean up as thoroughly as possible, and be certain to remove the odor, because the pup will assume that it is alright to go where there are signs of previous usage. (Diluted white vinegar is an excellent deodorant.)

The crate is an effective adjunct to housebreaking, because even the youngest pup will usually not soil his own bed unless he simply cannot hold it.

Centauri's Eros at 7 weeks old.

Physical Conditioning

Proper physical conditioning is important for your Bouvier's health. Lack of exercise can be just as serious for your dog as it is for you. Incorporate exercise into the daily routine. If you jog, by all means take your Bouvier along. Jogging is an ideal solution both for the dog and for you. Naturally, don't take a pup twenty miles — he must gradually build up stamina. As a general rule, six to ten months is a good age to start. Let the dog set his own pace. If he wants to go and does not hold back or seem excessively tired, you are probably not overdoing it.

Always take even the best-behaved dog on a leash. You can't expect a dog to be near traffic off lead and not at some time make a tragic mistake. Also, you will inevitably meet other dogs, and you don't need your dog following them home to finish an argument. If you are approached by an aggressive dog, slow down, get a good grip on your leash, and face him. If he perceives you as running away, he may come after you. Very few dogs will attack you if you face them and make a show of confidence unless they perceive you as encroaching on their territory. At night I carry a long, cast-aluminum flashlight, the type used by police officers, because as a last resort it will be of some use for defense.

In summer, do not overextend the dog when the temperature is high, because he is more vulnerable to heat and humidity than a person in good physical condition. An effective approach is to run dogs very early in the morning, just after sunrise, or late in the evening, an hour or two after the sun has set and the temperature has dropped.

It is generally safe to take your Bouvier out in cold weather. My rule of thumb is that it is safe down to about five below zero (Fahrenheit) if the wind is light. (This means going out with you for exercise or training, not being left out in a run or yard.) Dogs that are not acclimated to such weather should not be left out for extended periods when they are forced to be inactive. They have no problem going out into the colder air when they are allowed to exercise and thus generate body heat. The Bouvier enjoys the colder weather; ours sleep by the draftiest door or window in the winter and worship at the air-conditioning vent in the summer.

As a last word of advice, avoid force. If a dog is reluctant to exercise, he should not normally be forced, at least until a thorough medical evaluation has eliminated physical problems.

Mad Dogs and Englishmen

Due to its coastal location and the influence of the Gulf current, the European low country is a land of moderate temperatures and overcast skies. The Bouvier is well adapted to this damp, cool weather, and allowances must be made when the Bouvier is kept in other climates. There is an old saying that only mad dogs and Englishmen are to be found out and about in the heat of an intense summer day. I will leave it to the English to defend themselves and note that the Bouvier will normally retreat to the coolest place that he can find during the middle of a sunny summer day and sleep it away. You are wise to respect this inclination and not engage in outdoor

training, vigorous exercise, or other strenuous activity in the hot sun. These precautions are particularly appropriate to the Bouvier because of his dark color. Bouviers on the whole are lethargic in warm weather.

Never "clip down" a dog with the idea that it will make him more comfortable in the summer. On the contrary, the outer coat is his best protection from the sun. (Desert inhabitants often wear light-colored, loosely fitting clothing rather than running around naked.) You will, of course, want to brush and comb out the undercoat, which will shed in the warmer weather.

Schedule training when the temperature is most appropriate. This means in the morning or in the evening on hot days. If you are fortunate enough to have access to a suitable lighted area, training at night is delightful in the summer. Have a hose or at least five gallons of water available to douse the dog in case he reacts badly to the heat.

Feeding Your Dog

Proper diet is important in maintaining your Bouvier's health. If the pup's rapid development is retarded by inadequate diet, the losses may never be recovered entirely. On the other hand, excessive protein levels, a too-rich diet, or oversupplementation can also be harmful. In particular, calcium added to the diet can accelerate any tendency toward dysplastic hips and should only be used under close medical supervision. On the whole, dogs in America probably suffer as often from too much as from too little calcium.

The basic component of most diets is dry dog food or kibble. This is a relatively economical way to provide good nutrition, and it also cleans your dog's teeth. A diet of all meat and soft food allows deposits to accumulate on the teeth and fails to provide proper balance. Avoid "moist" foods because of their sugar content and lack of teeth-cleaning action. Avoid any food with significant amounts of sugar.

When selecting a brand of kibble (or any other food), look for at least 24 percent protein. Seek advice from your pup's breeder or from other experienced people in your area. Most knowledgeable people tend to feed brands with a high-quality reputation that are available in feed stores rather than heavily advertised supermarket brands.

Incorporate a portion of meat into your Bouvier's diet, because it makes his food more palatable. A few dogs are not especially into eating and may be underweight if they find their food boring. Canned or freshly cooked boiled beef are desirable. Again, read the label on the can carefully, because it should be all meat and/or meat byproducts. An adult Bouvier needs a can, or a cup and a half, of freshly cooked meat per day. The bitch in whelp or rapidly growing youngster can require a great deal more.

The amount of food required depends on the dog's age, condition, activity level, and metabolic rate. The Bouvier is not an especially big eater; the adult nor-

Only when this fails and the animal shows a definite tendency toward becoming overweight should you consider stepping in and limiting consumption. The amount of food consumed by the pup will gradually increase, reaching a peak at six to twelve months and then leveling off into the young-adult pattern.

When a Bouvier is in proper trim, you can just

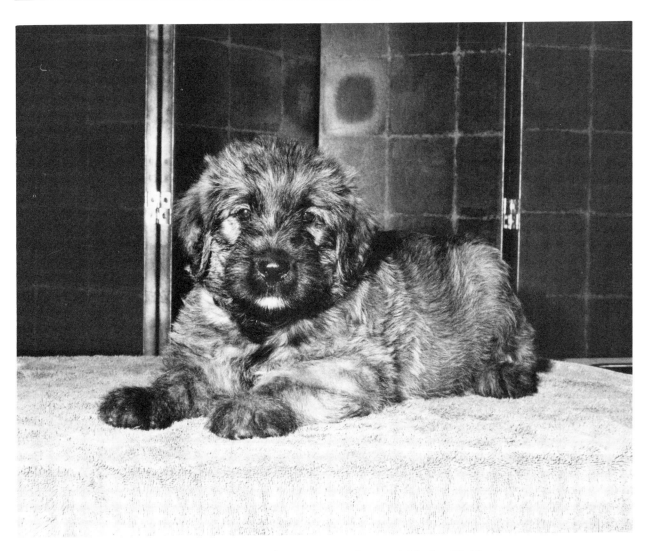

An adorable puppy. *Photo courtesy Ray and Marion Hubbard.*

mally consumes from two cups for the sedentary animal to six or more cups for the active individual, particularly those undergoing rigorous training.

How much should a pup eat? Unless he is overweight, as much as he wants. Differences in metabolism among different dogs are best accommodated by letting the pup's own system regulate intake.

barely feel the backbone. The animal that is chronically underweight should be examined by a vet for internal parasites or other physical problems. If he is healthy and active, accept his tendency to be on the lean side as a natural consequence of his genetic heritage.

Obesity in dogs is not unusual, but before you put

your obese dog on a diet, investigate the possible causes of his condition. Perhaps the most common causes are lack of physical activity and boredom. The dog confined to a run, as in a kennel situation, may eat because he simply has nothing else to do. Dogs in such circumstances are almost always fed a specific, measured amount. If Bouviers who live as home companions have similar problems, the most desirable solution is for him to spend more time with his people in vigorous activity, such as a training program or at play.

When and how to feed your dog depend on your life-style and common sense. The most important thing is that your dog eat when he is calm and relaxed. *It is vital that vigorous exercise or excitement not occur before or after a heavy meal.* An hour of inactivity before and three hours after is a reasonable guideline. Thus, the ideal dinner hour is when the dog is naturally quiet and relaxed. Unless it causes him to wake you up for trips out in the middle of the night, late evening is a good time for the main meal.

Many owners wish to supplement their pup's diet with minerals and vitamins. In doing so, they are no doubt motivated by a natural desire to provide the very best of care. However, supplementation may not be wise. In fact, excessive supplementation, particularly of minerals, can be harmful. Oversupplementation as a causative or exacerbating factor in hip dysplasia is strongly supported by research and by the opinions of most veterinarians. Many more dogs are probably damaged by oversupplementation than by a lack of proper vitamins or minerals. Your money is generally much better spent on a high-quality food.

If you are inclined to supplement, discuss this with your vet and follow his or her recommendations. Resist the temptation to up the dosage "just to be sure." If you cannot agree with one vet's advice, then find another with whom you can work. Do not change the dosage or type of additive without the vet's knowledge and still expect the vet to be responsible for your dog's health!

A number of health disorders, such as skin problems, "hot spots," and irritation, have been relieved substantially by switching from kibble with soybean content to one free of this ingredient. This is not scientific proof, but if you have persistent problems with several dogs, a little experimentation with diet may work wonders. If you are consulting a vet at the same time, be sure that he or she is aware of and approves the dietary changes. Behavioral problems may also be related to diet. In particular, the persistently determined chewer — the dog that will consume an entire rawhide bone without stopping — may be suffering from a nutritional deficiency. (See Koehler's basic obedience book listed in Further Reading.)

It is often beneficial to incorporate one tablespoon

of vegetable oil or cod-liver oil per day to improve the coat and help prevent dry skin. This may be necessary only in winter in cold climates.

Leftover human food can be incorporated to make the dog's food more interesting if the overall diet remains in balance. The practice of scraping out a pan from a roast into the dog dish, along with the dry food, provides a special treat. Cooked eggs and meat, cottage cheese, and small amounts of bread, rice, or noodles are acceptable, especially for the underweight dog. Avoid excessive amounts of sugar.

Never give a dog bones that can break up and lodge in the throat or intestine. Chicken or pork bones are an open invitation to disaster.

Breaking the rules once in a while does not do any particular harm. We like to buy an especially good dog a Dairy Queen. The joy of seeing a Bouvier eating the cone is magnificent!

Many groceries carry pet-food liver that can be boiled in slightly salted water for twenty minutes and then baked in a 325-degree oven for twenty minutes or until dry. It is then cut into pieces and kept in the refrigerator to be used as a special treat or as a reward in training. It is also a standard "bait" in the conformation ring.

The advice given here is general, and if you have any reason to doubt its applicability to your situation, consult your vet.

Working with Your Veterinarian

A sound working relationship with a good veterinarian is a key to success with your Bouvier. Good medical care is vital for the pup. Periodic health maintenance involves going in for whatever inoculations are necessary and at least semiannual stool checks for internal parasites. Bring any abnormality in physical function or behavior to the vet's attention. Good medical maintenance is not cheap, but it is an *obligation* when you acquire a dog.

The vet's task is much more difficult than that of the physician, because the vet's patients have no direct means of communicating what is wrong. Your dog depends on you to perceive a problem and to take him in. Your role should never be that of the passive bystander but rather the active participant, for your ability to accurately observe and report the dog's symptoms plays a major role in the vet's ability to quickly diagnose the cause of the problem.

Be aware of canine heartworms, parasites that live in the dog's bloodstream and that damage the heart, liver, and lungs. Previously confined mostly to the southern United States, heartworms have become common in many other regions and can occur any-

Ch Cayce du Clos des Cerberes, bred by Bowles & Jacobsohn at Belco Farm and owned by Christine Neves, was Best of Breed at the North American Championships in Detroit in 1984.

Vulcain du Clos des Cytises Ch
Lutteur de Val de Rol Ch; OFA '75
Tamise de Val de Rol LOF.13986 '70
Ch Cayce du Clos des Cerberes OFA '78
Dax du Clos des Cerberes Ch; '70
April du Clos des Cerberes OFA,TT '76
Ishtar du Clos des Cerberes Ch; '73

where. Do not assume that because you are not aware of a heartworm problem that they are not a danger to your dog. They are killers, and the first clinical sign may be a dead dog. Heartworms can be prevented; it is your responsibility to take the steps necessary to do so under your vet's guidance.

Cropped Ears

By long-standing tradition, the breeder delivers the Bouvier pup with the ears cropped and tail docked. Apparently, dogs with natural ears were taxed; also, the herd dog thus had an advantage when encountering a wolf or other predator. The cropped ears also contributed to the alert expression and to the prevention of various medical problems. Basically, however, Bouvier ears are cropped because the farmers who created the breed did so and because the modern founders of the breed created a tradition of cropped-eared dogs.

Advances in veterinary technology have rendered the ear cropping a minor surgical procedure, one causing relatively little pain or danger. The ears are generally done at about seven or eight weeks of age. In some instances, the ears are completely healed on delivery and no special care is required. At other times, the pup goes to his new home within a couple weeks of cropping and some care may be required. In this case, complete instructions should be provided by the breeder. In some instances, the pup will come with ears supported in order to ensure correct, upright carriage. Remove these supports according to the instructions given at the time of delivery.

If the ears drop over and stay down for more than a couple of days, contact the breeder for assistance. It is normal for some problems to develop during teething. In the event that further support becomes necessary, it should be done by a person with experience. A botched taping job, particularly one that cuts off circulation, can result in badly deformed ears and ruin the appearance of an otherwise handsome animal.

In the early eighties, no Bouvier in Europe attracted more attention than Theo de Wagenaar's Dutch Specialty winner, Halvar Bretta. Litter mate Jordina also did well in the ring, and, most importantly, in the welping box.

Tino van het Vonderke HD+ −
Ardan Zerna van het Vonderke HD+ − NHSB.886543
Zerna de la Thudinie NHSB.805247
Int Ch Halvar Bretta v d Boevers Garden Sch III Hd-
Oscy van Dafzicht D Ch; HD+ −
Bretta v Hoeve Bouvier SchH I HD- NHSB.888128
Borina van Hoeve Bouvier SchH II

One Big Happy Family

Puppy Training: Building Your Own Bouvier

An excellent dog results from a breeding program based on a sound genetic basis and from the pup growing up in an environment that enables him to fulfill his genetic potential. Hopefully, you have selected a breed, then particular lines, and finally a litter and pup according to your needs and desires. If so, then the die is cast with the odds in your favor. Much is predestined by genetic makeup, and only time will tell which of the ancestral traits predominate. But much is also in your hands, because the character of the adult remains for you to mold. In the first few months, your actions will shape much of the disposition, manners, and reactions of the adult.

If you are inexperienced and are primarily interested in a stable, confident family companion, your breeder should have selected a moderately active, middle-of-the-road pup suitable to your desires, and you should carry this out in your training. Your friend who is looking for a pup to train for serious obedience, police, or protection work will look for the most outgoing, aggressive, active pup he can find. He may go through several before he finds the one that can become the dog that he wants and needs. He will raise the dog with minimal restraint and maximum confidence building. There will be corrections to overt handler aggressiveness but a general avoidance of situations that require discipline. Tracking and preliminary obedience ideally begin at five to six months, emphasizing inducive methods and rewards. If the dog goes beyond the limits of acceptable behavior, he is brought back into line with minimal correction, to the point where many would consider the training overly permissive. Such an approach is appropriate to those with the requisite experience to know where to set the limits or the guidance of a competent instructor.

The point is that you should conduct your training program from the beginning according to your experience and objectives. If your goals are obedience or Schutzhund competition and you are a novice, seek the guidance of an experienced instructor. If you are primarily interested in a family companion, then you should be a little less permissive.

Just as the wolf pup learns through interaction with pack members (his extended family) to take on his role and responsibilities, the young Bouvier takes his place in the family and learns to respect the prerogatives of others if provided the proper environment and training. He will, of course, try to dominate as he becomes older, that is, as he becomes sexually mature. It is not unusual for a dog to take over and virtually run a family. It is his nature to do so. You must establish and maintain the leadership position in order not to wind up a follower. As we shall see, this is not a matter of brute strength but rather of attitude and training.

A child's intimate relationship with parents, siblings, and perhaps a few others from birth to five years of age immutably solidifies much of his or her character, temperament, and potential. Before even entering school, horizons are expanded or contracted according to the quality of personal relationships and shared experience. The Bouvier temperament and potential are similarly molded by early environment. Indeed, the only real difference is that the crucial period is measured in months rather than in years.

The child who is isolated and kept from contact with other children or adults fails to develop properly and has a great deal of difficulty in coping with the world. It should not come as a surprise that the same principle applies to a dog. The early weeks and months of life are critical to proper development. Puppies that reach twenty weeks of age isolated from human contact often have difficulty fitting in throughout their life. Experience denied at this stage can probably never be replaced in total.

By the time you bring your Bouvier puppy home, much of the formative process has already occurred through interaction with the mother, littermates, and hopefully, the breeder's family. To continue positive development, provide your pup with routine contact with new people and places. Examples include walking him in a park or through a shopping center and allowing your pup to go to training classes with the older dogs. Assuming that his inoculations are up-to-date, take every opportunity to bring the pup into close contact with people, other animals, and situations so that self-confidence can develop through familiarity with the world. This critical process is commonly referred to as socialization.

The pup should occasionally go along for an automobile ride and come to have pleasant associations with such excursions. When this is done, the dog is unlikely to be prone to car sickness.

Because the Bouvier was drawn from working stock dogs and was purposefully converted into a protection breed by the addition of guard-dog stock, it is natural that he take on the role of the family and household protector. As a young adult, he will begin to take his responsibilities seriously. It is essential that he learn to understand the circumstances under which an aggressive response is required. While the pup should be praised and encouraged when he barks at a stranger approaching the door, once the person is invited in, he becomes a guest whose rights must be respected.

It has sometimes been believed that by isolating the young dog, the protective capability is enhanced; the opposite principle in fact applies. The self-assured, confident animal that relates well to people is likely to be on hand when the time comes, while his isolated brother will likely be locked away when his services are needed. Also, the dog damaged by isolation may well lack the self-confidence to be of use even if he is present. If protection is to be part of your Bouvier's role, it is important that he be well socialized as a prerequisite to temperament evaluation and protection training.

Although the tone here has been a bit serious, actually applying the principles is most efffective through play. By getting down to the pup's level, literally and figuratively, rolling a ball to chase, tugging on the other end of a burlap sack (being careful of puppy teeth!), and roughhousing, you are building the confidence in both you and in your dog that is vital to future stability and training success. In fact, play periods can naturally evolve into training sessions. And play should actually remain a major element in even the most advanced and serious training. Tugging on the burlap sack evolves easily into protection training, games of hide-and-seek gradually become track-

Ch. Ciscoldo, shown with Della McNeilly

Brdr: Everet van de Pol
Sire: Dutch Ch. Basco Aleida v d Zaanhoeve
Dam: Silta
Whelped in 1947
Photo courtesy Marion Hubbard.

ing exercises, and ball playing remains a permanent and important element in obedience training. The pup will regard many of these games as contests, and you should see that he perceives himself as the winner.

When your pup is four to six months of age, you must apply an element of discipline, but with patience and with a light touch according to the maturity and nature of the individual dog. In order for your Bouvier to earn his niche and fulfill his role, you must respect his heritage and dignity. Your objective should be to establish a good working relationship based on mutual respect, not to force the dog into passive submissiveness.

In introducing the leash, you must help your pup to understand that rather than being a physical restraint, the leash serves as a guide and limit. The very young pup is encouraged to explore and develop confidence and is not really expected to respect the leash very much. But as he approaches six months of age, he must gradually be taught restraint. This is done by gently tugging or popping on the leash and then leaving slack. The pup will, of course, continue to lean into the leash, but by persistently popping it, you will teach him to keep it slack.

The idea that harsh discipline must be imposed on the pup in order to keep control of the adult dog is self-defeating. While it is essential that you learn to control your dog and teach him good manners, this is best accomplished through positive, constructive training rather than through harsh discipline. Teach your dog correct behavior patterns rather than waiting for boredom or isolation to produce bad behavior and the need for punishment. I seldom need to punish one of my adult dogs, and when I do, a verbal rebuke is generally sufficient.

Discipline: Living With The Beast

Discipline is a difficult area in which to give advice, because techniques that have always proven effective for me may not work well for others. The man/dog relationship is complex, and subtleties of application and attitude make tremendous differences in the effectiveness of disciplinary actions. The person who is especially close to his or her dog can often inflict a devastating reprimand with a brief verbal rebuke, while another who is less close may virtually scream his or her head off with only a "so what else is new?" reaction from the Bouvier.

Before dealing with discipline as a behavior-modification and training process, make sure that the undesirable behavior is not due to a physical ailment. If your dog's behavior changes suddenly or is pronounced without any apparent reason, it is essential to first eliminate a possible physical condition as the cause. A thorough physical examination by a veterinarian can often solve what was originally perceived as a behavior problem. The dog, after all, can't take you aside and explain that he is hurting, and the sooner you observe the beginning of a problem and deal with it, the better. For example, if an adult dog suddenly begins to be aggressive toward the owner or toward other family members, and there has been no history of this behavior, then something as serious as a brain tumor or pain from severely dysplastic hips is a strong possibility.

Most physically caused behavior problems are much less serious and can be dealt with relatively easily. For example, the compulsive chewer — the dog that will devour an entire rawhide bone without getting up — may suffer from a deficiency in diet. In fact, on one occasion when we had this situation, it was cured virtually overnight by supplementing the diet.

The literature on canine training and discipline falls basically into two camps — the mechanistic approach, and the dog psychology approach. The chief problem with "understanding your dog" is that once a viable theory is developed regarding the root of a problem, an action plan is necessary. It is not enough to tell your dog that you understand his problem and love him just the same. The drawback to the mechanistic approach is that it tends to be applied like a cookbook — look up the problem and apply the prescribed procedure. If the cure fails to address the causative factors, it cannot be effective in the long run and may do much damage by covering up a serious fundamental problem.

Over time, I have become more lenient with pups, perhaps to a fault. A lot is expected in both conformation and working competition, and the desire for enthusiastic, aggressive, confident dogs has led to a toleration for a certain amount of puppy insolence and assertiveness. When a pup less than six months old bites me in the leg or hand, I do not slap him in the head but rather make a game of it and gently push him away, showing him that this is not the time and place, but I do not cower or intimidate him.

An older dog is generally corrected by grabbing him by the ruff (the loose skin and hair on either side of the neck), making eye contact, and telling him what it is that has aroused my anger. He may not understand all of the words, but the message generally is clear. In a serious case, the dog is put in an isolated room to contemplate his sins. This is an extremely effective approach. However, do not confine a dog in his crate or normal sleeping place as punishment. He should be put in a place where he never goes otherwise and that is as totally cut off from the family as possible.

Jordina Bretta vd Boevers Garden.
This beautiful bitch is litter mate to Halvar Bretta. Shown with breeder Theo De Wagenaar. Jordina is the dam of Spencer Jordina, imported into the U.S. by Martha Hochstein.

The object of discipline is training rather than punishment — teaching the dog that he must refrain from certain activities such as chasing cars or chewing on your shoes. In order to discipline effectively, your anger must be under control. It is good that the dog perceive that you are angry, because this will convey to him the importance of the situation. But while your emotion will enhance the impact of your actions, your actions must be guided by reason rather than by emotion. If you cannot act dispassionately, let the situation pass and deal with it another time. For example, if you find your shoes chewed, it is pointless to find the dog and beat him. He will have no idea why you are abusing him. If, however, you catch him in the act, showing dominance and making a strong verbal reprimand will associate the undesirable action (chewing the shoes) with something unpleasant (your anger).

When teaching a dog to do an exercise such as an automatic sit or to retrieve an object, use both positive and negative inducements. In other words, correct your dog when he fails to respond properly, and praise him when he does right. However, when teaching him *not* to do something, such as lunging at a car or chewing the furniture, it is essential that no praise or positive reinforcement follow the correction, for to do so will confuse the dog. If a young male marks the end table, a quick, open-handed swat (not directed to the face), and a verbal rebuke are appropriate. If he becomes sad and unhappy, resist the temptation to comfort him, which would teach him that urinating on the furniture is an effective means of getting attention.

A correction should be sufficient to get the job done the first time. If you inflict an escalating series of ineffective corrections, the dog's tolerance for them is going to increase. Ultimately, more severe actions may be required, unpleasant measures that could have been avoided by the timely application of an adequate correction.

Therefore, a disciplinary correction for a forbidden action must have three elements in order to be effective:

1. It must be timely, that is, done while the dog is in the act or immediately thereafter.
2. It must be sufficient so that escalating repeat performances are not required.
3. It must be dispassionate and must not be followed by affection or praise, which would confuse the dog and negate the effectiveness of the original correction.

A particularly important example is preventing death or injury under the wheels of a car or truck. Many dogs have no fear of moving vehicles and will chase into the street to challenge them. With the pup, safety is mostly a matter of keeping the animal away from traffic. As the animal matures, it is essential to provide general obedience training so that you will have control.

When we road work our dogs, we find that at twelve to fifteen months of age, the dogs will often take to lunging at a passing car — particularly at night. The dog is severely reprimanded, with a pinch collar if necessary. If verbal and pinch-collar corrections do not prove adequate, the radio-controlled shock collar is used — one of the few situations where the routine use of this device is appropriate. In general, it is desirable to instill an element of healthy respect for a moving automobile into a dog, and fairly severe methods are appropriate if necessary.

Long before the dog became associated with mankind, his ability to search out and kill game was necessary for his survival, and the instinct is still strong. The Bouvier is large, agile, and canny enough to be an effective hunter, capable of chasing down and killing a rabbit or your neighbor's cat. Although natural, this chase instinct should be strongly discouraged because of the danger of the dog's being struck by a car in the process and because it can lead to bad relationships with your neighbors.

For these reasons, I train my dogs so that they will not chase even a rabbit. If a dog does go after one when not on leash, the situation is difficult to deal with effectively, because by the time you catch up

expert guidance is not inappropriate if lesser methods fail.

It is common for us to find a rabbit sitting in the middle of the backyard when we go out to do a little obedience work. My practice is to heel the dog slowly and deliberately toward the rabbit so that we get as close as possible before he breaks. If the dog does not remain in the "heel" position, further corrective training is devised. It's kind of the ultimate in distraction training!

Dutch Ch Tino Faisca van de Vanenblikhoeve, one of two sons of Dayan Claudia van Hagenbeek to win the Dutch National Specialty, in 1990. (Tino's mother is Faisca Danny van de Vanenblikhoeve.)

with him, he may not understand why he is being reprimanded. If you believe that he will understand, grab him by the ruff and jerk him home, all the while telling him what a bad dog he is in an angry voice, then confine him. Do not call the dog, because to do so and then punish him only teaches him to run when called.

Deal with individuals that persist in chasing rabbits or other small animals by "setting them up." Take them to a place where temptation is likely to occur and have them on a long line and a pinch collar. Just before the dog hits the end of the line, call him. When he hits the end and yelps, calmly pull him in as if you did not notice his little problem. A pair of leather work gloves can prevent a nasty cut on your hand. On the whole, I have had less trouble with rabbit chasing with my Bouviers than with the Shepherds I have owned and trained, but on occasion you do run into a really hard case. Use of the shock collar under

The principle of catching a dog in the offending act can be difficult to practice when a dog barks persistently or does damage when you are away from home. Fortunately, the Bouvier is not inclined to endless, purposeless barking. Damage to the home is most effectively prevented by confining the young dog. As he matures, the inclination will in most instances dissipate. The older dog that persists in destructive behavior is likely reacting to what he perceives as a lack of attention, and the root problem may well be simple boredom.

If you are firm and consistent as the pup grows up, you should have no need to strike him with an object or a closed fist. The old rolled-up newspaper routine for housebreaking is in general ineffective and counterproductive. In particular, striking a dog about the face or head is dangerous and is likely to make the animal hand shy, not really teaching him anything. I will swat an adult on the rear with an open hand if he starts to mark in an inappropriate place or for some similar infraction, but this is far enough for everyday discipline and training. I will also strike with an open hand a dog that shows aggression to another family dog.

The only just cause for really striking a dog in an aggressive manner is to respond to inappropriate aggression on the part of the dog. Unfortunately, on occasion it becomes necessary to resort to physical force in order to correct an animal that has come to believe that he can harass human beings, neighboring dogs, or other animals. I have used a piece of rubber hose, about eighteen inches long, across the bridge of the nose of adult dogs that would repeatedly go after other dogs in a class or dog-show situation. The correct technique is to get a good grip on a strong collar and bring the hose down across the bridge of the nose, being careful to stay away from the eyes. The cases where I have had to resort to such techniques have involved older dogs with poor training in their own homes rather than animals that I have trained from puppyhood. Unpleasant? Yes, of course, but much better than putting down an otherwise good dog.

It must be emphasized that such methods are reserved for the most serious transgressions on the part of mature adults dogs and must be applied literally when the dog is caught in the offending act. You must assess the situation very carefully before taking such serious action and should not act when angry.

I own and use on occasion a radio-controlled electric-shock collar. It can be useful in dealing with inappropriate aggression, car chasing, and barking, among other things. In general, I do not recommend the use of such devices for the ordinary companion-dog owner, because the cost is several hundred dollars and because the collar can be easily abused. If you are not an experienced dog trainer, only resort to such severe measures under the direction of an experienced trainer. In general, you should take the dog through a complete obedience-training program before resorting to such measures, and in most instances, you will find that they were not necessary after all.

At twelve to eighteen months of age, the young male may decide that in addition to being top dog, he will have a shot at becoming head of the house. A variation of this is the dog that belongs to one adult trying to be dominant over another person so as to maintain a favored position. Such situations, while serious, are not unusual and can in most instances be dealt with effectively. While sufficient discipline must be used to make it plain who is boss, the corrective

Ch. Jasper du Clos des Cerbers comes out of the Open class to win the American Club Specialty at Westchester in 1971, as a 14 month old. Bred & owned by Edmee Bowles, handled by George Edge.

action must be measured so as not to damage the dog's spirit and initiative. One way to deal with this is for all adult family members to participate at least to a token extent in the discipline and training of each dog.

When a dog growls at a family member, you must take action. A brief verbal rebuke is usually sufficient, but in more serious cases, grab hold of the dog, roll him over on the back, and hold him until he quietly submits to your authority. For the dog, this is a complete loss of face. As with human beings, humiliation can be a much more severe punishment than the simple infliction of physical pain. I can't recall doing this in the last ten years, but if a situation required it tomorrow I would not hesitate.

If you are afraid of the dog, he will know it and will press his advantage. You must get help in dealing with such situations. Seek out a professional trainer and explain your problem. Do not be embarrassed; even veterans are afraid when they know that they or some other person may be bitten. I have run into several situations where a person was simply not able to gain the psychological upper hand. Usually the dog ends up being "placed" or put down. In general, the dog is within the normal range and is simply unfortunate enough to end up with a human being unable to handle him.

The police-style breeds such as the Bouvier, the Doberman, and the Rottweiler generally have become too popular. An "owner's license" requiring both a written examination and a practical handling test as a prerequisite to the purchase of such a dog would eliminate many problems. A big factor in America is that most lines have been bred down to produce much less dominant dogs for people who like the image but who have trouble dealing with the reality. When an especially weak person ends up with a throwback to the underlying character or with a dog out of serious working lines, problems can develop.

As a general rule, the experienced Schutzhund or protection-dog trainer delays "establishing who is boss." To be frank about it, we love the challenge of bringing out the best in a spirited dog or bitch and are willing to tolerate a fair amount of pushiness in a youngster. On the other hand, general-obedience and companion-dog trainers are much more likely to make the younger dog toe the line. The "park-district trainer" who deals primarily with novice owners and all-breed companion situations will in many instances put the greatest emphasis on psychological dominance of the dog.

My advice is to read and listen to as much as possible and then adopt the general approach of those who are accomplishing with their dogs what you want to do with yours. An open mind and a continuously improving rapport with your dog are your best guides.

Prominent Dutch stud:
Bonaparte Zierce v d Cerberushof NHSB.1073603 '79

Sire: IntCh Halvar Bretta v d Boevers Garden Sch III
Dam: Zierce ten Roobos NHSB.950013
 LOSH.354094
Bred by: Henk and Gerda Harmers

Perhaps the greatest wisdom is in understanding that the Bouvier is a working dog and that bad behavior is often a sign of boredom. Provide a constructive outlet for the energy, one that involves spending time with the dog. Training the dog to do something useful that will enhance his role is the best way to accomplish this. While every Bouvier should be trained in basic obedience, more advanced work such as a Schutzhund program would be even better.

The subject of training is covered elsewhere, but it must be understood that these are artificial distinctions. Training and disciplining are merely different facets of your relationship with your Bouvier. You are actually training your dog every day according to what you reward and punish or simply ignore.

Children, Motherhood, And Apple Pie

The advocates of each breed always refer to their dogs as "good with children;" it just goes along with motherhood and apple pie. While I would not necessarily recommend a Bouvier (or any other dog) as a child's personal dog if that child is to have responsibility for training and discipline, the Bouvier generally gets along well with children of all ages. Many individuals seem fond of very small children. They are gentle and seem to understand and account for the limitations of the individual child and are concerned about the child's welfare.

Because the Bouvier is relatively large and powerful, he has no reason to fear the child who will grab handfuls of fur or the ears. If the child persists in rolling on and mauling him, the dog can simply stand up and walk away. This is not always possible for the small dog that may feet trapped, perhaps with some justification, and that may need to snap or nip to get away.

Your attitude and discipline will play an important role in how well your animals and children mix. The pups and kids must both understand the rules and respect the rights of others. Teach the puppy from day one that any member of the family, adult or child, may take away a food dish, bone, or toy at any time. However, the children need to be taught that such actions are not for their amusement and that they should do these things only under supervision as a training exercise. They need to understand that the dog that is eating or otherwise occupied should be left alone and that sleeping dogs should by all means be left lying. This approach provides two levels of protection: if a child takes an unwarranted liberty, the dog may nevertheless be expected to tolerate the offense and simply move out of range.

Every dog is entitled to a place where he can be left absolutely alone, without the bother of children. Although you must discipline the children to enforce this, it is worth it in terms of domestic tranquility. In our house, the sanctuaries are under large end tables that form natural caves.

Running The Menagerie: The Multi-Animal Family

Many owners enjoy their Bouvier so much that they begin to think about another. Before bringing a second pup into the home, there are a number of things that you should be aware of ahead of time rather than finding out by experience. Because of the wide diversity in individual personalities and histories, there are no universal principles — every observation and statement made on the subject of multiple-dog relationships will have its exceptions, and every rule will on occasion be broken with impunity. Someplace out there in this strange world is the fellow with several stud dogs and brood bitches in the house, oblivious to the fact that according to everybody else's experience he should be dealing with at least one dog fight a week.

The gender of the dogs that are to live together is especially significant. The most volatile combination is two males. Although in some instances this arrangement is feasible, it must be handled with great care, especially if a bitch is present or either dog is used at stud. Most success stories involve introducing a male puppy into the home with an established adult that is able to maintain the leadership role as the pup matures. Introducing an adult male Bouvier into the house where one is established is an almost certain disaster.

Several bitches are somewhat more practical, although problems may still arise, especially when one is bred and approaches her time to whelp. The dog-and-bitch combination has by far the highest probability of an easy, trouble-free relationship and should be considered seriously by anyone contemplating a second Bouvier. In addition to the prospect of domestic tranquility, many subtle differences compliment one another when both sexes are present. Consider neutering one or both unless you can take on the responsibility of your bitch having puppies.

There is much to be said for taking the current family dog along when picking up a new pup. The introduction can occur on neutral territory, and the older dog may have a sense of participation in a new venture. The adult often develops a strong attachment for the newcomer; it is not unusual for them to play together, with the adult being gentle in consideration for the pup's physical limitations. When you arrive home with the new pup, pay particular attention to the senior dogs rather than to the newcomer. Walking in with the pup and giving all available time and attention to him is sure to create jealousy and resentment.

The dogs in a household will naturally sort themselves into a social hierarchy. One dog or bitch, generally the most senior or oldest, will hold the leadership position. Support rather than interfere with this, for when each dog knows his or her place, there will be few problems. Letting the young dog have his own ideas on what to do and when to do it is inviting chaos. In a properly run home, encourage the senior dogs to keep order. The correct social arrangement is a benign dictatorship rather than a democracy. The bitches and dogs may have their own individual pecking order, with a senior dog and bitch seeming to share power.

A fight is most likely to occur when a dog seeks to move up a notch. The pup by nature starts at the bottom but seeks to move up as he matures. Accept this as the natural order of things, and do not interfere unless an older dog is a bully (which is uncommon for a Bouvier in a household situation). Do not allow a dominant dog to abuse dogs of lower station. Be careful to maintain the ultimate leadership role for *yourself*. When two dogs play roughly, become involved and make it clear that if anybody is going to get rough and teach lessons, it's going to be *you*.

Common sense dictates that dogs should never be left loose together when you are not home unless you are very sure that there will be no friction. This is *very* important, even when you leave for a short time. We prefer not to leave more than one dog and one bitch loose in any portion of the house during our absence.

Bitches coming into season greatly increase the potential for a fight among males, especially if one or both are experienced studs. The bitch about to whelp is apt to decide that there is only room for her and the puppies in the house and may try to drive the rest of the dogs out. She may be particularly aggressive toward other females.

The real problems will probably occur when the unassertive but persistently forward dog refuses to take "no" for an answer. When the Bouvier lies down in the corner and gives out a low growl at the approach of another dog, he is best left alone. The dog that persists in such a situation is eventually going to provoke retaliation.

None of this should prevent you from the pleasure of having several Bouviers if you are willing to observe the elementary precautions. We have always had a number of dogs in the house, and the only serious incident involved an outside male that we were foolish enough to bring into the main part of the house.

Tory, our first Bouvier, was capable of being as aggressive as a situation might require. Although a successful and enthusiastic Schutzhund competitor, he never attempted to bite anyone off the sport field, nor did he show inappropriate aggression toward another dog. He never took food, a bone, or a toy away from another dog or pup and never nipped or barred his teeth at a child. He would tolerate a substantial amount of abuse without response and would, if possible, avoid a confrontation. If a pup would eat from his bowl or sneak up and grab a bone, Tory would be displeased but would not forcefully recover his property. When an older bitch was brought into the house, he even tolerated her increasing assertiveness. Finally, he used his shoulder to knock her down when he reached his limit. She rolled over once, stood up, and went about her business, accepting second place with no further question. This application of minimum but sufficient force is typical of the Bouvier and is truly one of his most admirable attributes.

If you have several adult dogs in the house, be prepared for the worst. Assume that you will eventually deal with a dog fight that could easily cause a serious injury to a man or dog. Your first instinct is

Unidentified Police Service Bouvier, East Coast United States. Circa 1955.

to wade in and grab a dog. The other dog will act as if you are helping and will take this opportunity to gain the upper hand. Do not do this, because you are extremely likely to be bitten severely! Try shouting as loud as you can. This probably won't work, but it doesn't take much time and may distract the dogs for a moment. Use what is available, such as a garden hose or bucket of water, to distract the combatants. If they stop, even for a moment, you may be able to regain control without further injury.

The ideal solution is the electric cattle prod, a battery-powered "shock stick" about thirty inches long. It generates a high-voltage, low-current discharge, similar to that created by the shock collar, which is painful but safe. Such units are available from canine-supply houses and also at most farm-supply stores. Stick it in the side of the most aggressive dog and give him a shock, then immediately go to the other dog. If this does not work, apply it to the genital area or wherever hair is at a minimum. If you have a quality unit and fresh batteries, this will almost surely stop the fight. This sounds violent, and it is, but it is by far the safest and most humane method of dealing with the situation.

Hoscy Dukke Bianca fan it Hanenhiem

A massive powerful Bouvier, a good case could be made to claim Hoscy Dukke to be the pivotal stud of the eighties, for his progeny in the first and second generation predominate in the Dutch show ring. There is a story about the breeding of this great dog: it seems that a well known judge happend to see his mother, Bianca Angelique, at the Dafzicht Kennel where she was to be bred. She was quite critical, for the bitch had rated poorly in the show ring. Annie Semler nevertheless persisted, and the result speaks for itself; sometimes the intuition of an experienced breeder, a knowledge of lines, can be the best guide.

Dutch Ch Hoscy Dukke Bianca fan it Hanenhiem
Bundessieger 1981 HD.Tc NHSB.1081385

Sire: Dutch Ch Hoscy Kata v Dafzicht
Dam: Bianca Angelique v Folkenhiem
Breeder: S. de Haan
Born: September 24, 1979

Grooming the Hairy Beast

Kathleen Engel

Much of the visual appeal of a handsome Bouvier is due to a good, neatly groomed, well-cared-for coat. As in any rough-coated dog, a certain amount of expense or work is involved in coat maintenance. While the Doberman or German Shepherd can be neglected and the situation made right by a good bath and brushing, a neglected Bouvier coat will require either hours of work or clipping off the entire coat. In the latter instance, it will take a year or more for the coat to grow out, and the texture may never be the same.

A regular maintenance program requires only a few minutes a week and provides other benefits besides a handsome appearance. Every dog sheds hair that is then replaced by new growth. In the Bouvier, this loose hair is held in the coat until it is either brushed out or is pulled loose as the dog moves through brush in the course of his work. Short-coated dogs do not retain this loose hair — it is shed and comes to rest in the surroundings. When we had one Shepherd and four or five Bouviers in the house, 90 percent of the loose hair that had to be cleaned up regularly was from the Shepherd! It is much easier to spend ten minutes once a week brushing the dog out than spending the entire week trying to clean hair off of the floors and furniture.

Maintaining a correct Bouvier coat need not be a burden. It is true that the long, soft coat fashionable in some segments of the show set can be a serious maintenance problem, but this is not a correct Bouvier coat. The correct coat is harsh and about two and one-half inches long. We continually train our dogs, including tracking in all sorts of cover, and show them on weekends. No matter how dirty they might get, and no matter how many burrs we need to remove, a good bath and grooming can get the dog ready for the ring. The summer that Leah went second overall in the nation in the show ring, she was being trained heavily for her Schutzhund III, which she achieved.

The Bouvier Coat

Growing a really good coat is more than a matter of genetics. It also involves correct diet and grooming. Some coats are oily, which is a blessing in disguise. If you brush your dog regularly to distribute the oil, you will rarely have to use supplemental conditioners. However, you will have to bathe your dog more frequently, perhaps as often as every six weeks, to keep him socially acceptable.

Harsher coats need frequent applications (probably several times weekly) of conditioner or diluted cream rinse to keep the furnishings on the legs and face intact. Those of us who work and show our dogs at the same time face exceptional challenges in keeping enough coat to satisfy the judges. Even though the standard says two and one-half inches overall on coat length, the winning animals often have a lusher and much lengthier coat, encouraging breeding for incorrect soft coats that more easily maintain excessive length. This problem comes and goes according to local trends. The popularity of the Dutch imports is to a certain extent promoting more correct coats and moderate styles of ring presentation.

The Bouvier's overall health is reflected in his coat. Fleas and internal parasites strongly affect coat growth and condition. Some medications, such as long-term use of cortisone, adversely affect coat condition and growth rate. Other physical problems, such as a thyroid condition, can first show up as deterioration in coat quality.

Diet can play a major role in your dog's health and can therefore affect coat growth rate and quality. Quality feed is a sound investment, because you simply cannot expect your dog to look or feel his best when given low-quality feed. Even when your dog is on good-quality rations, you can fine-tune his diet with careful supplementation. Since commercial supplements vary considerably depending on the time of year and the region, specific recommendations are not practical. Consult your breeder, experienced groomers, or fellow enthusiasts in your area. We sometimes add one teaspoon of brewer's yeast and/or one tablespoon of vegetable oil. During times of especially high stress, we may use both, gradually introduced into the diet to avoid flatulence or diarrhea. In northern regions, the dry, indoor heat of winter often requires supplementation in order to avoid dry skin and associated problems such as "hot spots."

Weekly Maintenance Grooming

The key to an effective grooming program is regularity. The following items should be attended to weekly:

1. Check all of the nails to see if they need trimming. (They should not touch the floor or ground when the dog is standing.)
2. Check between the toes and pads of the feet for mats, and trim or shave them out.
3. Check and clean ears, and pluck out any excess hair. (Ears may be wiped out with an alcohol-dampened pad.)
4. Look in the mouth of the dog, and scale the teeth if necessary. Your veterinarian can show you which tool to use and how to do it.
5. Brush and comb out your dog thoroughly.

Special circumstances, such as getting out burrs, naturally require immediate attention.

When brushing out your dog, start at a rear foot, brush all of the hair up with a slicker brush (or a pin brush if you are trying to save coat), and gradually comb out from the skin with a coarse comb. Work one leg at a time, and be especially careful at friction points, such as the armpits and around the testicles. (In general, it is probaably better to shave these areas with a clipper rather than try to comb them out.) Also, carefully comb the beard. It is essential to get right down to the skin so that the comb can be pulled freely through the entire coat.

If you are preparing the coat for show, apply a good coat conditioner *before* brushing so that it is thoroughly worked in and can prevent, at least to a certain extent, the needless breakage of hair.

Grooming also provides the opportunity to check for sores, cuts, and dandruff so that you can take care of small problems before they become serious. Keep an eye out for ticks and fleas. Once you learn the procedures, keeping your Bouvier in good condition should take about twenty minutes a week.

The Bath

Dogs do not need the regular bathing that human beings find necessary, basically because they do not perspire but rather pant to keep cool. Excessive bathing, either too frequently or with overly harsh shampoos, can cause dry skin and other problems.

The type of shampoo that you use depends on your reason for shampooing. If you just wish to freshen up the coat, a number of professional-quality shampoos are available, but stay away from heavily scented ones. Some have color brighteners, and some are medicated. Experiment to see which meet your preferences. Regardless of what you use, it is essential to rinse thoroughly to prevent skin irritation from residual shampoo.

In general, a bath is necessary as part of show preparation. As a final rinse (which is left on), we dilute one pint of white vinegar in one gallon of water. It helps to maintain coat texture and is an excellent odor neutralizer.

It is very important to not bathe your dog until he is completely brushed and combed out. Those who ignore this will find that bathing will tend to "cement in" the mats and thick spots, making them impossible to remove without cutting them out.

Fleas and Ticks

If you are troubled by fleas, some excellent citrus-based organic products are effective. Fleas and ticks can be a difficult problem, one that may require a complete control program involving several thorough sprayings of the house and yard. If the infestation is especially severe, you may need an exterminator. We avoid the use of flea collars, but the final authority on this should be your veterinarian.

Tick problems vary according to region. Even though our dogs are constantly out in fields and wooded areas, we seldom find a tick on a dog in northern Illinois. They are common farther south and, at the right (or wrong) time of year, are incredible farther north or in the Canadian and western woodlands. Beyond being a nuisance, ticks can carry Lyme disease, which is a serious danger to both humans and dogs.

There are a number of methods for removing ticks. I prefer to drop rubbing alcohol on the head of the tick, wait several minutes, then remove the tick. Always remove the tick with tweezers. Be sure to pull out the head. Be careful, because the head can easily break from the body, and if left imbedded it can cause serious problems and infection. Your veterinarian will be familiar with the best methods of dealing with ticks.

Slicker Brushes

A rubber pad holds a number of closely set metal pins. The ends of the pins may be straight or slightly bent, and the pad may be flat or curved. Wooden or plastic handles are acceptable. The curved model is about three by four inches and is excellent for taking

Grooming Equipment

First Row: Greyhound-type combs; *Second Row:* left, Bouvier rake; right, curved slicker; *Third Row:* #7 blade, pin brush, center stripping knife, curved scissors, mat splitter (front), German Shepherd rake (back); *Fourth Row:* thinning scissors, clip-on plastic blade; *Fifth Row:* electric clippers.

Grooming Equipment

Think of your grooming tools as an investment — don't select only on the basis of price! Choose tools with the best construction and materials. Quality brushes, rakes, and scissors should last for years. Quality scissors also hold a sharp edge longer and often have better alignment.

hair out of thick spots. The flat version is approximately two and one-half by four inches and plays a vital role in a regular grooming program.

Combs

The "Greyhound"-style comb has teeth about one and one-half inches long and is usually imported from England or Belgium. It has a fine-toothed end and a medium-toothed half on the other end. Another comb that has teeth about two and one-half inches long with both medium and wide spacing is useful for getting right down to the skin.

Shears

The following shears should be included in your grooming equipment:

1. Regular straight-blade, eight-inch grooming shears.
2. Seven- to eight-inch, curved-blade grooming shears with rounded points.
3. "42-toothed" thinning scissors, with one blade plain and one toothed.

Rakes

These rakes are the most useful:

1. A "German Shepherd" rake — "T"-shaped with one row of metal teeth, short, blunt, and fairly widely spaced. (Be careful not to use this too vigorously.)
2. A "Bouvier rake" (if you can find one) — four rows of sturdy metal pins set in a hardwood frame and handle. (Those with two rows are not as effective.)

Ear-Plucking Equipment and Nail Clippers

Keep these items on hand:

1. Forceps and ear powder for plucking ears.
2. Nail clippers — either guillotine or scissor type.
3. Blood-clotting powder in case you cut too close.
4. You may also wish to use a nail file to round off rough edges.

Electric Clippers

You will need electric clippers with the following blades:

1. #10 or #15 blade for the outside of ears and genital area.
2. #40 or #30 blade for the inside of ears and between pads of the feet.
3. #8½ blade for the top of the head.
4. #7 or #7F blade for assistance in shaping and setting in the pattern.

Mat Splitters

If you need mat splitters, use the following:

1. A metal six-toothed comb with twisted teeth. It is very effective with mats and thick spots.
2. A metal comb with five or seven removable metal blades set perpendicular to the wooden handle. The blades can be resharpened.

Stripping Knives

We have an assortment of five knives with blades varying from one-eighth inch apart on the center of the teeth and one-fourth inch deep (this is very coarse and is useful for blending) to three blades or teeth per one-eighth inch and approximately one-sixteenth inch deep. The intermediate sizes are used like a comb to remove excess undercoat. The finer stripping knives are used as cutting tools for shaping the coat, and the very finest knives are used for detail areas like the head and for shaping the eyebrows.

Pin Brush

The pin brush has fine metal pins that are spaced fairly far apart and set in rubber on a wooden base. It is excellent for fluff drying and spares the coat as much as possible when you are working with it.

Grooming Procedures

It is best to get a puppy accustomed to grooming as early as possible. A grooming table and arm that has a noose with which you fasten the dog to the table is certainly a great asset, but you can also teach the pup or adult to lie down on his side. The pup must learn to be still and accept the procedure. The older dog will eventually become accustomed to the procedure and will likely fall asleep until you hit a snag. *Never* leave an animal unattended on the grooming table while attached to the noose! He may try to jump off while you are gone and hang himself.

You will need a grooming arm either forty-two or forty-eight inches long depending on the height of your dog. There are various styles of nooses with which to attach the dog to the arm. Nooses with metal slips seem to work best. I like to work on a grooming table that is forty-two to forty-eight inches long and about twenty-six inches wide. It is easy to make your own table even if you are not very handy with tools. The collapsible legs are available in the large Sears catalog. The top can be made of three-fourth-inch plywood or particle board. Cover it with rubber matting available at most large hardware stores, or you may use nonslip material available at some boat-supply stores. It can be applied to the top with large-headed tacks by wrapping around the top edges and tacking it on underneath.

Work on one area of the dog at a time, and do it thoroughly rather than jumping around doing this area and then that area in a random pattern. If you begin in the rear, the animal will have a chance to settle down by the time you reach his head. Experience has taught me the advantages of a systematic ap-

Coupling or Loin

Anus

Breastbone

Angulation

Stifle

Hock

Parts of the dog's body.

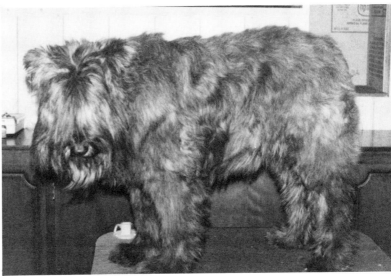

Untrimmed Bouvier.

proach, especially when you groom every dog in the same order. In this way, nothing will be missed.

Let us begin by going over an "imaginary" dog in my accustomed order.

1. With your dog on the table or on his side on the floor, begin on the rear leg nearest to you. Presuming that the dog is not matted, take your regular slicker brush (the one with the flat base, *not* the curved base), and, beginning near the top of the leg, vigorously brush all hair upward toward the spine, making certain to get all the way down to the skin. Be as thorough on the inside of the leg as on the outside.

2. When all of the coat is thoroughly brushed upward, then, starting at the toes, use your Greyhound comb to carefully comb the hair back down a small layer at a time. This will remove all loose hair. If you are thorough in brushing the coat upward (making sure that you are getting down to the skin all over), no matter how thick the coat, you should be able to brush so that you can see the base of the hair at the skin.

3. If your dog is shedding a gread deal, you may prefer to replace the slicker brush in this operation with a Bouvier rake. If you are happy with the balance of the coat, use a pin brush, because it will have the least effect on coat texture.

4. Next, work with a coarse comb to save as much coat as possible. Also in the interest of preserving the coat, you may with to spray the animal before you begin combing. Dilute canine cream rinse (one part cream rinse to three parts water), place it in a spray bottle, and mist on the dog.

5. Continue in a like manner on the side and belly, then on the front leg and on the chest. This is followed by working on all of the neck and the head, being doubly careful with the beard. You may find the neck especially thick, because the Bouvier grows a natural ruff of fur about the neck. Therefore, plan to spend extra time on that area.

6. Then restart on the other back leg, on the side, and on the other front leg.

To summarize, the recommended order is:

1. Rear leg
2. Side
3. Belly
4. Front leg
5. Chest
6. Neck
7. Head
8. Other rear leg
9. Other side
10. Other front leg

If the dog is to be bathed, this is the correct time. Wet the dog down thoroughly, soap vigorously, then rinse completely. Repeat the process. Be especially thorough with your last rinse! The beard may need additional applications of soap to clean it.

Never cream rinse a coat for show! This will soften the coat and seriously degrade the proper texture. A final rinse of vinegar and water is optional. After the dog is rinsed, blot the coat as dry as possible with towels. Then, entirely fluff-dry the animal with a blow dryer while brushing with a pin or soft slicker brush so that the coat will stand out evenly for trimming.

Make certain that the dog is perfectly dry, including the feet, before starting the next step. Cutting wet or damp hair quickly dulls scissors and clipper blades.

The Feet and Nails

Cut the nails so that they clear the floor when the dog is standing. If your animal has dewclaws on the front legs, trim those as well. If you are uncertain at what point to cut the nail, ask your veterinarian to show you where and how. Because most Bouviers with good pigment have black toenails, it is difficult to know where the quick is and how far back to cut

Figure 6-1: The Feet

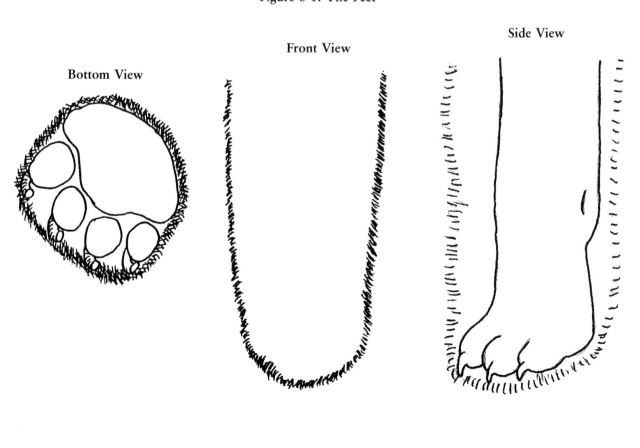

Bottom View   Front View   Side View

the nails. That is why it is a good idea not to cut nails unless you have a blood-clotting powder on hand to stop the bleeding should you misjudge where the nail is cut. Nails can bleed profusely if you cut them too short. It is very effective to round off the rough-cut edges of the nails with a nail file, making them less likely to snag your clothes and hosiery.

Have some experienced person instruct you on safe clipper use before you begin on your dog.

on the toe pads. All clipper work on the feet is done from the bottom of the foot. If there are mats between the toes on the upper portion of the foot, take them out with your thinning scissors and a fine-toothed comb. If you leave the hair unshaved, check for mats between the pads during your weekly grooming, because they can make a dog's feet sore to the point of lameness.

Around the bottom of the foot, trim close to the

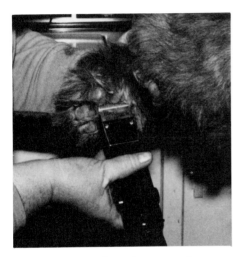

Shave out hair from between the bottoms of the pads using a scooping motion around the large single pad off the foot. *Photo by Linda Schneider.*

Around the bottom of the foot trim close to the pads with a stright blade scissor. *Photo by Linda Schneider.*

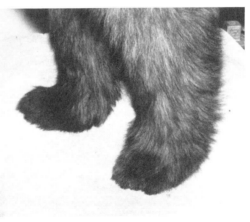

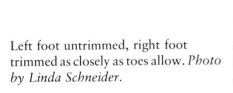

Left foot untrimmed, right foot trimmed as closely as toes allow. *Photo by Linda Schneider.*

Scissor the hair flush with the pads on the bottom of the feet. As an alternative, shave out from between the bottoms of the pads with a #40 or #30 blade. (Please be very careful using the #40 blade. This is a surgical blade and could cut or burn the pad.) This is accomplished by using your clipper blade in a scooping motion around the large single pad of the foot. Be especially careful to have the feet clean and dry, because the surgical blades should be applied with minimum pressure. As always, sharp, well-lubricated blades are essential.

First scoop away from the large pad toward the toe pads, then turn the clippers around and clip back toward the large pad, resting the back of the blade

pads with a straight-blade scissors. Then put the foot down and have the dog stand squarely on it. Take the curved blade scissors and, resting the lower side on the grooming table, angle away from the foot at a forty-five-degree angle (see photos). You are trying to cut as close to the foot as possible yet still maintain proportion to the overall appearance of the leg. Therefore, if the leg has extremely abundant hair, you would leave slightly more circumference to the foot to keep it in proportion. If the front feet toe out slightly (not uncommon in puppies), the offending foot or feet can be rounded in such a manner to minimize or conceal the fault. The overall cut is a rounded oval. The front and rear feet are trimmed in the same manner. However, as shown in the figures, the front and rear legs are handled differently.

The Hind Legs

Brush the hair all the way up on the hock, them comb away from the leg horizontally. If you pick up the foot by the two foremost toes and shake slightly, the hair should puff out around the hock so that you can trim it to approximately two inches in length (Figure 6-2). You may notice that the hair at the back of the hock is also thick and will take more work both to make it stand out properly and to trim it evenly. This is one of the points at which you can alter the appearance of angulation (the angle at which the hock attaches to the stifle), leaving more hair at the back of the hock for the appearance of more angulation or leaving less hair if you wish your dog to appear less angulated.

The front and side hair of the back leg is then combed horizontally away from the leg and evened off (Figure 6-2) with the thinning scissors. You may also use one of your short-toothed stripping knives as a cutting tool. Place the offending hairs a few at a

Figure 6-2: Hind Legs

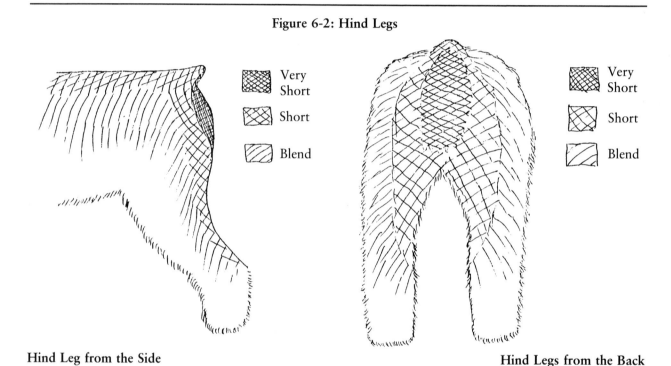

	Very Short
	Short
	Blend

Hind Leg from the Side

Hind Legs from the Back

Trimming the Hock

time between your thumb and the stripping blade and use a quick, sharp twist of the wrist to cut off the hair. This takes practice. Don't try to make it too perfect.

We prefer to keep the hair short on the back of the thighs, very short around the rectum and genital area both for sanitary reasons and for appearance (Figure 6-2), and shorter on the inside of the legs. Here you can use your regular scissors if you wish. You will make fewer mistakes with the thinning scissors, because they cut more slowly. If you do use your regular scissors, be extra careful. If your dog should sit down suddenly or jump around, you could do him serious damage with the sharp scissors blades.

With the dog standing squarely, comb the hair so that it stands out horizontally. Look for hairs that are sticking out too far, and even them out with the scissors. Hair on the outside of the legs is usually left longer (two and one-half inches), while the hair on the inside of the legs is shorter (about two inches long).

As you approach the genital area, trim the hair shorter and shorter on the inside and back of the legs until it is short at the genital area and around the rectum — perhaps as short as one or one and one-half inches — and stripped out underneath enough to lie flat but not enough to be bald (Figure 6-2). It should be neat but not shaved except around the testicles, which are safer shaved than brushed. If you do shave in this area, be extra careful, because you can easily cause clipper burn to tender parts. A #10 or #15 blade is recommended.

The overall effect is supposed to be neat and cared for but not overly groomed. In essence, you spend several hours just subtly touching up the overall appearance of the dog — taking off the shaggy spots and removing hair that would distract the judge. You can also greatly change the overall appearance of the dog by considering where the faults are and minimizing or concealing them and/or by setting off the good points with expert grooming.

The Body

Before you begin grooming the dog's body, step back and take a good long look at your dog from different angles. What you do next can make or break the entire effect that you wish to create.

Consider the topline. Is the back too long? Is the topline properly level with the tail as an extension of the backbone, or is there a dip before the tail? How is the body length? Leaving excess hair on the chest and rump can give the illusion of inches of unnecessary body length. Are the ribs flat or nicely sprung? Is the chest well let down? Where is the neck attached to the back, and is it nicely arched? Is the neck too long or too short? What type of coat are you dealing with in terms of abundance and texture?

Before you cut a single hair, formulate a plan of attack. Decide where you wish to improve on mother nature and what you wish to show off to good advantage.

If there is excessive hair, so much that you really can't see what you are doing, try this if your dog is steady and accustomed to electric clippers. Have him hooked up and standing on the grooming table. Comb his body hair out away from the body as much as possible. With a #7 blade on the clippers, *lightly* skim over the topline and top third of the body. Stay away from the body by at least three inches. If the coat growth is really excessive, this will make the next step in trimming much easier for you to handle. If the coat is not excessive, skip the clippers.

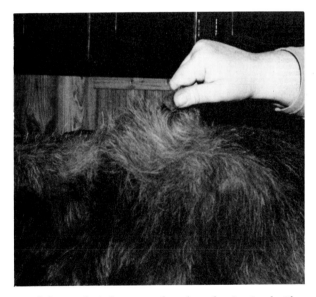

Catch longer hair between thumb and stripping knife and pull knife toward you. Work in direction of hair growth. Do only a small amount of hair at a time. *Photo by Linda Schneider.*

On the first pass, you will set the pattern for the entire process. Do this with the thinning scissors. For maintenance, use stripping knives. However, if you are already proficient with stripping knives, it is fine to set the pattern with them rather than with the thinning scissors.

Starting on the topline, comb the hair up away from the back. Step back and look at the dog. Is his back

Figure 6-3: The Body, Side and Front Views

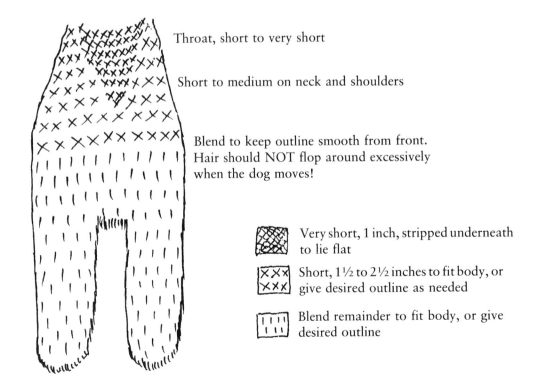

Leave a little longer at back of neck for a nice arch of the neck.

Breastbone →

	Very short, 1 inch, and stripped underneath to lie flat
	Short, 1½ to 2½ inches to fit body, or give desired outline, as needed
	Blend remainder to fit body or give desired outline

The finished coat is carefully blended to look natural. There is NO line of demarcation between coat lengths.

Throat, short to very short

Short to medium on neck and shoulders

Blend to keep outline smooth from front. Hair should NOT flop around excessively when the dog moves!

	Very short, 1 inch, stripped underneath to lie flat
	Short, 1½ to 2½ inches to fit body, or give desired outline as needed
	Blend remainder to fit body, or give desired outline

too long? If so, start his neck at the shoulder blades. Leaving longer hair at the back of his neck will make his back appear shorter.

Does he have a dip before his tail? When trimming that area, leave extra hair so that the topline will appear level.

Now, with the thinning scissors or stripping knife, take down the legnth of hair just on the back so that it is even all the way across. You will have to experiment with coat length, because so much depends on thickness and texture, but it will probably be around one and one-half to two and one-half inches. Trim straight across the back so that when the hair is combed up from the back, the cut is straight, not curved, until you are at the sides where it is gradually blended in.

at a time with the thinning scissors until you get the right look. You can also alter the illusion of where the shoulder is set by "cutting it in" where you want it. Subtly using stripping knives or your thinning scissors, take out a little extra hair at the line where you wish the shoulder blade to appear.

The hair on the bottom of the body (the ribs) is left fairly long. Therefore, just trim off the uneven hairs unless hair growth is in excess of four inches (then you may want to use the thinning scissors to trim it off somewhat). The belly hair is left longest toward the front legs and is tapered shorter as you approach the stomach. If your dog seems to have extra-long legs, leaving this hair longer will minimize the length of leg. On the other hand, if your Bouvier's legs are a little short, you may wish to keep the body

Thinning scissors are used to trim straight across the back so that when the hair is combed up from the back the cut is straight.

Next, work on the sides. The top one-third to one-half of the body is cut shorter. At the topline, it will match the length of what you have just cut and will then gradually lengthen until it blends into the natural coat length about halfway down the ribs (Figure 6-3).

As you are grooming, you may wish to ask an assistant to help you by periodically taking the dog off of the table and moving him in a show trot so that you can see where more trimming or blending is necessary. Watch for areas that are flopping round and distracting the eye. Try blending them in a little

hair shorter to keep him from looking like a Daschshund!

When the sides are blended in to your satisfaction, blend in the back legs and rump, keeping the hair shorter around the anus for sanitary reasons. The tail, when held in a horizontal position, is treated as part of the topline. Combing the hair toward the end of the tail, trim off the excess with the curved blade scissors so that it is almost even with the end of the tail. Be careful not to cut it too short, especially if the end of your dog's tail stub is bald. The underside of the

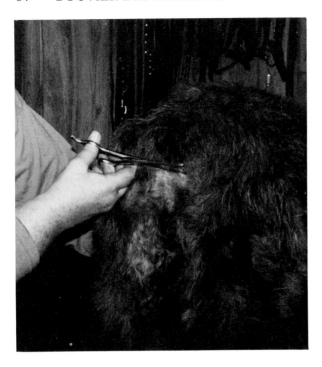

Combing the hair toward the end of the tail, trim off the excess with the curved blade scissors so that it is almost even with the end of the tail.
Photo by Linda Schneider.

tail is cut very short with scissors for cleanliness — you may even wish to clipper it with a #10 blade. If so, be careful not to nick the area, because it is tender. Continually comb the hair up and outward to make sure that it is blended smoothly, taking off any uneven ends as you go.

When a dog is first groomed, it often takes a few days of touching up until the pattern that shows off the animal to best advantage evolves. There is no pattern that makes all Bouviers look their best. Rather, you must tailor the grooming to the individual so as to minimize his faults and emphasize his good structure. If you intend to show, attend some shows and see how others are grooming their dogs. You need not be a copycat, because what looks good on another dog may not suit yours. But don't be above picking up a new trick or technique.

Remember that the Bouvier is supposed to look neat but natural and *not overgroomed*! When getting a dog ready for the show ring, it can take many sessions over a period of weeks to get the dog in top form. If your dog has a good coat, maintenance should be a matter of twenty to thirty minutes weekly once the pattern is set properly.

The Front Legs

Brush the hair thoroughly upward toward and including the elbow using a slicker or pin brush. Make certain to get down to the skin. Then, grasping the two foremost toes firmly, shake the leg several times. The hair should stand out from the leg. Take your thinning scissors and even out the ends of the hair all around the leg, just cutting off protruding strands and generally neatening.

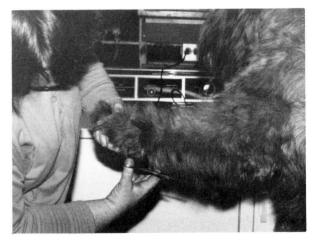

Take your thinning scissors and even out the ends of the hair all around the leg, just cutting off protruding strands and generally neatening.

If you are dealing with a particularly lengthy coat (more than four inches on the back), take off some length as well. By using the thinning scissors, no scissors marks will be made on the coat the way they would be with ordinary scissors. Therefore, the end result will look natural — just much neater. Pay particular attention to the elbows, because the hair seems to grow faster and thicker there. You will have to judge how much coat to leave. Taking off the wisps of hair does seem to bulk up the coat and make sparse furnishings look fuller. Depending on the rate of growth, a trim once a month to once every six weeks should keep your Bouvier looking neat.

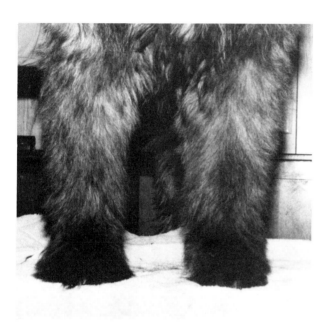

Untrimmed foot and leg on left, trimmed foot and leg on right. Trimming off whispy ends can make the trimmed leg look fuller than the untrimmed one. *Photo by Linda Schneider.*

If the dog has a narrow front, you can trim the hair on the inside of the legs a little shorter to give the illusion of more width. If the dog tends to be out at the elbows, you can take more hair from the outside of the leg to make the fault less obvious.

If you grasp the front leg by the two foremost toes and shake the legs firmly several times, the hair will puff out around the leg so that you can trim it off all the way around with your thinning scissors. Pay particular attention to the elbow area, because the hair grows much thicker there.

The Neck

On the neck, I usually use my clippers with a #7 blade for the first cut, because the hair is very thick around the ruff and is hard to trim with the thinning scissors. Comb the hair on the front of the neck and chest outward. By feel, determine where the breastbone is and make note of it, because you will cut no lower than this.

Now, lifting up the dog's chin, feel where the jawline meets the throat. Hold the beard up with the chin and start your cut at the jawline, going downward. Take the blade right down to the skin at the throat (Figure 6-4), and gradually lift it as you travel downward toward the breastbone so that the hair is blended in as you go. Cut the entire front of the neck in this manner — very short immediately at the jawline and gradually blending in when it meets the breastbone and shoulders.

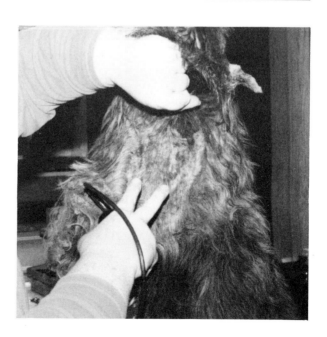

Front view of clipped area of neck before being blended into the shoulder area.
Photo by Linda Schneider.

Figure 6-4: The Neck, Front and Side Views

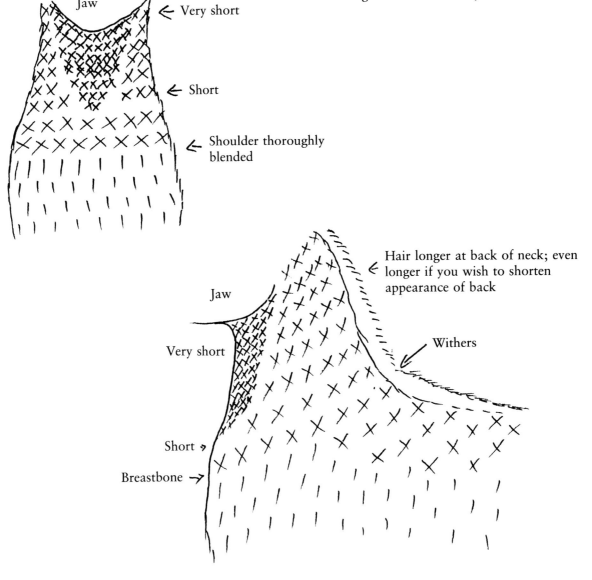

Hair on side of neck medium length, but well blended.

Now put away your clippers and go back to your scissors or stripping knife. Standing in front of the dog, comb outward on the hair at the side of the neck and shoulders, trimming and blending as you go The hair above the foreleg and elbow area will tend to flip as the dog moves, so you may wish to blend more thoroughly here. Blend around the neck, leaving the hair on the back of the neck slightly longer at the base and slightly shorter as it approaches the skull.

Pick up your stripping knife that has the longest teeth. Holding the blade at right angles to the skin and starting at the head toward the body, comb downward vigorously. This will take some muscle. Go all the way around the neck, because this will be an excellent aid in blending. (You can use this same technique on the backs of the thighs and along the topline and the top third of the body.)

Do not finish blending the neck until you have done the head, because you may wish to leave more or less hair depending on the overall effect of the head. If the dog is tired or restless, give him a play and potty break before starting on the head.

The Head

Begin the head by clippering the outside of the ears, going in the direction of the hair growth with a #10 or #15 blade, depending on the thickness of the hair. Use the #15 if the hair is really thick, the #10 if it is not. The effect should be neat and close-cut but not scalped. Clipper from the tip of the ear all the way to the base, pulling on the tip of the ear to stretch it for smooth cutting. If you are very careful, clipper the edge of the ear as well. Remember, though, that the blades can cut flesh, especially the #7 blade, which has distance between the teeth. So if your dog is restless with the clippers so close to his head, trim the amputated edge with scissors instead, having someone help you hold his head steady.

The inside of the ear, along the uncropped edge, is shaved extremely close with a #15 blade. The ear canal is dusted with antibiotic powder (there is some available especially for dog ears), and the hair is plucked with your fingertips or with forceps, if you can handle them without poking your dog. Ask your veterinarian to show you how to use forceps. If the ear is greasy, wipe it out with a paper towel dampened with alcohol, or peroxide.

Clip the skull with a #7 or #8½ blade (Figure 6-5). Then go over that area with a medium stripping knife used in comblike fashion to blend in the cut edges. Make certain to clipper in the direction of eye to occiput, the direction in which the hair grows. Clip

Figure 6-5: The Head — Direction of Clippering

just past the occiput so that there is a place for the show lead to rest — approximately one-half inch maximum. The skull is clipped down the sides to a line from the outside corner of the eye to the outside corner of the ear. As you approach that imaginary line, lift the clipper slightly so that there is not a distinct line.

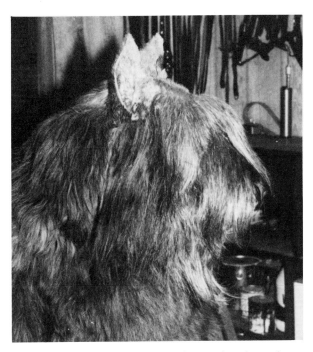

The skull is clipped down the sides to a line from the outside corner of the eye to the outside corner of the ear. As you approach that imaginaray line, lift the clipper slowly so there is not a distinct line. *Photo by Linda Schneider.*

If your Bouvier has bushy cheeks, giving him a chipmunk look, strip out the coat from underneath, *never* from the top. If that still does not do the trick, very carefully use the thinning scissors close to the skin on the bottom two-thirds of the cheek. It will take a maximum of three or four "V"-shaped cuts with the thinning scissors. Don't get carried away. You can always take out more hair later, but losing control and taking off too much can mean waiting months for the coat to grow out.

The grooming of your Bouvier is just about complete. Keeping the ideal in mind, stand back and walk around your dog. Don't rush. If you are not sure whether some of the hair belongs there, live with it for a few days. It is always a simple matter to take off more hair. If you have assistants, have them take the dog outside and gait him for you at a show trot.

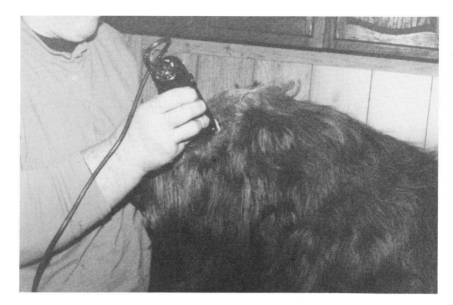

Shave top of head from eye socket towards back of skull with #8½ blade. Leave adequate hair for eyebrows.

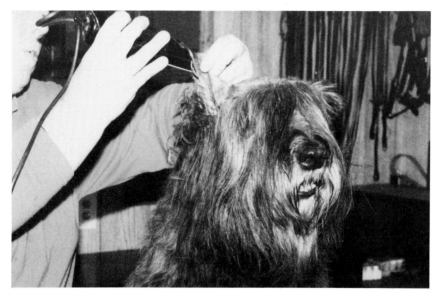

Outside of ear is shaved from skull toward tip with a #10 blade. Inside of ear is shaved from tip toward skull with a #15 blade.

Hair for eyebrows and center fall are combed forward before skull is shaved. Here, left ear is trimmed, right ear is untrimmed.

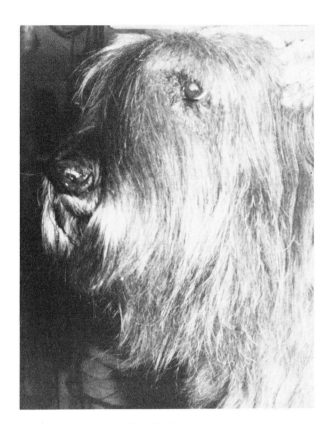

Eyebrow is trimmed with thinning scissors at one angle, closer at outside corner of eye, longer at center fall. It is not cut straight across, but with a slight arch. Center fall is NEVER trimmed.

Get down on your knees if you can to see the dog at eye level. Is hair flopping around? Is it distracting to the eye? If so, you may wish to blend more thoroughly with your thinning scissors. Remember your written standard. This is a rough-coated animal with a tousled coat. He should look neat, cared for, clean, and healthy — a dog that you wouldn't mind petting. He should *not* look overgroomed or coiffured, like he has a can of hair spray applied to keep every hair in place. The coat should move with the dog. Some show dogs are so covered up with hair dressing and baby powder that their coats are fixed in place like suits of armor — nothing moves naturally in the breeze. This is definitely *not* the look that you want.

Other Thoughts

There is no single correct way to groom your Bouvier. Watch other exhibitors groom, try out different techniques, and develop the methods that work best for you.

Sometime ago I had the pleasure of attending a grooming seminar given by the most prominent Dutch Bouvier groomer. He used scissors and thinning scissors exclusively. He was outspoken about his beliefs that stripping and plucking make the coat feel too soft.

On the other hand, our professional handler, who also is an expert groomer, insists that the coat must be plucked. She uses rubber fingertips from the office supply on her thumb and forefinger, and thus equipped, she "plucks" all coat that sticks out too far. She will go over a dog, plucking as she goes, every few days. Alternately, the coat is brushed with the German Shepherd rake to keep the undercoat in balance.

It takes three to six months for the coat to "roll over" (grow out from the skin). Plucking throughout

Using rubber fingertips from the office supply, you can pluck out coat that stands out too far.

this period of time can improve coat texture in some dogs.

The Utility Cut

The previous section covered grooming suitable for conformation presentation. If a dog is six months away from the show ring or is retired, you may want to adapt utility-style grooming.

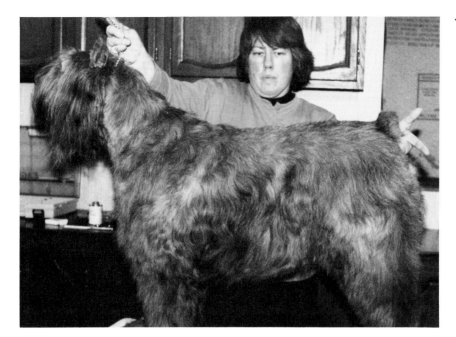

The utility cut.

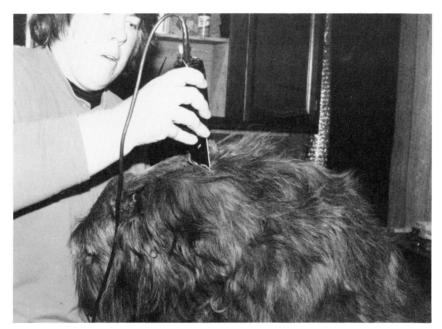

Doing a utility cut with a plastic clip-on blade over a #30 blade on the clipper. If the dog is not perfectly combed out, this won't work. *Photo by Linda Schneider.*

To do so, purchase a set of plastic combs that clip onto your electric clipper blades. With the dog completely brushed out and fluffed, clip on one of the plastic blades and clipper the dog instead of scissoring. I would use the shortest blade (clipped on over your #30 or #40 blade) on the back and front of the neck, and the medium blade halfway down the sides and on the rest of the neck. Use the longest blade on the stomach and legs. You should still show groom the head. Never, ever clip off the beard! Remember, this clip will take some time to grow out, so don't do it unless you are sure. Clipping may also adversely affect coat texture — consider before you cut!

You may prefer to use a #5 blade on your clipper for the back and on the front of the neck. Blend in what you can, then scissor the rest of the animal. Either technique can leave you with an animal that still looks like a Bouvier.

Unless your dog has a medical problem or a hopelessly matted coat, never "cut down" your Bouvier, that is, clip him very short all over. The rough coat is natural insulation against heat and cold and protects the skin from bushes, briars, thorns, and the sun.

Coat Maintenance

Now that you are done with the initial grooming, the worst is over. However, carefully consider what needs to be done to maintain your Bouvier in superb condition with minimal work.

It is important to keep the coat texture in balance. Every dog and every coat is a little different, so there are no hard-and-fast rules. Some of our animals keep a balanced coat naturally and are never stripped except for the purpose of blending. Some grow excessive undercoat and stripping is a routine matter, something that must be started seriously three to four months prior to show-ring competition. With such an animal, use the medium-toothed stripping knife like a comb. Comb very thoroughly over a section of coat every week. This combing-over process takes out a good deal of soft cottony coat. The German Shepherd rake can also be used to pull out excessive undercoat, but be careful with this tool because it can rip out too much coat. I know of more than one instance where a dog was left with nearly bald patches in a matter of a few minutes of overenthusiastic brushing. The stripping knife is the tool of preference.

As the initial grooming begins to grow out, use one of your finer stripping knives to take the tips off of the outgrowing hair. Place the offending hair between your thumb and the blade of the stripping knife and, with a twist of your wrist, cut off the ends. Progress along the body, combing the hair outward. In this way, you can see what is sticking out and take it off with the knife. Coat growth is erratic. It varies on parts of the body and overall during different seasons of the year. If you are doing your job properly and the dog maintains good health, it should not be tedious to maintain your dog as the handsome Bouvier that he was meant to be.

A fine example of the finished product of the groomer's art: Madrone Ledge Nuka of Fogbank with the groomer and handler, Judy Higgins.

"Old Dutch" has in fashionable American circles often been a code phrase for "crude, low class, and ugly working dogs" with "working" being the most disparaging term of all. But for me the traditional Dutch police lines are the purest and most noble of all, the very essence of the Bouvier heritage. Here we have Bart Krist's Duko van Mereveld, holder of the Dutch Police certificate and perhaps the quintessential specimen of his line and heritage. Agitator in photo is Mr. Rein Beumkes.

The Ring and the Trial

Although most Bouviers today serve primarily as companions, many owners become involved in competition. Broadly speaking, this means either confirmation exhibition, that is, an evaluation of the structure and appearance of the dog, or working trials in which the dog's performance of various exercises is evaluated.

In America, most shows are for the purpose of attaining an AKC or CKC Championship. The North American Working Bouvier Association (NAWBA) conducts annual evaluations with European judges where written critiques of the individual dogs are taken down and published. Although these are not AKC sanctioned, they provide the North American community with a view from the homelands and an opportunity to experience European procedures and practices. Other working trials include AKC and CKC obedience, the German Schutzhund training, and the Ring Sport, originated in Belgium and later extended into France.

Until a few years ago, competitive dog training meant preparing for the AKC obedience and tracking titles. "Protection training" was mostly a professional service to provide personal protection but offered little opportunity for amateur participation. It was generally accepted that the civilian dog owner should have nothing to do with protection work and that such training should be left to the police and military. The Bouvier was not thought of as a police-style dog, and many people were content to leave such work to the German Shepherds and Dobermans.

In Holland, Belgium, and France, however, Bouvier training has involved police training or closely related sport training for three generations. Nowhere is this more true than in Holland, where for almost a century many police dogs have been trained by amateurs. Once the Bouvier has earned a Police Certificate (KNPV title), he can be sold to a police department. The amateur police clubs in Holland use methods that are virtually identical to those observed at training sessions for active police dogs.

Americans have always had an affinity for the police-style dog. Over the past twenty years, Americans have been drawn increasingly to this European style of training. Protection work is exciting and rewarding, and the dogs enjoy it enormously. Indeed, much of the attraction for the trainer is sharing the joy of his or her canine partner.

Traditional AKC and CKC obedience competition has for the past fifty years provided an arena for a dog to execute obedience exercises and to have his accomplishments recognized. This work leads, in order of increasing difficulty, to the titles Companion Dog (CD), Companion Dog Excellent (CDX), and Utility Dog (UD). There are also tracking tests, leading to the Tracking Dog (TD) and the Tracking Dog Excellent (TDX) titles. The AKC has recently developed trials for the hunting and herding dogs but so far has refused to recognize the functionality of the protective breeds. This has led to a proliferation of other organizations, some of which are setting up registration and conformation programs. The recently formed American Working Dog Federation hopes to fill this void left by the AKC and thus ensure the long-term integrity of the police-style breeds.

Obedience Competition

The AKC Companion Dog (CD) program is a series of straightforward exercises involving simple "heeling" patterns both on and off lead, a "stand for examination," and a "recall." To obtain the title, the dog and his handler must perform the exercises with a sufficient number of points and without a complete failure in any single exercise, at three different trials. This type of training should be considered the minimum for any large dog. It would be much better if the license fee for a dog without such a title was perhaps $100 and the fee for a dog with the title was one dollar. Although attention tends to focus on the advanced work, the Novice exercises are the most important in that they allow families to integrate a dog into their household as a safe, reliable, pleasurable companion.

The CDX exercises introduce the dumbbell retrieve. The handler throws an object that the dog must fetch and then present to the handler by sitting before him or her and waiting for a command to give up the object. There is a retrieve "on the flat," where the object is simply thrown out about twenty feet, and one "over the jump," where the dog must jump over a barrier, pick up the object, then return over the barrier. The entire test is conducted off lead.

The UD involves a scent discrimination exercise, where the dog must pick one object that has been held by the handler from among a group that the handler has not recently touched. There is a "go out," a directed retrieve, and a jump over a bar. The latter is more difficult to teach because the dog will naturally tend to go under the bar. Perhaps ten Bouviers have achieved the UD in the United States and Canada together in the past forty years.

In addition to the obedience titles, the AKC offers a Tracking Dog (TD) and a more advanced Tracking Dog Excellent (TDX) title. In the tracking test, a dog must follow the path that a "track layer" has taken through fields and wooded areas and find an object, usually a glove, which has been placed at the end of the track. The dog is taken to the beginning of the track about an hour after the object is placed and works on a harness and twenty-foot lead. For the TDX text, the track is at least three hours old and has more turns. In general, it is a much more demanding test. These tracking tests are on a pass-or-fail basis; no point score is involved.

The obedience trial as it exists in America was originally introduced from England. Credit is due to a breeder of Standard Poodles who wanted to demonstrate the intelligence and capability of her dogs. Mrs. Walker naturally selected a form of competition well adapted to her breed and to her perception of the proper place of dogs in human society. It is a tribute to her foresight that Standard Poodles continue to be among the very best AKC obedience competitors. She has performed a great service for her breed and for dogs in general.

The Bouvier is neither a numerous nor especially successful AKC obedience-trial participant. While there are exceptions, very few of the two thousand or so Bouviers whelped each year participate, and, more to the point, the influence on breeding selection has been nil. Even the better-working Bouviers are reserved and less demonstrative than is currently fashionable in the obedience ring. In competition, they tend to lack the quickness, apparent enthusiasm, and

artificial precision that are increasingly necessary for high scores.

Overall, the Bouvier is otherwise a good obedience dog, and if all breeds could be rank ordered, the Bouvier would be toward the upper end but not at the top. I do not see this as a shortcoming of the breed, but rather of a system that lumps all breeds into one generic "obedience sport." There certainly is a need to breed the Bouvier toward more energy and willingness, which will produce better obedience-trial performances. It would also be possible to select for attributes that make breeds such as the Golden Retriever so successful. But would such dogs still be Bouviers? I think not.

Until the advent of the TDX and the Obedience Trial Championship (which no Bouvier has ever held), the highest level of working distinction has been to hold the UD and the TD, that is, the "UDT." To my knowledge, two Canadians and one American have reached this level with a Bouvier — Thea Bossart and Bernie Blair in Ontario and Martha Hochstein in California, three accomplished and successful trainers. These three people have become primarily Schutzhund trainers rather than seeking a Bouvier with which they could be competitive at the top level in the AKC sport.

If you are a Bouvier owner with a desire to get more involved with your dog, participate in one of the various training sports. Probably the best approach is to visit as many of the clubs or other organizations within a reasonable distance and watch their training. Look for emphasis on happy, "up" performances and for instructors who are able to compete with and title their own dogs. If there are Bouvier trainers in your area, seek out their advice concerning the merits of the individual training programs. A representative selection of German Shepherds and Rottweilers doing well in a class indicates an open attitude toward the protective breeds. Your Bouvier will probably also do well if you are willing to work with him.

Schutzhund

Beginning in the early twentieth century, when the police-style breeds were being formalized, a number of training and trial systems were devised in Europe to qualify breeding stock, to provide practical training for service dogs, and to provide a sporting outlet for training enthusiasts. At this time, the best known of these in America is the German "Schutzhund" (Protection Dog) trial, which was developed in the early 1900s by the creators of the German Shepherd. Simi-

Ch. Woodbine's Hurricane Breeze UD, for several years top obedience Bouvier, also placed in the Group. Owned and trained by Sally McBride, bred by Judy Odom. Out of Ch. Nack du Clos des Cytises/Ch. Woodbine's Demelza CD.

lar tests were utilized in many other nations during the same era, including the Police (KNPV) trials in the Netherlands and the Ring Sport of Belgium and later France. These tests require a dog to demonstrate proficiency in tracking or searching, in obedience, and in protection on the same day.

The German Schutzhund trial is in the slow and painful process of becoming an international canine sport and may eventually become part of the Olympics. For many years, it was widely adapted by other breed organizations in Germany and the German-speaking areas of Europe. Fifteen to twenty years ago, Schutzhund trials began to be held in other nations, such as the Netherlands, Belgium, America, and France.

In the 1970s, American dog enthusiasts began to develop a serious interest in Schutzhund training. By 1988, about 200 clubs existed in the United States. Many of these clubs are still in their early stages and do not yet provide regular first-rate instruction. Although progress continues to be made, only small numbers of North Americans have practical access to participation in this sport. However, some clubs have gone from sleeves made out of carpet remnants to the highest levels of European competition.

The elementary title is Schutzhund I, with more difficult exercises leading to Schutzhund II and the most advanced title, Schutzhund III. At each level, tracking, obedience, and protection exercises must be passed. In tracking at the Schutzhund I level, the handler lays his own track. The track has two turns and two objects (or "drops") to find and is run when it is twenty minutes old. For the III, the track is laid by a stranger, has four turns and three objects, and can be an hour old.

The tracking test measures the dog's ability to utilize the sense of smell, which is fundamental to the utility dog and essential to his usefulness in many working roles. It also is an effective test of the dog's working willingness and initiative, because although a dog may to some extent be coerced to perform obedience exercises, he must in the tracking test work independently, essentially beyond direct handler control.

In obedience, the Schutzhund I dogs do part of their exercises on leash and do retrieves on the flat and over the high jump very much as in AKC open obedience classes. The III dogs do a much longer set of exercises entirely off lead. There is a gun test at each level to demonstrate impartiality. The obedience exercises are a test of the dog's willingness to participate, to interact, and to be a member of the team. They also measure agility, stability, temperament, and handler control. A dog must be a strong obedience performer in order to achieve distinction in Schutzhund, because 100 obedience points are at stake and he must be in the nineties to compete for high-in-trial honors and be within a couple of points of a perfect score to win a major championship.

The protection test, which is only one brief portion of the trial, is what typically comes to mind when Schutzhund is mentioned. Not only is it the most exciting and dramatic segment, but it also measures courage, stability, restraint, and control. The dog must respond to an attack with a vigorous defense, but he must also search and hold without biting, guard

A guard of object exercise in France, circa 1950. In later years, French training would emphasize the leg or thigh bite. *Photo courtesy Justin Chastel.*

Bart Krist's "Duko v Mereveld" in Dutch Police competition. Agitator in photo is Mr. Rein Beumkes.

Sire: Nerodan KNPV m.lof NHSB.347143
Dam: Coraah v Sevenheym NHSB.394484
Born: November 18, 1969
Owner: Bart Krist (Pleinzicht)

Duko was purchased from Bart's mentor Coen Semler, who had received him as a stud puppy for the use of Nerodan.

The case of the disappearing sleeve. (I think that Gambit has it!) Under the stick of Mike Reppa, with Jim Engel in the background.

Select Champion Centauri's Gambit, SchH III CD

his leader from a surprise attack, and guard a stationary adversary. The dog is tested with a stick (in reality a length of bamboo) by being struck twice across the back to ensure that he is willing to persist in the face of a determined foe.

In Schutzhund I protection, the dog goes to a single blind and, finding an agitator with a sleeve, barks and guards the man. The dog then does an off-lead heeling exercise during which he is attacked by a man who comes out from a hiding place. The dog must bite firmly without hesitation and accept two blows from a bamboo or padded fiberglass stick without showing fear or releasing his grip. When the agitator ceases to fight the dog, the handler commands the dog to release his hold on the sleeve. If at any point the dog shows fear by failing to bite or by running from the agitator, he is dismissed. Finally, the handler holds the dog by the collar while the agitator runs away. At the judge's signal, the handler sends his or her dog after the fleeing man. Once the dog is in pursuit, the agitator turns and advances toward the

dog, threatening him with the stick. At the actual point of impact, the agitator should be threatening but not actually running at the dog. After the release command, the dog and handler escort the agitator to the judge.

In Schutzhund III, there are five bites, two sets of blows from the stick, and considerably more obedience. The distances are greater, and the agitator is as aggressive and intimidating as possible so as to fully test the dog.

In Europe, the Bouvier was until a few years ago virtually never a Schutzhund participant, simply because this form of competition was unknown in his native regions. Rather, he participated primarily in the Dutch Police trials and the Belgian Ring, which are described in the next section.

As the international popularity of Schutzhund became more apparent, the Federation Cynologique Internationale (FCI — the world canine organization) established a set of international (IPO) rules almost identical to the German Schutzhund rules. However, most competition continued to be according to German rules. In 1985, nations such as the Netherlands, Belgium, and France ceased recognizing the German rules and only allowed titles gained according to the international process to be recorded in the breeding records and to appear on official forms and pedigrees.

In Holland, this led to much strife, with German organizations conducting trials locally, much to the displeasure of the Dutch establishment. This was not really an issue in the Bouvier world, because since 1985, no Schutzhund titles have appeared on official (Raad van Beheer) Bouvier pedigrees. Rather, IPO titles have taken their place. Bouviers now participate exclusively in this version of the sport. German Shepherd fanciers have been much more involved, and there is immense German pressure to recognize the Schutzhund title as the primary breed working standard. These conflicts are much more than a matter of procedure and semantics, because the Dutch and French resent the common German assumption of the God-given German right to control working-dog affairs worldwide.

The Ring Sport and Police Trials

During the past few years, Americans have shown increasing interest in the French Ring Sport. Although the sport originated in Belgium about the same time Schutzhund was emerging in Germany, it is the French version, distinctly different in rules and even philosophy, that has attracted American interest. Although the Bouvier was once a serious and respected competitor, the breed is unfortunately not seen today at the higher levels of Ring competition.

I was fortunate enough to be in Lorient, on the Atlantic coast in France, for the 1987 *Coupe de France du Chin d'Utilite* (the French Ring Championships). It was an incredible experience, a whole new world of working-dog excitement. Unlike Schutzhund, where the dog is taught to bite only the padded arm, a complete body suit is used, and the dog may bite anywhere. In practice, most dogs are trained to go for the legs and thighs. The dogs must release on command before the agitator ceases aggressive behavior and must either return or stay and guard on command. The handler must, in some instances, call the dog off of the attack before the dog reaches the agitator.

One of the most fascinating exercises is guarding the object, where the handler must place an object (such as a wicker basket) on the ground in the center of an eight- to ten-foot-wide ring. The handler then goes away, out of sight, no doubt to worry quietly. The agitator then approaches from the distance, mak-

ing no overtly aggressive moves but wearing the full body-style ring suit. The dog wants to attack but knows that he must stay at his station. The agitator circles, showing disinterest, but moves continually closer. Finally, when he detects a moment's lack of attention, the agitator reaches for the basket. At this point, the dog must bite, and, when he does, the basket must be put directly on the ground. If the dog leaves the basket or allows the man to remove it from the circle, many points are lost. It is a fascinating battle of wits between man and dog, between agitator and trainer, played out mostly in slow motion with an occasional flash of action.

The Belgian Ring is in many ways different from the French, but the chief one is that the judge has a great deal of latitude to change the procedures so that the handler never knows exactly what will happen in the trial. At one trial near Liege, the object presented for the retrieve was a large sponge in a bucket of water. The handler was required to take it out, throw it, and send the dog to bring it back. In the protection exercise that day, the agitator had a rope attached to the lower of two stacked plastic barrels. As the dog came in to bite, the agitator pulled on the line so that the dog had two big, bouncing barrels behind him, out of sight, as a distraction!

Although the Belgian Ring seems to be the forgotten European sport, as far as Americans are concerned, it is one of the most interesting sports to watch. The fields tend to be small and intimate, and the creativity of the judges in devising new situations adds greatly to the overall interest. This sport has not received much international attention, perhaps because there are several Belgian sanctioning organizations. This is not all bad, because something can be said for having a dog sport truly devoted to local people training their own dogs, without any big-money interests. If you visit Europe, seek out a local trial and spend the afternoon drinking beer and leaning on the fence that usually surrounds the field. It will be like stepping backward in time to an older, slower-paced, simpler world.

"KNPV," seen as a suffix on the names of many Dutch dogs, is an abbreviation for *Koninklijke Nederlandse Politiehond Vereniging*, or Royal Dutch Police Dog Association. This organization conducts police-dog trials and offers certificates that are among the most coveted and respected in the world. This test requires a dog of great character, physical strength, agility, and stamina. It involves heavy protection work with distant attacks on a remote adversary who strikes the dog with a stick before the dog actually bites. Realistic gun tests are also conducted. The dog is required to take a man down off of a bicycle, the desired procedure being to leap high and grab the man's upper arm so as to avoid entanglement in the wheels. There is a search for dropped objects rather than the tracking common in America. Overall, the KNPV trial demands very hard, tough dogs.

The Dutch Police trials are distinctly different in procedures and philosophy from the Ring of Belgium and France. Although many amateur trainers are involved, the purpose is to produce functional police dogs and to identify worthy breeding stock. A number of police-titled Bouviers have been imported for breeding, particularly by Erik Houttuin in St. Louis. (I am aware of no Belgian– or French–Ring-titled Bouviers ever being brought to the United States.)

Unfortunately, the Bouvier is no longer seen in the Belgian or French Ring sport, and the breed today is in a severe state of decline in Belgium and France. In Holland, the Bouvier is seen in the Police trials with much less frequency than in former years.

Although the Europeans originated the protection breeds and created marvelous sports to maintain and enhance the character of the breeding stock, the Bouvier faces serious problems today. Fellow enthusiasts have in many ways fallen short of their ideals, dramatically lowering their standards. In Holland, there is no working requirement for the championship, and in both America and Holland, the working stock and the show stock are fragmented. In Belgium, the Certificate of Natural Qualities is a requirement for the championship among protective breeds. But the test is not especially demanding, it has not been required consistently over the years, and it is not required as a breeding prerequisite.

The practical problem with the Ring and Police trials is that they are geared for the competitive trainer rather than for the breeder. The typical KNPV entrant is owned by an individual with only two or three dogs, and the dog is usually four or five years old when he begins competition. This is simply too demanding a test as a breeding prerequisite, because the breeder cannot spend this much time on each dog or wait that long to start a breeding program. Because of this conflict, the police stock has to a large extent been separate from the conformation stock for many years. The same is true in Belgium, where many breeders have devoted total attention to the show ring, thus widening the gap between Ring dogs and show dogs. This is a tragedy for the Bouvier breed.

In Europe, however, Bouviers are increasingly active in the IPO sport. Nowhere is this trend more pronounced than in Holland, where Bouvier participation is extensive and growing. Halvar Bretta van de Boevers Garden, perhaps the most spectacular show winner over the past decade and an FCI World Champion, is also Schutzhund III. (His title was earned before the previously mentioned switch to IPO rules.) There are annual FCI European Championships, in which a Bouvier, Ria Klep's Donar, placed

as high as third.

Dutch fanciers and breeders have in the last few years formed many "Bouvier Only" IPO clubs. In the April 1988 issue of the *Bouvier Nieuws*, forty-six exclusively Bouvier clubs were listed in a nation whose population of fourteen million is roughly comparable to that of Illinois. Because Holland is such a small, compact nation, it would seem that virtually everyone has reasonable access to a Bouvier training club.

Perhaps the greatest hope for the Bouvier in Europe lies with the Dutch IPO trainers. Dutch conformation judges tend to favor the working-class dogs, and hopefully the Dutch will introduce a character test as both a championship and breeding prerequisite. Increasingly, kennels that have been successful in the show ring are also training and trialing their dogs. Many seek to add police potential to their breeding lines.

The Belgians are also tightening up by requiring the Certificate of Natural Qualities (the CQN) for the championship. This test involves elementary obedience such as heeling and a retrieve, and a reasonably comprehensive protection test.

People tend to think that the difference between European and American training is the protection-work, especially the aggression exercises. In my opinion, this misses the real point, which is that in the homelands, the working trial was intended first and foremost as a breeding eligibility test.

Herding

Herding is a complex and subtle subject, mostly because the herding-heritage breeds form a diverse group ranging from the short, stocky Corgi to the massive Komondor. This wide variation in structure and character is due to the vastly different functions that evolved in different regions.*

Livestock dogs fall into a number of categories, ranging from the pure herd-control dogs of the British Isles (as represented by the Border Collie) to the guarding dogs on the central plains of Europe (such as the Komondor and the Anatolian Shepherd). The Bouvier and German Shepherd form intermediate types. They are, because of their background as combination herd protectors and controllers, among the most versatile and utilitarian breeds.

Herding as a trial system in the United States has largely been limited to one extreme end of the spec-

---

* For those who wish to see what modern working-dog breeders can gain from a knowledge of the herding heritage behind the protective breeds, read the work on Lorna and Raymond Coppinger, especially their article in *Smithsonian* magazine (April 1982).

trum, that is, the quick, agile, British-style sheepdogs. A Komondor, for instance, is unlikely to do anything that is even regarded as herding at such a test, yet the breed is among the best in the world for its niche. Continental cattle dogs, such as the Rottweiler and Bouvier, clearly had a much different working function from that of the British sheep-dogs — so much so that it must be asked whether it makes sense for them to compete in the same working trials.

In Britain, sheepherding trials featuring primarily the Border Collie have become popular spectator sports. In this country, similar trials have been held for many years, again featuring mostly the Border Collie and the Australian Shepherd. More recently, efforts have been made to popularize herding as a competitive event, with emphasis on drawing in individuals from a more diverse set of breeds. Herding Instinct Tests are being held, where a dog is evaluated and perhaps awarded a certificate declaring that he has a herding instinct or shows natural interest.

During my visits to Belgium and Holland, I inquired as to whether Bouviers served as active herding dogs and was consistently told that they did not. It is clear (as indicated by Louis Huyghebaert, a judge, writer, historian and breed founder, and other authorities) that larger, more powerful dogs such as the Matin were introduced into the native lines of cattle dogs to produce more of a police-style dog in the early years of the twentieth century. This occurred because the need for herding dogs in Flandres diminished due to mechanization. This is particularly true of the "type Roulers," the predominant genetic wellspring of modern Bouvier breeding.

Therefore, compared to many of the other breeds considered herding dogs, the Bouvier is relatively distant from his herding roots, both in terms of genetic background and in the number of generations that have passed since real selection for herding effectiveness has been practiced. The establishment of the Bouvier as a truly functional herding breed, to the extent that lines would again be bred specifically for this purpose, would require enough dogs actually in practical service to form a viable genetic pool.

If herding training and trialing are to become relevant to the Bouvier breed in America, the standards and methods of necessity must be those found appropriate to such dogs. Perhaps some of the German Shepherd trainers could be brought over for educational purposes and their methods emulated. I don't believe that anyone in North America or Europe is currently conducting training and trialing systems relevant to cattle dogs such as Bouviers and Rottweilers. Only one or two Bouviers have been trained for even the lowest levels of herding competition.

Thus, if you are interested in reestablishing the Bouvier as a serious herding dog, there is good news and bad news. The bad news is that the road will be long and difficult and you will essentially be starting at the beginning. The good news is that you are venturing out on uncharted waters. And, if a group of enthusiasts bands together and establishes Bouvier lines of serious, functional herding dogs, they will have literally turned back the tide of history.

Carting

The Bouvier has been mentioned as a carting dog, and many would have you believe that this function is an intrinsic part of the heritage. However, this is simply not supported by fact or by common sense. The very attributes that make a good, general-purpose herding dog — speed, agility, quickness, and aggressiveness — are contrary to the description of a serious draught dog. The European standard discusses various aspects of physique in terms of how they relate to "the power of attack of the Bouvier" but nowhere mentions suitability to any sort of draught function. In fact, using a dog to pull a cart is illegal in Holland on the grounds that it constitutes abuse.

In the October 1983 Southern California Club *Bulletin*, the French judge Dr. André LeLann commented on the carting function in a long letter:

> This is perhaps the place to help discard a belief that has gained ground over the years. It is true to say that some dogs have been used, especially in Belgium, as draught-dogs. But they were built for the part, most often smooth-coated and big-headed, of the type commonly called "Matin." Most well-informed people, like Justin Chastel, have great doubts about the Bouvier originating in any way from such an animal. It is unfortunate that this belief may have influenced, and still does, the thinking of some fanciers, who identify the Bouvier with a bulky draught-dog.

This is not to say that training a Bouvier for carting is in any way undesirable, because carting in the sport sense is simply a specialized form of obedience. However, the idea of breeding Bouviers suited by structure for heavy loads or long distances would be a serious deviation from the historical working function of the breed. Dogs are not now and most likely never again will be an effective and efficient means of transportation, and tying a breed's purpose to an obsolete working function would be a sure ticket to oblivion.

Flandersfield Bilbo Baggins, owned by Rosemary Lewis. Winner of the carting competition at the first Working Championship, Labadie, Missouri, October 1980.

Conformation Competition

The purpose of exhibiting dogs should be to provide, in conjunction with a working test, an impartial and dispassionate evaluation of each dog presented, so as to serve as a guide to the breeding program. In spite of this conceptual simplicity, in practice, significant difficulties in implementation have not been unusual. In considering an individual dog, many detailed aspects of physique must be weighed relative to each other in the process of reaching an overall determination of his value. Much judgment and a deep feeling for a breed and its heritage are necessary to render a proper critique. Rank ordering a number of dogs, each with his own assets and shortcomings, is even more complex and demanding.

Beyond the intrinsic complexity of the task, the frailties of human beings acting under the intensive pressures of what is an inherently political process become evident. Judges do not exist in isolation. They typically are or have been breeders or exhibitors and are often well acquainted with the dogs and the people in the ring.

No system is perfect, and honest differences of opinion are a natural and not undesirable part of the process. Judges come to different conclusions about the relative merits of individual dogs, and a dog can present an entirely different picture when not in top condition. In spite of this, it is nevertheless possible to conduct an evaluation that serves the overall purpose of guiding breeders and thus advancing the breed.

One characteristic of a sound system is relatively few judges and a rigid and lengthy qualification process. In Belgium in 1976, there were ten judges of the

Bouvier des Flandres, including Justin Chastel, Felix Grulois, and Victor Martinage. Four years later, in 1980, there were still only ten judges. Only one name had changed, because Martinage had passed away and Annie Verheyen had become a judge. In Holland, where the Bouvier is the most numerous breed, there were in 1986 twelve men and women listed as eligible to serve as judges. In America, more than this number become AKC judges every year.

Another European feature is the mandatory written evaluation of each dog, published for public scrutiny. This prevents a judge from just selecting familiar faces, which in America usually means professional hand-

there are also numerous cases of unqualified judges handing out meaningless championships. The primary problem in America is that so many judges are licensed for so many breeds that their expertise becomes diluted.

Although this system is imperfect, people continue to show their dogs for two basic reasons. First, they enjoy the social and entertainment aspect. And second, people show their dogs because they want to breed them, and to gain the recognition necessary for breeding success, they believe that they must compete and win in the show ring. Like it or not, the person intending to breed his Bouviers is under significant

Left: Ch. Woodbine's Hurricane Breeze UD, for several years top obedience Bouvier, also placed in the Group. Owned and trained by Sally McBride, bred by Judy Odom. Out of Ch. Nack du Clos des Cytises/Ch. Woodbine's Demelza CD. *Right:* Grove's Grover of Kroankel, American and Canadian Champion. Bred by James Wheatley, owned by John Tummers of Alberta. Among the best known Canadian Show dogs in the mid-1980s.

lers. The combination of relatively few judges and mandatory published evaluations means that each judge is held accountable.

Conformation shows in North America bear little resemblance to this ideal. Those with a number of years of experience in the conformation ring can no doubt recall the disappointment when it was realized that while there are many good, competent judges,

pressure to participate in show-ring competition. Breeders have a continuing need to subject their work to outside review, because each individual can get off the path without knowing it and may need a gentle reminder to step back and take a fresh look. Even when the show system is not perfect, we should still participate and make efforts to eventually change it for the better.

Conformation Exhibition in America

When most Americans refer to a "dog show" they are thinking of a conformation competition where the physical appearance and structure is evaluated and the dogs rank ordered according to their relative merits in these areas. The purpose of this section is to explain how this system works, how to prepare your dog for competition and the practicalities of engaging the services of a professional handler.

Since there is such growing interest in the European scene, and so many imported dogs coming over, a

Class," and then as "Winner's Dog" or "Winner's Bitch" when all the class winners are brought back into the ring. A "Reserve" also is selected in each sex and is awarded the points if the winner is subsequently declared ineligible. (The most common reason for a dog to lose the points is when he is entered in a class for which he is not eligible.)

Zero to five points are available, depending on how many dogs are in the competition. The number of points available for beating a specific number of other dogs varies according to breed and region of the country and is based on the number of dogs that have been shown per show in that region during the previ-

Ch Rocheuses Singular Sensation, Best of Breed at the 1990 American Club Specialty in North Carolina. Owned by Doug and Michaelanne Johnson.

brief comparison with continental practice is included.

The first objective of the dog show is to "finish" the dog, which means attaining his championship. To do this, a dog must obtain fifteen points, including at least two "majors" under different judges. At a show, only one male and one female in each breed can obtain points by first being selected as "Best in

ous months. The process is complex, but the point schedule is printed in every show catalog. A major is obtained when three or more points are won.

The classes are "Puppy" for animals from six months to a year old, "Novice" for dogs with little experience and no majors, "Bred by Exhibitor," "American Bred," and "Open." Any dog, including finished champions, can be entered in the Open class,

Quiche's Gabriel, American and Canadian Champion, whelped in 1982. This dog, bred, owned, and shown by the Paquette family, was number one in American conformation in 1985 and 1986. Best male or highly placed at many specialties.

Sire: C/A Ch Quiche's Barrier
Dam: Ch Quiche's Extra Ruffles

although champions virtually never are. Foreign-born dogs may be entered only in the Open class.

After the Winner's Dog and Bitch are selected, they are joined in the ring by all of the champions of both sexes. The judge then selects a male or female as "Best of Breed" and then a "Best of Opposite Sex." Either the Winner's Dog or the Winner's Bitch is designated as "Best of Winners," and either or both may be selected as "Best of Breed" or "Best of Opposite" over the champions present. Additional points may be obtained in this way.

Etiquette for ring procedure is elaborate, established as much by custom and tradition as by the rules themselves. Its purpose is mostly to keep things moving, because the judges must evaluate a lot of dogs in a relatively brief time. If you haven't had the pleasure, attend some shows. At first, the procedure will be totally confusing, but you will soon get the hang of it.

In Europe, ring procedures are much less rigid because the judge is expected to do an in-depth evalua-

tion that takes considerable time. During this lengthy procedure, the judge sees each dog under a number of circumstances. This makes it difficult to conceal or divert attention away from a fault. Much of the American handler's bag of tricks is not available, because "stacking" a dog is in effect admitting that the animal's structure is so faulty that he cannot be presented as he naturally stands. There is a lot of barking in the European ring, and shows of aggressiveness are to a large extent tolerated or even encouraged. Double handling (when someone outside the ring gets the dog to stand attentively) is accepted as a matter of course.

Showing the Beast

Once you commit to showing competition, you must devise an effective strategy that allows you to achieve the most success for the amount of money that you can afford to spend. Make no mistake — the show ring is expensive, and if your financial resources are limited, you must be very careful to avoid breaking the family budget.

Although many dogs are shown effectively by their owners or breeders, the American show world revolves around the professional handler. This is a man or woman who makes a living by showing dogs for owners who lack the time, knowledge, or desire to show their own dogs. The professional handler is virtually unknown in Europe. It is practical for a European to show his or her dog a number of times without spending an undue amount of time or money. As a result, many successful show dogs in Europe are owned by men and women of relatively modest means.

Before the dog actually goes into the ring, much preparation has to be done. No matter how good the dog is, it is foolish to send him out until he is well prepared. This means that he must be in good physical condition with a well-maintained and groomed coat. He also must be trained to respond to the judge and to the handler. Perhaps the worst mistake is to take a dog into the ring before he is ready. By doing so, you detract from the dog's reputation and correspondingly from that of the owner and from the kennel whose name he carries.

Generally, it is a good idea to start out showing your own dog. Sure, you'll take your lumps, and you might lose because your dog isn't that good after all, or you simply may lack the skill for effective presentation. The pros are likely to give you a tough time; on the whole, they probably have better dogs than the novices in the ring, because enough of them know a good dog and have clients experienced enough to spend their money on showing only reasonably good dogs.

Eventually, however, the novice with a reasonably good Bouvier, a willingness to learn, and a little natural ability will succeed. The system is set up to produce roughly the same number of champions in each breed, which means that it is easy to finish (show to a championship) a dog in a less numerous breed, somewhat more difficult in a moderately popular breed, and very difficult for the newcomer in a really popular breed such as the German Shepherd.

Regardless of who shows the dog, success in the ring is based in large part on good preparation, such as physical conditioning, coat maintenance, grooming, and training. The well-prepared dog will achieve the championship much more quickly. If the dog goes with a handler, having the dog trained and in condition will save you lots of money. However, the handler generally is willing to condition the dog, get the coat in shape, and train him.

Considerable training is needed to prepare your dog for the ring. Because American conformation-shows require stylized and production-line rapidity in presentation, the dog must give an alert, confident impression in the ring and must go immediately into the "stacked" position and hold it.

There is a well-entrenched belief that show dogs should not be obedience trained because it detracts from the dog's enthusiasm and animation. In many instances, this belief has a solid basis in fact. Unfortunately, much of the training inflicted on Bouviers today is not suited to his nature and spirit and thus can do considerable damage and reduce his effectiveness in the show ring. Correct training applied to a sound dog, on the other hand, can be an asset to conformation exhibition. Professional handlers who have worked with our dogs have had no difficulty, because they don't exhibit the browbeaten reaction typical of Bouviers subjected to heavy-handed obedience. Some Bouviers are simply not sound, and the undesirable reactions to training are due to fundamental defects in the dog's character.

As a general rule, I like to get a dog performing well in protection, biting hard and with confidence, and into the high jump, wall climb, and go out before emphasizing precision heeling. In this way, the dog is not inhibited by the corrections that precision obedience requires. This is important with a dog of moderate or slightly deficient confidence.

Generally, the person doing serious obedience training is likely not to be the best one to present the dog in the show ring, because the dog's attention is most likely going to be on the handler. There are, of course, great variations among dogs and people, so find what works best for you.

Finally, don't put a lot of time and/or money into showing a dog until you have him radiographically examined to ensure that he is free of hip dysplasia. Better yet, have your dog certified by the Orthopedic Foundation for Animals.

Handling the Handler

A breeder, especially one involved in serious training, may simply not have enough time or energy to show his or her own dogs. Showing your own dog is expensive due to travel costs. The handler can be the appropriate choice and, if managed properly, can be the most cost effective.

The dog going out with a handler should always be a competitive animal in optimum condition. When these conditions are met, the handler should be able to finish the animal for less money than you would spend doing the job yourself.

Many handlers conduct conformation-training

Thea Bossart's "Yggdrasil Brethil" is to the best of my knowledge the only North American Bouvier to hold the UD and the TDX, both earned in Canada. She is also Canadian Champion and was Select Number Two at the North American Championships in Detroit in 1984.

classes during the week, where people bring their dogs to practice ring procedure. In a good class, both dog and handler learn together. Even if you never actually take your dog into the ring, it is important to get him used to the procedures, to learn to accept the stacking process, and to learn to be examined by a stranger. The price is usually reasonable, and it is a good way to become familiar with the procedures. One of the reasons why handlers conduct such classes is to acquire clients, and the class provides a good way to get to know the handler without making a major commitment.

In spite of some problems inherent in the handler system, the fact remains that handling requires a great deal of skill. The AKC ring process is very rapid, and if a dog is not properly presented, he might well get lost in the crowd. Also, considerable skill is necessary to consistently present many different dogs well. Handlers may be part-time or full-time. Many people show dogs for others on weekends and during other free time. Usually, they became handlers by showing their own dogs, then began taking in a dog of a friend once in a while. Because they still retain a full-time job, they usually are not under undue financial pressure and can be selective in the dogs that they show. The disadvantages of part-time handlers are that they are not always available and they are not in general as well known by the judges. The full-time professional handler generally has a whole string of dogs to show and is under significant pressure to keep the string large because this is how he or she makes a living. This, of course, means that the clients must be convinced that the handler is worth the money — which means winning.

If you are going to employ a handler, take your time and do as much research as possible. Talk to many dog owners and see who they recommend. Although most of what you will hear will be little more than idle gossip, it is possible to gradually get a feel for how well the various individuals are doing.

If your dog is involved in protection training, you must be forthright with the handler and make certain that he or she is comfortable with this aspect of the dog. We like for the handler to see the dog in his protection exercises and even work him a little to make sure that the handler understands what is involved. We have sent a number of strong Schutzhund dogs out with handlers with no problem.

To a large extent, the relationship is a matter of chemistry, so it is important to deal with a professional in whom you have confidence. A successful handler will not have to scrape for every possible client in order to put food on the table and may thus tell you that your dog is simply not of championship caliber. Such advice should be given serious consideration, for the successful handler makes a living by knowing how well he or she can do with a dog.

When you find a handler with whom you can work, keep up your end of the relationship by keeping the dog in condition and by following instructions on maintenance. And pay your bills promptly. Although the life of the professional handler may seem glamorous, like being paid to have fun, a lot of hard work and drudgery are involved. More hours are spent cleaning up after dogs than accepting Best in Show trophies. Also, a gift at Christmas or after an unexpected win is a nice gesture.

Ton Peeters' "Marco" has been one of the most successful Bouviers in the Dutch Police trials. He was fifth in the 1987 all-breed championships with 470½ points out of a possible 475. He was also the Champion of Limburg provience in 1987.

Sire: Rudy NHSB.1172680
Dam: Walda Tjoerzicht
NHSB.1010088
Brd: C. Xhofleer

Kathy Engel's Donar daughter "Hantal" was the first female to gain the FH, the advanced Schutzhund tracking title, and one of the first SchH II females. Shown here with the heavy Schutzhund dumbbell.

Sire: Donar SchH III, FH, NAWC'82 '79
Dam: Brenda Peggy v Casa Petrosa

Training For Companionship, Sport, and Service

The purpose of dog training should be much more than teaching the dog to sit or heel or even obtain this or that title. Rather, it should be to enhance the human/canine relationship so that the partnership can be effecive, productive, and pleasurable. There is much more to a well-trained dog than mere obedience in the sense of subservient compliance to the whim of "master." The dog should gain increased confidence and enhanced ability to perceive and do the right thing on his own, whether that be preventing a child from leaving the yard through an open gate or dealing with the mugger who attacks the human partner from behind. What good is a dog with an impressive obedience-competition record that has in the process become so inhibited and handler-dependent that these natural canine instincts are blunted?

"Training" and "obedience training" are synonymous in many minds, which does much to explain the fact that while a great deal of lip service has been paid to training over the years, very few Bouviers have really been trained to do much of anything. Training a dog to execute a simpleminded sequence of "obedience" exercises that are little more than stunts is ultimately a sterile experience. Yes, obedience is an important attribute of a well-trained dog, but it is not the highest or the most important for this breed; responsibility and courage are certainly more significant.

When training is perceived in a broader perspective, encompassing, for instance, tracking and protection, it can become an effective means to develop and enhance the whole dog. In this way, it can become the vital and fulfilling experience that it should be. It is essential that the training objectives and methodology *enhance* rather than detract from the essence of the Bouvier character.

Working with sound methodology and a good Bouvier can be enjoyable and rewarding, for there is much satisfaction in bringing out the potential of the correct working dog. Perhaps the greatest gratification is in the close relationship that evolves with your Bouvier as you become partners and companions rather than a person who happens to possess a dog. It is a tremendous experience when the dog indicates the object in tracking competition, a fit reward for the time and effort. When the protection exercise goes well, it is thrilling to send the dog to the blinds, where he searches for and then holds the evil agitator at bay and attacks him should he dare to attempt an escape.

Although motivations and methodologies are as diverse as the people involved, the basic goals of dog training are to enhance the dog as a personal and family companion by installing habitual good manners and to prepare the dog for work or sport competition.

Training For Family Companionship

Training in manners and social behavior is not optional. The only question is whether good habits and desirable deportment are to be established or whether the dog is to become a spoiled, self-centered malcontent. Make no mistake — whether you realize it or not, training commences the day the dog comes into the home. Certain behaviors are rewarded and others are discouraged. If the pup is fed from the table or is allowed to sleep on the sofa, the adult will be expected to persist in these things as well.

It is not my place to dictate acceptable behavior. If you come to my house, you are likely to see an old bitch comfortably asleep on the sofa and a dog sprawled out on the bed. The point is that you must decide what is to be allowed and then consistently enforce your rules.

The dog is entitled to consistency. It is not fair to punish today what was tolerated yesterday. Teach him that he has to bark twice and roll over before entering the living room if that is what you want — just start it early and allow absolutely no exceptions. Adapt from the very beginning your own house rules, appropriate to your circumstances, preferences, and lifestyle, then consistently enforce them.

Detailed training methods are covered in books listed in Suggested Reading. But even the best texts will leave you uncertain as to exactly what it is you are to do when you finally walk out on the field to train your dog. There is a lot more art than science to dog training, and efforts to record effective procedures are not very satisfactory. So much depends on the subtle details — attitude, timing, reading the dog. You can study a text and go out to the backyard and do precisely what it says, and yet the dog's perception may be very different because of variations in timing, emphasis, and nature of the individual animal. A split second can measure the difference between an effective correction that the dog understands and merely abusing a confused dog. When it comes right down to it, no book can contain words that extend the gifts of perception and timing.

In reading and listening, be aware that very few things, beyond the necessity of respecting your Bouvier and his heritage, are known absolutely. Much is in the murky realm of the art, the experience, and the gut feel rather than of science. Sometimes the beginner has exceptional success with a dog because he or she is not aware of how difficult it is supposed to be, just as most of us raise our children without consulting books by the "experts." Just as it is questionable if the various child-care books are a help or a hindrance, a book on dog training can cause problems as well as provide help and insight.

While the year-old dog in some breeds may in many ways be an adult, the typical yearling Bouvier is often still essentially a pup and in need of being treated as such, regardless of how large he may be. Many problems are caused by the failure to perceive that emotional maturity can greatly lag physical development. The trainer must be sensitive to the significant variations in the maturation patterns of individual dogs. This does not mean that training must be delayed until the dog is mature but rather that training must always be according to the maturity of the dog. For instance, the five- to eight-month-old should be learning to walk on the leash without pulling and should learn the idea of staying on the left side.

Training As Sport Preparation

Perhaps the most consistent trend during the past few years has been toward more intensive training at

Centauri's Gambit clears obedience high jump.

a younger age. The principle is that "firm but gentle" allows you to establish correct behavior patterns in the young dog without the heavy-duty corrections that might be necessary to convince the older dog to do it your way. Even traditionally coercive exercises such as the forced retrieve are being used effectively with relatively young dogs.

The people who have been the most successful with this method are firm but gentle and fair. My overall opinion is that the better the trainer, the more that can be accomplished with a young pup. The dangerous opposite side of the coin is that mistakes made at an early age, especially relating to harsh methods, can inflict serious and long-lasting damage. My advice is to move toward earlier training but under the guidance of a good instructor or as your own knowledge, confidence, and experience increase.

Over the years, I advocated relatively late training of the Bouvier. As the benefits of earlier training became increasingly apparent, my ideas gradually changed along with everyone else's. Overall training methods are getting better, and the necessary coercion is being applied with more sophistication and understanding.

Puppyhood is the time to grow, to develop, and to have fun. Most of the activity with the pup — and the pup should have a lot of time with the trainer — should be essentially play. The confidence and self-assurance necessary for stable, responsible adult dogs take time to develop. To accelerate the growing-up process by putting pressure on the pup to perform beyond his maturity is perhaps the most foolish thing that you can do.

Ten or fifteen years ago, conventional wisdom was that "serious" obedience training should be reserved for the mature dog, and many Schutzhund trainers believed that the dog should be biting seriously and hard before the real obedience work began. The concern was that the coercion of the obedience would make the dog "soft." This was not entirely without foundation, because much of the obedience work was overly harsh and much less sophisticated.

A harsh correction of a Bouvier pup that is confused but is trying to please can have a lasting negative effect. Reprimand a dog only when you are sure that he fully understands what is required and then refuses to obey. Early training applied with a heavy hand is likely to result in a resentful, sullen dog and will set the stage for long-term training problems.

Today's approach puts much more emphasis on building up the young dog, but at the same time training the young dog to accept commands and to be precise. Even the "out" for protection work is increasingly built up from a young age. Properly introduced, tracking is particularly appropriate to the youngster. Several Bouviers have achieved the AKC tracking title

within weeks of the six-month minimum age. This means that they certified — essentially did a TD-level track for a judge — at about five months. Tracking is suitable to the pup's limited development. He is capable of doing it and usually is willing to do it.

The eight-month-old can go along to the Schutzhund training and watch the older dogs train; the ten- to twelve-month-old can work on the fence and learn to bark at the bad guy. At perhaps a year, always according to the individual, it is time for the first real bite on a sleeve.

It is difficult for the novice and experienced trainer alike to know when to be lenient and when to insist on adult standards of behavior. It is perhaps better to allow the smart young adult to get away with puppy tricks for a few extra weeks or months than to force responsibility on a dog that is not quite ready.

The danger in pushing protection work too fast is that apparent success and the resulting overconfidence on the part of the handler may cause the youngster to be pushed too hard and to consequently break and run. A young dog can show tremendous progress and strength in one location, working with a particular agitator, and falter in another location or when facing another person. A trainer who pushes a Bouvier pup can do damage that may take months to repair and may in fact diminish the pup's ultimate potential.

Wilson van Pleinzicht, KNPV, SchH III, OFA, NHSB.780763 '74, imported by Erik Houttuin, was the first Bouvier to hold both a Dutch Police certificate (KNPV) and the Schutzhund III.

Sire: Duko v Mereveld
KNPV NHSB.495738
Dam: Lisca v Dafzicht
NHSB.529544 '70

Facing a large and aggressive man with a stick is meant to be a test of the courage and character of the adult dog; it takes time and maturity to build up the young dog to face hard protection work.

Training the Bouvier — Special Considerations

On the whole, a good Bouvier is a little more difficult to train at a competitive level, but his potential is great if the trainer is sensitive and perceptive enough to master the art. The biggest problem is the lack of experienced people to lend guidance. A German Shepherd owner can find plenty of people who have been successful in training and who are willing to share their experience. The Bouvier trainer, on the other hand, must often learn the subtleties by trial and error, which can be a lengthy and frustrating process.

Most Bouviers enjoy tracking and protection work, and there is normally no need to motivate them beyond getting out the sleeve or the harness. In fact, if they are not ready to go, a trip to the vet may be in order. Obedience training, on the other hand, can become boring for the Bouvier. Therefore, it is especially important for the handler to use methods that maintain interest and an alert, positive attitude.

The avenue to success is through firm but gentle training of the young dog, keeping the training sessions short and crisp, varying the routine, and working under pleasant conditions, such as in the evening or at night during hot summer weather. If a dog *correctly* executes an exercise once or twice, such as a barrier retrieve or a recall, praise him and go on to something else. If you run the exercise into the ground and cause a problem to surface, then a positive experience is turned into a negative one. Correctly timed praise, when the dog has done really well, is vital. Men in particular tend to be insufficiently demonstrative — they are too reserved to praise their dog properly for a good performance.

Fundamental aspects of the Bouvier character can render dealing with him difficult. He can be stubborn — there is simply no other way to say it. The correct way to deal with this is *not* to break him of the characteristic but to *use* it to your own ends. Once you start something and fail, the Bouvier has the upper paw. The next time around, the situation will be even more difficult. You must proceed with deliberate caution, one step at a time. Never give a command unless you are prepared to do whatever is necessary to ensure compliance, as long as you are sure that he understands what is required.

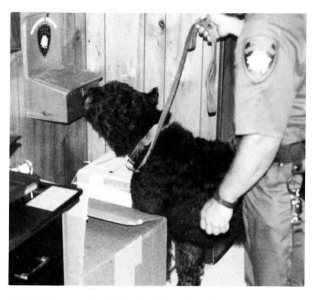

Officer Bruce Griffin's Bref du Clos des Jeunes Plantes, bred by Gerard Gelineau of Le Blanc in France, is a certified drug detection dog and all-purpose police canine for the Cocoa Beach Police Department.

An element of force, and sometimes infliction of pain, are inherent in every effective obedience program. The dog must come to accept that you are at various times going to give orders that require compliance. On more than one occasion, I have stayed up until the early hours of the morning working on a stand or sit exercise, engaged in a patient test of will with a dog. On one occasion, the dog, on doing the stand for examination, was perfect right up to the end, and then he slightly moved one foot. It was defiance, pure and simple. To have lost my temper would have been a major setback, because the next time the situation would have been worse. It was a simple matter of waiting it out, repeating the exercise until the dog finally did it correctly twice in a row, then praising him and going to bed.

By being patient and persistent, you teach the dog that doing what you want is the easier way. Thus, the plan is to do the exercise as many times as necessary, without impatience or excess pressure, to make the dog understand that he can't get out of it by playing dumb. Then quit after one or at the most two correct executions, being certain to praise the dog. In this way, he is rewarded for correct action, and hopefully next time he will do it correctly right away in order to avoid the hassle.

Such confrontations should be the rare exception,

however, because if you and the dog are not having fun most of the time, something is seriously wrong. When you encounter problems with your training attitude or methodology, resolve them before proceeding. Little will be accomplished unless both the person and the dog are willing participants.

While the Bouvier's stubbornness can be frustrating, on the other side of the coin is his courage and tenacity. Other breeds may be easier to train, but a good Bouvier is a real working dog. Those training

training, your primary objective should be building up your ability to communicate. These comments are especially appropriate to the Bouvier. Other breeds can to an extent be "programmed" in specific reactions by rote training, but the Bouvier is likely to rebel at such an approach and refuse to participate. In many instances, no amount of "correction" can force real compliance, and any grudging acquiescence will in the long run be of little practical consequence.

For me, the most important objective of training a

F Ch Uberty de la Thudinie, well-known working Bouvier in France in the 1970s, owned by Dr. Andre LeLann and bred by Jusin Chastel. (Tapin de la Thudinie x Quina ten Roobos).
This is a typical "Guard of Object" exercise, the object here being the box at the lower right typically used in training. *Photo courtesy Justin Chastel.*

such a dog should expect to deal with an equal, should know that there will be give and take, and should have respect for the dog and merit respect in return.

A number of skills and procedures are requisite to success in training, such as using the collar and leash as correction tools. Timing and technique must also be developed by experience and practice under the eye of an individual who can point out faulty execution. But training procedures and tricks are ultimately of secondary importance. The essence of effective training is *learning to communicate with your dog.* You must be able to understand his motivations, his desires, and his fears and use this knowledge to make him understand what you require and to motivate him to act accordingly. Whatever your goals are in

dog is not obtaining this or that title, or even obtaining good behavior, but the pure joy of participating in the fulfillment of his potential. It is a pleasure to follow him as he works out a difficult track, persists even though changes in ground cover or cross tracks are momentarily confusing, and works out the problems. The execution of a set of obedience exercises by a good team is a pleasure to behold, calling for maximum rapport between a person and his or her dog. The protection work is, of course, the most spectacular and makes the greatest impression on the casual audience. When done well, it is a tremendous demonstration of what a good human and a good dog can do together.

Specific Characteristics of the Protective Breeds

Significant differences exist among the protective breeds that influence their selection for specific applications. The good Doberman is quick and aggressive but not well adapted to extremes of cold or warm weather. This limits his usefullness in police applications in many climates. The German Shepherd is a remarkably versatile dog and the beneficiary of a strong, long-term promotional effort by the breed club in Germany. He is the predominant working dog throughout the world. The Rottweiler is powerful and strong but is also headstrong and sometimes lethargic. As bred for the show ring, he is often more bulky than necessary for practical applictions. The Giant Schnauzer tends to be a sharp dog, requiring an especially experienced and capable handler. Each of these breeds has its place according to its special qualities.

The Bouvier also has distinctive characteristics that should be primary considerations if you are interested in acquiring a working dog. He is agile and capable of great acceleration, as compared with the German Sherpherd's grace and efficiency. Running a Bouvier and Shepherd together demonstrates the other side of this structural trade-off — the Bouvier must labor to cover the ground that the Shepherd covers with effortless grace. Another consequence is seen in the go-out exercise, where the dog is sent away and then commanded to "down." Once the Shepherd is in motion, he can hardly turn his long body before covering the necessary distance. The Bouvier, on the other hand, hardly ever seems to travel twenty feet without darting to the left or right, taking a quick look over his shoulder.

There are also consequences of the cattle-herding heritage for the sport dog. The Bouvier learned, no doubt by harsh lesson, to be wary by responding to a threat with a quick jab of the foot or blow by the shoulder and then ducking quickly out of range and deciding on a next move. The bite is inhibited, reserved for serious provocation. This is well and good but is a slight problem in training for the Schutzhund trial, where the correct response to a threat is to take the offered sleeve and then hang on. Thus, natural reactions must to some extent be overcome by training in order for the dog to succeed in the sport.

One of the most desirable characteristics of the Bouvier is his slow fuse — the fact that he is not quick to anger and thus not apt to snap or bite an innocent person because of a perceived offense. It is a tremendous advantage to have a dog that can attack on command or in response to a clear-cut provocation but that can also have routine contact with diverse people without undue danger of an inappropriate bite.

On the whole, the Bouvier should be bred for more suspicion and aggression, but it is equally important that the "equitable nature" called for in the Belgian standard be maintained. It is a hallmark of the breed and a key element in his special desirability as a working dog. Many of the police departments that use the Bouvier do so because he does not have the "vicious attack-dog" image so often (unjustly) associated with the Shepherd or the Doberman.

Differences in training the various breeds are a never-ending topic of discussion. At one extreme is the "pure trainer," who holds that a dog is a dog is a dog, and that talk about breed differences is just sniveling and whining by those who for one reason or another can't cut the mustard. At the other end of the spectrum are those who confide that their breed is unique and that only those with long experience really know anything about how to train it.

What is the truth? Rather than try to answer this question directly, I advise you to take the attitude of the trainer. Accept that a dog is a dog, and approach the individual candidate with a minimum of preconceived notions and total respect. Do not start out to train Rotties or Bouviers or Dobies differently from Shepherds. But when you look back over many dogs, you will find that, yes, certain attributes and propensities tend to be characteristic of a breed.

So, there are breed differences. But when you get down to basics, the variations are more in the sense of the distribution of tendencies within a breed than fundamental, breed-specific characteristics. Perhaps the area in which you find the most variation is "dominance," that is, the tendency to be hardheaded, to challenge the handler, to hang on to the prerogative of "doing my own thing." Especially dominant dogs can be very difficult to force into an "eyes-only-on-the-handler" attitude in obedience and can be difficult to bring to the point of tracking reliably and "outing," that is, releasing their bite, in protection work.

The totally dominant dog would be impossible to live or work with. However, the dog with no dominance tendencies, while safe, would be useless. On the whole, balance is the key, with a tendency to prefer dogs on the upper end of the dominance scale for protection sports.

Broadly speaking, the breeds with which I am familiar can, in my opinion, be rank ordered in terms of dominance as the Rottweiler, the Bouvier, the German Shepherd, and the Malinois, with noticeable overall differences at all levels. Within each breed, the males are more dominant than the females. Thus, if you look over a thousand Rotties or Bouviers and pick out the five or six most independent, self-centered individuals, training is going to be a rough row to hoe. Similarly, if you look for the most submissive female Shepherds, you are going to have a hard time

The Zevanaar (Netherlands) riot squad, ready for action, circa 1980.

building up their confidence to produce a reliable performance.

Basically, when you seek out a really good, well-balanced training candidate, the general attributes that you look for are more or less breed independent. But where you find them relative to the breed *as a whole,* they are very much breed dependent. Thus, the really good Rottie prospect is not going to be as high up the dominance scale of male Rottweilers as the good Shepherd is going to be within his breed. Similarly, the tendency when picking among females in any breed is going to be toward the upper part of the dominance range.

Let me now attempt to describe the general Bouvier tendencies as working dogs. The need of a real bond with the handler, while important in any training situation, is especially important in the case of the Bouvier. Bouviers take significantly longer than other breeds to acclimate to a new owner or to a new training situation, and the training process tends to be longer and to require an especially patient and even-handed trainer. Administrators of Dutch Police programs and Dutch KNPV Club instructors have stated that roughly twice the training time goes into a Bouvier as a Malinois, which is an especially quick dog to train. When asked why they still included a number of Bouviers in their program, the reply was, "We have a need for some especially serious dogs in our work, and like the Bouvier for these applications." In general, the Dutch Police Bouviers have over the years had the reputation of being especially strong and aggressive, and apparently there is a need and desire for such dogs.

Consumer's Guide to Obedience Classes

Although much of a dog's training occurs as a natural part of day-by-day living, formal instruction also has a place. If you are a novice selecting a class, consider your level of experience, the time that you are willing to devote, and what it is that you want to accomplish with your dog. The highly competitive AKC obedience exhibitor who offers classes to others is perhaps not a good choice if you are an inexperienced dog owner who doesn't really understand what it's all about. The pressure is likely to be incompatible with your needs and desires.

On the other hand, if you have done some training and want to compete, seek out the instructor who has been successful. You should understand and accept the pressure and hard work that preparation for serious competition demands. You must also be prepared to accept that the instructor may inform you that your dog is just not good enough and that in order to be competitive, you should get another one. (A second opinion is definitely in order here!) This is

American and Canadian Ch Centauri's Marco Polo, Best in Show son of Centauri's Gambit and Dutch import Natasja.

Owner: Karen Saunders
Brd: Centauri

simply the nature of things, for just as relatively few people have the potential to be first-rate athletes, not all dogs are good candidates for top-level competition.

One serious problem is that the typical dog-training class instructor has never seen a Bouvier and has no idea how to train one. The methods used are apt to be appropriate to the Golden Retriever or to the Cocker Spaniel and are often less than effective with the Bouvier. The Bouvier generally requires more patience and sensitivity on the part of the handler. Be particularly wary of the text or instructor that insists that all breeds are essentially alike and can be trained effectively by identical methods. There *is* a fundamental set of universal canine principles, but there are also strong breed and individual characteristics that must be understood and accounted for in training methodology. The exceptional dog that does not fit the instructor's preconceived perception is likely to be lost in the crowd of the class.

In many urban areas, you will find a number of options. Classes are run by park districts, by obedience clubs, and by private individuals with varying degrees of competence. (Anyone can "hang out a shingle" and be an instant obedience-training instructor.) You will find a wide diversity in class size, quality of instruction, philosophy, and program objectives. Regardless of the organization involved or the philosophy espoused, the most important factor is the capability, experience, and enthusiasm of the instructor, who should be seen in action if possible before a commitment is made.

Try to avoid large classes of more than ten or twelve dogs. Such classes tend to result in a mechanistic approach, with the instructor demonstrating an exercise and mass confusion following as the class attempts to duplicate it. It is unfortunate that such an approach is almost a necessity when dealing with an excessively large class. If you are a novice, consider private or small-group sessions with an experienced instructor. You may think that this will be more expensive, but when you consider that in a class situation you spend 70 or 80 percent of the time standing around, individual instruction may well be more cost effective. The ideal format consists of four or five dog/leader teams that meet for an hour or less two or three times a week so that the instructor can give individual attention and a faulty technique is not practiced for an entire week before being corrected.

The most serious problem with many obedience programs is the emphasis on total obedience through harsh correction and repetitive drill. In addition to the ability to execute simple commands, other essential attributes of a good Bouvier include initiative, willingness, and courage. What can it profit you to make your Bouvier mindlessly obedient to commands such as "Sit" and "Heel" if in the process the other essential attributes are blunted?

Nobleair's Apache, Canadian Ch. To the best of my knowledge, the only Bouvier to hold both Schutzhund III and the Utility Dog degree. Bred and owned by Bernie and Lillian Blair, Spencerville, Ontario.

Sire: Ch Nobe de Bolshoy CDX
Dam: Ch Victoria's Honore CDX

Bouviers "de la Thudinie" in the early 1960s. From the left: Kaline, Irca, Job, and Kelly.
Photo courtesy of Justin Chastel.

The Propagation of the Race

What Makes A Successful Breeder?

Being a breeder is not just a matter of mating a bitch and selling the puppies. It requires commitment in terms of time, dedication, and disruption of lifestyle. Bitches must be bred when they come into season, and pups are born when their time comes, even if it is in the middle of a planned vacation. The commitment requires 365 days a year, twenty-four hours a day. A breeder must carry on through the lows as well as through the highs, patiently persisting through times of misfortune and disappointment.

Prominence and publicity do not a breeder make. Many people involving many breeds buy (in the United States or abroad) animals of such repute and quality that random matings cannot help but produce good or outstanding dogs. But this does not establish their credentials as breeders, because that requires a demonstration in the second, third, and subsequent generations of the production of better dogs than existed in the initial stock.

Usually those contemplating the breeding decision already have a bitch. Never mind that this is backwards — that you should decide to breed and then select a bitch — because the evaluation principles are the same in any event. If you have her and she is good enough — if she stands up well to the tests proposed here — breed her. Otherwise, get rid of her or spay her and keep her as a pet. Then look for a really breedable bitch. (This is easy advice to hand out but can be exceedingly painful to live up to!)

The best approach to a first litter is to evaluate the established breeders and select one whose dogs you admire and whose purposes and ideals match yours. Don't be unduly impressed with the number of championships accumulated, the possession of imported dogs, or extensive advertising claims. Put off breeding involvement until you feel confident that you can reasonably evaluate the dogs being produced rather than be taken in by the opinions of others. Once you have identified an appropriate kennel, approach the proprietor, explain your intentions, and ask for his or her help. In this way, you may hope to produce well-bred litters from the beginning.

According to the Standard

The person seeking to become a successful breeder is traditionally advised to "know the standard." The truth is that words on paper are a less-than-ideal means of communicating the concept. Most of us have difficulty matching the written description in a standard book (without breed identification) to dogs at a show or on the street. Thus, while the formal breed standard serves as the guide to breeding selection and should be seriously studied, it is only a starting point. A standard is a complex document, requiring an enormous amount of background information and experience to properly interpret. The novice will find that it takes several years of hard work to really grasp the concepts underlying the standard.

The best approach to forming a personal perception of type is to see and examine as many Bouviers as possible. You can attend dog shows, visit kennels, and in general go wherever there are Bouviers to see. It is especially worthwhile to spend time in Europe and see the Bouvier judged in his homeland by those who have helped to establish the breed. Watching Justin Chastel or Annie Verheyen evaluate Bouviers at a major Dutch or Belgian show can teach you more in four hours than a hundred North American shows. The North American Working Bouvier Association brings over a European judge for the championships each fall, at which critiques are taken down and published. Usually a seminar is presented that allows questions to be asked and the evaluation process to be explained.

When evaluating dogs, keep an open mind and concentrate on form, structure, and movement rather than on profuse coats and elaborate grooming styles.

If every Bouvier was dumped in a swimming pool immediately before entering the ring, structure and gait would be emphasized in selection.

You should gradually form an impression of which dogs possess overall quality and note the relationships among them, that is, see if the animals have common backgrounds. Collect pedigrees of the animals that you find interesting and learn about bloodlines. Seek out the advice and help of the people in the breed who you believe are truly knowledgeable.

Genetic Inheritance

We are all aware that a pup is normally going to grow up to have a resemblance to its parents in type and character. The reason for this is genetic inheritance — the fact that the "instruction set" of the sire is combined with that of the dam to produce a new and unique code, but one that will share many fundamental properties with those of the parents, grandparents, and more remote progenitors.

Barring a genetic accident (a mutation), a pup out of a particular sire and dam is limited in form and character variation by the combinations of genes that can be made up from those of the parents. There are literally billions of possible combinations, but there are so many more codes that *cannot* be produced because the genes to construct them are not present in either the sire or the dam. You just don't find a horse in a litter of Bouviers!

The study of genetic inheritance has made tremendous strides in the last thirty years. Every serious breeder should learn the general principles of genetics and become familiar with the terminology. If it is the function of the genetic scientist to discover how the process works, it should be the function of the breeder to act as genetic engineer, that is, apply the knowledge so as to produce better dogs.

The most fundamental and important aspect to understand is that even the most detailed physical analysis and examination of an individual cannot reveal the total content of his unique gene set. A large amount of "extra code" that is not manifested in the outward realization is nevertheless carried in every cell of the body but not used. Therefore, pups can exhibit physical properties and character traits that are present in *neither parent* but that perhaps *are* apparent in a grandparent or more remote ancestor. This is one reason why great dogs throw poor offspring and why animals can sometimes produce better than themselves.

A couple of genetic terms need to be explained — "phenotype" and "genotype." Phenotype is the physical and mental essence of an individual animal — the observable realization of that portion of his total genetic heritage that makes him what he is. Genotype is the total content of an animal's genes, both the characteristics that manifest themselves in an individual and the latent information that can only have external realization through his offspring and future generations.

In the American show ring or working trial, the phenotype is a determining factor in how well a particular dog performs. Breeders, however, are concerned primarily with gaining an accurate and complete knowledge of an animal's genotype, because a dog's genotype determines his potential to produce. This information can be gained by learning about the dog, about his parents, and about more remote ancestors and siblings. Tremendous insight is also obtained by observing his progeny, which is why a stud dog with a proven record as a good producer is so much more valuable than a prominent show winner that cannot reliably replicate the properties that make him good.

This hidden genetic potential makes a knowledge of bloodlines and pedigrees so important to the breeder, because the clues to what this generation's breeding stock can produce are hidden there. And while breeding "pedigree to pedigree" when the animals themselves are not of adequate quality is not advisable, you must also understand that breeding two apparently excellent animals can be disappointing if there is not good genetic reason for the perceived quality. As always, a balanced view is the key to wisdom.

Breeding Strategies

In order to establish and maintain a breeding program, you must have a plan that is more sophisticated than running off and mating a bitch to the current show-ring star. Breeding is an inexact science, and plans will need to be altered when a promising young breeding animal exhibits unexpected defects as he matures or when a mating produces a lesser quality than anticipated. Every new development requires a revision of the plan. The continual process of evaluation, comparison, and selection leads to the depth of understanding on which a sound, long-term breeding effort is based.

A distinction needs to be made between genetic defects, which can be passed on to the progeny, and congenital defects, which may be acquired during development in the uterus and not through heredity. Drugs that are normally safe can deform the pups in a pregnant bitch. This points out the need for the bitch to be in the best possible health before being

Miss Edmee Bowles, founding breeder in Belgium and America. Her line, "du Clos des Cerberes," stood in the forefront of the Bouvier world for half a century. Photo taken at Belco Farm, September 1979. *Photo by Jim Engel.*

bred. Congenital defects will not be replicated in future generations and thus will not necessarily prevent the afflicted animals from being bred. Unfortunately, it is not often known whether a defect is due to genetics or to some other factor during pregnancy. Deciding what to do in the face of such uncertainty is one of the most difficult problems in breeding.

Breed type is usually established and maintained by "breeding tight," that is, by mating closely related animals in order to diminish the gene pool and thus produce more commonality of appearance and temperament in the group of animals that constitute the breed. This can be a double-edged sword, because the same process that consolidated desirable traits can do the same for the undesirable traits, and the limited gene pool can make it very difficult to rid a breed of an entrenched problem.

There is a lot of close breeding behind the Bouvier. Chastel bred incredibly tight from 1960 through 1975, when he and a couple of cooperating Belgian breeders were the predominant force. They supplied the bulk of the gene pool in France and a substantial portion in the Netherlands and Belgium. This did much to consolidate the Bouvier type but also made further close breeding more treacherous than it would be if a more diverse gene pool were available.

In planning a breeding program, it is advisable to restrict yourself to some sort of limited background. Decide which lines to work with, and select stock accordingly. If a new, unrelated outside stud dog is used for every breeding, you will soon end up with such a diverse background in your stock that every breeding will be totally open and will likely produce diverse and unpredictable types and characters. Even when an open breeding produces an outstanding specimen, the value of the animal as a stud or brood bitch is often much less than would be expected from the show record, because the diverse background naturally produces diverse offspring, and the animal may never come near to reproducing himself. Look back over the years to see how the big winners really stack up in pedigrees of the dogs that are relevant today. You may be surprised to see how little they mean in the long run. Certain animals in particular lines will predominate and will stamp their mark on the flow of the breed because of their inherent worth and solid background and because they were in the hands of knowledgeable and dedicated breeders.

In the long run, most breeding programs are kept relatively tight to conserve and replicate desired attributes, but they eventually get boxed in. The point comes when essential traits are lacking that are simply not available within the confines of the line. The usual solution is an out-cross, that is, a breeding to a dog with few if any common immediate ancestors and a strong background in the desired attributes. This is usually best left to the more experienced breeders. The novice is advised to work with more conservative line breedings. Every mating is a roll of the dice, but the unpredictability of the radical out-cross makes it a gamble in a class by itself.

An outstanding animal of diverse background may tend not to replicate himself and may throw progeny as diverse as his own background. If the dog has any tendency to consistently throw new and desired properties, the progeny inheriting them can be bred back together so as to consolidate the gain, that is, produce animals more capable of consistently reproducing the desired attributes. Out-crossing is not for the faint of heart or the impatient, because it can take generations and years to consolidate the gains.

To perpetuate a breed of strong, useful dogs, a vigilant effort must be made to eliminate dogs that are not pleasing to the eye as well as those with genetic weaknesses. It is necessary to have a sufficiently diverse gene pool to be able to eliminate the offending dogs and use for breeding stock animals that are remote enough genetically to allow the reproduction of the breed to continue while breeding out the problem. Overly tight breeding can make this very difficult.

The kennel that breeds tight and adopts a "see-no-evil" attitude toward fundamental problems can breed itself into oblivion in short order. If there is a general deterioration in the vigor of a line (reduced longevity, lessened fertility, and repeated incidence of specific problems), perhaps Mother Nature is telling us something. Thyroid problems, dysplasia, bloat, and a hundred other degenerations are with good reason believed to have genetic causes or predispositions. The problem is that animals that can be kept alive to breed would be quickly "selected out" in nature or have such a low social position as to be precluded from breeding. In keeping dogs in kennels and determining which are to be mated, man has largely disabled the natural process of selection for vigor. This is one reason why a demanding working test and physical criteria such as provided by OFA for hips as

breeding eligibility criteria are so important for the maintenance of a working-dog breed.

The creation and maintenance of a line is a complex and difficult process involving many years and numerous animals. Since very few of us will ever have the resources to maintain a complete breeding line, you should not view your program in isolation, but rather as related to those of selected breeders with compatible ideals and objectives. The key to success is to find the right people to work with and then establish cooperative relationships.

The International Perspective

Many novice breeders are anxious to own imported dogs. While it is true that a carefully selected import and the knowledge of how to use it in a breeding program can offer great benefits, many import for the wrong reasons. Many beginners become impatient and go overseas to buy dogs, or arrange a purchase through others, before they are mature enough as breeders. Often they pay too much for dogs that are inferior to breeding stock readily available in the United States. At other times, they end up with worthwhile dogs that cannot be used effectively because the breeders do not have enough experience to produce really good pups. Although the possibility of eventually importing breeding stock is an important reason for the beginning breeder to become familiar with European lines and trends, this knowledge is equally important when looking for breeding stock on this side of the Atlantic, because most top-rate dogs in the United States have relatively recent European ancestors.

Breeding-Stock Selection

To be worthy of being bred, a dog must be a good overall specimen of his breed. He must be free of serious genetic defects and adequate to very strong in all fundamental physical and moral attributes. He must be sound, athletic, and free of physical defects. He must be strong in type, which means that he must exhibit the physical structure and moral makeup that define his breed. Finally, his character must be strong and correct, enabling him to fulfill the traditional breed functions.

There is a great deal of art in breeding, and even the most rational and thoughtful breeder is unable to totally articulate the reasons for his or her selections. No book or computer program can give you a

Ch Rostan du Clos des Cerberes, whelped in 1958, shown at left taking Working Group First in 1964. This large, but correctly short-coupled, male is perhaps the pinnacle of the early Bowles lines. Handler is Pat Marcmann.

Sire: Bel Ami du Clos des Cerberes '52
Dam: Si Jolie du Clos des Cerberes '54
Brd: Edmee Bowles
Born: 1958

checklist that enables you to crank out the answers like you do for your income taxes. There is something to the celebrated "eye for a dog," although many more claim it than have it. You need to develop this ability to quickly form an overall impression, but then you must be able to relate it to the specifics. If a dog looks good to you but you find serious deficiencies when you look at the specifics (skull proportions or coat texture), then you are deceiving yourself. An experienced, knowledgeable person can quickly evaluate a dog and discard a large percentage as obviously faulty in character or conformation. To be a breeder, you must train yourself to this level.

As you gain experience and confidence, you will discover that certain breeders are using dogs that you don't think stand up very well to your criteria. In some instances you may be correct, but in others you may not understand the reasons behind the selection.

The reality of the Bouvier world today is that the winning conformation dogs and the top working dogs are coming out of different lines. Many breeders are not concerned about this. Some regard the Bouvier as a show dog and pet and regard the working function as obsolete or irrelevant. On the other hand, some people whose primary interest is training and working their dogs could care less about what their dogs look like, or even if their dogs can be registered.

In my opinion, both of these one-dimensional approaches to breeding are shortsighted and destined for mediocrity. Many kennels in Europe, and a small but increasing number in America, are making a serious attempt to bridge the gap. When the conformation-oriented breeder comes to understand that more is involved than merely training a couple of dogs, that he or she must bring working-character dogs into the program, friends and enemies are likely to wonder if that breeder has lost touch with reality. In a similar manner, when the working enthusiast starts looking for dogs of reasonable potential in show lines in order to improve the type of his breeding stock, friends may suspect that he or she is about to defect to the enemy and may predict dire consequences.

The need to bring the breed back together is the reason why many kennels have some very nice-looking dogs that are not strong and hard enough for serious work, and working dogs of a style not currently popular in the show ring. These breeders are trying to force the metamorphosis in an attempt to

plan to reach this goal and seek out alliances with others who share these ideals.

If your long-term goal is to consistently produce competitive conformation dogs with serious working potential, you will have to make compromises. For many years, your kennel will have pieces of the puzzle and hope for the future but relatively few dogs that will approach the ideal of both worlds. If, however, this goal is realized, these visionary breeders will have reestablished the breed according to the original ideals of the founders. In my opinion, this is a goal worthy of a lifetime of effort.

Donar, SchH III, FH
1982, North American Working Champion at Niagara-on-the-Lake, Ontario

Ria Klep's "Donar," Working Champion in the Netherlands whose American visit in 1982 did so much to awaken interest in working Bouviers. Donar was a dog of immense presence, immediately the center of attention wherever he went. In working competition he captivated the audience with his enthusiasm and assertiveness. He regularly placed in European show rings, usually with the rating "Excellent."

eventually bring the breed back to one balanced whole.

Setting Goals

To succeed as a breeder, you must set your own goals. If you desire trophies (for work or for conformation) and the approval of others, then your course is obvious. Those who have a higher personal vision of the dogs that they want to produce must devise a

The Genetic Road Map

The focus thus far has been on developing your ability to evaluate the dog, that is, establish in your own mind that he is adequate in type, soundness, and character. Now it is time to look seriously at background evaluation — the other half of the breeding equation. Recall that much of a dog's genetic potential is hidden and that when two dogs are mated, attributes and propensities evident in neither parent come forth. OFA-excellent individuals mated together can produce dysplastic offspring. Washed-out pups can come out of parents of correct color. Weak, even dangerously fearful, dogs can come out of strong working dogs.

This tendency for hidden characteristics to appear is so strong that many breeds evaluate the pedigree before really looking at the dogs. It is easy to get carried away with the illustrious names from the past and imagine finding a pup that combines the best attributes of each — the cream of the cream. But it usually doesn't work out that way, because those same famous names are behind hundreds of dogs, some of which are not of good quality at all. If the parents and grandparents are not very good or outstanding animals, then more remote progenitors, no matter how illustrious, are most unlikely to "breed through" and produce a high-quality litter. The names of dogs more than two generations back should be thought of as interesting and useful as background information but not something on which to base a breeding decision if the more immediate ancestors are less than first rate.

On the other hand, it cannot be emphasized enough that only part of the genetic potential of an animal is revealed by external appearance and character, because genes come in pairs, only one of which may manifest itself in a particular dog. Only by knowing something about an animal's immediate progenitors, his siblings, and other offspring of his parents can his total genetic potential be evaluated properly.

Animals whose parents or grandparents exhibit serious defects or are simply mediocre should be suspect, because many attributes not apparent in the individual may surface in the progeny. Also, the general quality of the littermates is vital, for a good animal from a uniform litter may well be a better breeding prospect than a more outstanding animal whose littermates exhibit significant faults.

It is worthwhile to look four or five generations back, to note the overall background. Historically, significant differences have existed among the Bouviers in the various countries (primarily Belgium, Holland, and France), and distinct and largely separate traditions have developed within individual countries, such as the Dutch show dogs and the KNPV dogs of the 1940s and 1950s. When you look deeply into a pedigree, it is useful to understand the overall characteristics of these various breeding traditions. Yet, the presence of specific animals should not be decisive. Certain lines are predominant, because few Bouviers today do *not* have Soprano or Marc de la Thudinie in their background (the only possible exception being an isolated dog out of old Dutch stock).

In pedigree evaluation, the working character of the animals is no less relevant than the conformation. Working achievements such as the KNPV certificate and Schutzhund titles are important considerations, as are many of the European surveys, such as the Belgian "select" examination, which incorporate a character test.

Selecting the Stud Dog

Once a bitch has been selected for breeding, that is, fulfilled the spirit of the criteria outlined in previous sections, it is time to think about a stud dog. The males should be scrutinized against an even more demanding standard of soundness, type, and character, because the individual can produce so many more offspring, with only a relatively small number being used. Most of us are constantly seeking good potential stud dogs and find a limited number with proven character *and* credible conformation.

The place to start in selecting a stud dog is knowing your bitch as thoroughly as possible. Seek to understand her strong points and the aspects that you want to improve. Determine which dogs in her background are most likely the genetic source of the attributes that you are trying to enhance or minimize.

Seek a male with an established record of improving the specific qualities that you have the most need to enhance in the genotype of the bitch and in your program in general. This points out the advantage of using a dog with a significant number of previous litters, because his progeny (in combination with his ancestors and siblings) provide a reasonably complete picture of his genotype. These comments are especially pertinent when selecting a mate for the maiden bitch, because if she were bred to a novice stud, it would be more difficult to sort out what was coming from where in the litter. The use of a well-proven male will hopefully provide much information that will be useful in evaluating the quality of the bitch's value as a breeding animal. In the opposite situation — the evaluation of a young and unproven male — it is common practice to use him on several established bitches so as to compare the get with previous progeny and thus gain a good estimate of his value.

The conservative approach is to consider dogs "in the line," that is, with significant common ancestors. A stud that has been used with good results on bitches of similar backgrounds and attributes usually has the advantage of predictability because of the common genetic material. This is because the total number of possible progeny phenotypes is reduced by the common genes.

The disadvantage of linebreeding or any sort of tight breeding is that recessive characteristics, usually undesirable, are apt to crop up with increasing frequency. In addition to producing specific defects, many believe that tight breeding has a tendency to-

Marion Hubbard is truly an American breed founder. She has been a breeder, teacher, and leader for three decades. She is shown here with Ch Madrone Ledge Courage (Yago van de Buildrager x Madrone Ledge Zolla) in the early 1980s.

ward producing reduced vigor — genetic weaknesses that don't show up as specific problems but that lead to reduced overall health and stamina.

It is useful to have a good relationship with the breeder of your bitch so that you have better access to detailed information about the results of previous, similar matings. Ask for a candid opinion of your bitch and the mention of possible mates. The practicality of this advice is dependent on your confidence in the breeders. Some will always have a stud to push and the desire for the fee, which will influence the advice given. Finding people with whom you can work is essential to your long-term success as a breeder. Virtually no one in this day and age has the financial resources, time, and energy to run an entirely independent breeding program.

Seek strong relationships with breeders who are able to keep things in perspective. These are the people with whom you should seek to work and learn. When you select a stud (or buy or lease a bitch), you are heavily dependent on what they tell you about the animal's background. It is difficult to verify this infor-

mation up front, so trust and honesty are valued commodities.

As you become more experienced and able to make your own evaluations, your focus in selecting breeding stock should be more on the animals. The time will come when someone whom you do not like or respect has a stud dog that would benefit your program. Many fine breeding programs have been weakened because the people involved would not or could not deal with others who had animals that they needed to breed to or to buy. Avoid this self-defeating attitude! If you need something, go get it. You should, of course, be especially careful that your research is complete and that the dog paid for actually services your bitch.

When you find a potential mate, research as many of his offspring and littermates as possible, looking for consistent quality and a lack of serious defects. Don't overlook a young dog or one in the hands of a less financially able owner. Rather, develop the ability and the confidence to make your own decisions. This is a project for a lifetime.

Ch and W Ch Centauri's Gambit
SchH III, NAWC '87, '89,
CD, OFA/Ex

Sire: Dutch Work Ch Donar
SchH III, FH
Dam: Ch and W Ch Centauri's
Fleur de Lis SchH III
Brd: Dr. Erik Houttuin
Owner: Jim Engel
Born: 1982

A mother's work is never done! *Photo courtesy Marion Hubbard.*

The Breeding of the Beast

Kathleen Engel

The Heat Cycle and Its Variations

Female canines become sexually receptive and of interest to the male during a "heat" or estrus cycle. In wolves, this occurs only once a year, so that resulting puppies will be born when weather and hunting conditions allow the pack to remain in one area for many weeks while the pups become mature enough to travel. In domesticated wolves, that is, dogs, the heat cycle usually occurs twice a year, although the actual time of occurrence can come at any time of the year.

Bouvier females typically have their first heat cycle at about eight months of age. The first cycle will often be a "puppy" heat that lasts only a few days. A complete adult heat cycle normally lasts about twenty-one days, although an experienced stud will only be interested for a few days. After a puppy cycle, a normal heat cycle usually follows a few weeks or months later.

The heat cycle begins with bloody-red discharge from the vulva. As the cycle progresses, the vulva swells and the discharge lightens in color until it becomes pale pink or nearly clear, usually around the eleventh to fourteenth day. This would be the appropriate time to breed the female. If no breeding occurs, the discharge darkens again and disappears around the twenty-first day. The swelling of the vulva decreases as the discharge darkens and disappears. If a yellow, creamy, or pussy discharge appears, take the bitch to a veterinarian immediately, because this may indicate a serious infection.

The time between cycles may vary depending upon the bloodline. A bitch will often follow the breeding pattern and problems of her own mother. Just as your gynecologist or urologist would inquire into your family medical and reproductive history, so should you

inquire into the family medical history of your breeding animals. Some tendencies follow certain family lines, and you should be aware of all of them before you undertake a breeding.

The normal interval between heat cycles is about six months, although an interval of four months is not unusual. These short cycles are often associated with other problems, such as a failure to conceive or the incidence of pyometra, which is a severe and, if untreated, fatal uterine infection believed to be triggered by a hormonal imbalance.

Heat Cycle Mapping, Key to Your Breeding Future

Once your females are past the first heat cycle, it is wise to "map" all of them to be used as brood bitches. Mapping consists of keeping chronological and descriptive records of all cycles and related breeding information. It is an invaluable aid in the breeding process. Carefully and accurately note the date on which each heat cycle begins, then detail its progress, that is, the change in color of discharge and other factors. It is especially important to note the day on which the discharge is at its clearest. The best method is to wipe the vulva with a clean white tissue so that the color and texture can be noted. As the discharge begins to clear, tickle the area just above the female's tail and see how she reacts. If she tries to arch her tail stub over her back or off to the side, it is referred to as "flagging" and may indicate tht she would be receptive to a male. That also should be noted by calendar date.

For bitches with infertility problems, we take this a step farther by going to the vet at intervals for vaginal smears. When professionally interpreted, these can help to define the progress of the heat cycle. Cell structure changes as the heat cycle progresses. Also record these results in the mapping book. This is a guideline and is not infallible. I have known of bitches to conceive litters even when the slides said that conception was impossible. We had one litter of nine puppies when the veterinarian said that the bitch was not in heat and that she only had an infection.

Always note the reactions of your male dogs, because an experienced stud knows more about when a bitch is ready than even the best veterinarian with a box of slides. Mapping can be challenging if the female has little discharge or keeps herself very clean but can be an indispensable breeding aid.

Photo courtesy Marion Hubbard.

Some females are meticulous about personal hygiene, while other are casual about their bloody discharge and leave a considerable mess. Some owners have success using boys' jockey shorts of an appropriate size and a disposable sanitary pad on the inside, placed on the bitch so that her tail extends through the front opening. Some females accept this well, while others consider removing this device a challenge.

Some odor is also normal with the heat cycle. If the female is not to be bred, you may wish to check with a large pet supply, because tablets are available to give your dog orally to reduce odor. Or you may wish to try chlorophyll tablets handled by the pharmacist and often used by people with body-odor problems.

Occasionally, bitches have side effects from their heat cycles. Upset stomachs, diarrhea, and moodiness are common. More frequent urination is not unusual. Emotional changes and moodiness are apparent in some bitches up to three weeks before they come into heat. Emotional changes can range from crabbiness (this may be where the term "bitchiness" originated) to lethargy and excessive desire for affection. This can create real problems with the working bitch, who may become inconsistent and handler-dependent during this time, even before discharge occurs.

To add to the dilemma, false pregnancy is common in some lines. In this instance, even though the bitch is not bred, she will swell up at an appropriate interval after the heat cycle (five to seven weeks). Her udder will fill with milk, and mood swings will occur. She may adopt a toy as her "puppy." Once again, for working bitches this can be frustrating as they become clinging and uncertain. This stage passes in three or four weeks, usually without veterinary interference. With all of these hormonal emotional storms going on, it is easy to see why there are so few highly titled working Bouvier bitches.

Breed By Appointment

Breeding is not recommended before eighteen months of age, because the bitch is simply not physically mature enough for the stress of pregnancy and motherhood. In general, two years to thirty months of age is the ideal time for a first litter.

When you plan to breed your female, other research needs to be completed long before the heat cycle begins. You should have first- and second-choice stud dogs chosen in advance and have contacted the respective breeders to see what their breeding requirements are and what stud fees are involved. The stud fee is usually equivalent to the price of a puppy and varies with the quality and reputation of the stud.

The well-informed breeder is concerned with physical and mental soundness and genetic compatibility, plus the dog's ability to produce the desired attributes. The stud dog owner will ask for an extended pedigree of your female (one going back past her grandparents) so that his or her knowledge of genetics can be used to evaluate possible problems or pluses. This person may also request a photo of your female or may wish to evaluate her in person to see if the match would be mutually beneficial — remember that the betterment of the breed is at stake here. At the least, no harm should be done by producing puppies with probable genetic defects.

The stud dog owner should also require either an OFA certificate or other acceptable hip evaluation (something that you should also require on the stud dog). Radiographical examination of the hips should be done in advance and not close to the heat cycle, because some experienced breeders believe that the hormonal changes around the heat cycle can adversely affect the outcome of the X-rays. The hormones generated by the heat cycle may cause excessive looseness or laxity in the hip joint, making it appear faulty when the same X-ray taken several months later might show acceptable tightness.

In addition to hip X-rays, the stud dog owner should demand a brucellosis test on the female. You will need to know how much in advance this is required. Don't leave it until the last minute. The usual test generates a certain amount of false positives, and doing the test early enough will allow time for a more lengthy backup test if it is necessary. You also should demand proof of freedom from brucellosis on the stud dog. If he has not had pups fairly recently or is past middle age, a sperm count may be in order. You have the right to ask for this information, because you are paying the stud fee for live sperm. The stud dog owner may also ask for a vaginal culture to indicate that the bitch is free from infection. On all maiden bitches an internal exam should be performed by the vet. That way, if internal strictures would cause a problem with breeding or whelping, everyone is aware of the situation ahead of time and can proceed accordingly.

Get a written contract from the stud dog owner regarding policy on failure of your bitch to conceive. Do you get a repeat stud service? What if the stud dog is unavailable? How many pups constitute a litter? What if your bitch is unavailable but you would like to get your replacement breeding on another bitch? If everything is in writing, there will be no misunderstanding later if something goes wrong.

Make certain that your female is in excellent health and that she is not over or underweight. Get a thorough physical and have her checked for parasites to make sure that she is free from anything that can be transferred to the puppies. If your vet is agreeable, you may wish to do a chem-screen — a blood test that gives the status of many bodily systems, including some liver functions and the blood-protein level. That way, if something subclinically is wrong, you can take care of it or at least not put her life at risk by breeding her. This procedure is relatively inexpensive considering all the valuable information it can generate.

It is strongly recommended that the maiden bitch be kept relatively close to home for her first breeding. Even experienced bitches may not do well when shipped for breeding. The bitch that is a spoiled house pet is more likely to be troubled by this than a kennel dog. I have known of breeders desiring puppies out of a certain stud to have the stud (and owner) flown to the bitch so that she would conceive if attempts to ship her proved unsuccessful. The Bouvier is not always an easy dog to breed.

Think Before You Breed

Before you take the giant plunge and breed your female, there are several other important considerations.

Do you have homes for any of the puppies that might result from such a breeding? There are always people who will tell you, "I'd just love to have a puppy; just let me know when she has some and I'll take one." But when you call with the delightful news that your bitch has just dropped a litter of thirteen, that same person will have sixty-nine excuses why this is a bad time to take a puppy. Now what are you going to do with thirteen hungry mouths to feed?

Even well-established breeders with well-known stock go through periods when it is very difficult to sell pups. They have to be prepared to hold them for a long time. The longer you hold puppies past the cute, cuddly stage, the less salable they tend to be. Most of our pups are sold on reference from other breeders, to people who have purchased a pup from us in the past, or through other contacts made over fifteen years in the dog business. These contacts, built up over many years, are not available to the novice.

Plan ahead for puppy expenses and for advertising — even before your female is bred! Do you have a veterinarian who is used to dealing with breeders? You need to find one who has a good emergency service and who can deal with common problems, including a cesarean section if necessary. Also, which vet will be prepared to crop the ears on your puppies? This is an art form and if done improperly can ruin the looks of an otherwise spectacular dog, making him virtually worthless. In advance of breeding, it is advisable to establish a budget so that you will have an idea of the amount of cash needed before the first pup is sold.

Do your homework and fill in figures for these probable expenses:

Stud fee $_____

Veterinarian fees (brucellosis test, exams and tests during pregnancy and after whelping) $_____

Breeding travel or shipping expenses (breeding within one day's drive, overnight accommodations, and food — four days minimum) $_____

Extra food for bitch $_____

Tails, dewclaws, and physicals
for eight pups $_____

Advertising (several display
ads in a national dog magazine
at $_____ per inch plus other
local ads) $_____

Food for puppies for twelve
weeks (_____ pounds at $_____
per forty pounds) $_____

Ear cropping for eight or more
pups $_____

Three sets of shots and three
wormings for eight pups $_____

Emergency reserve in case of
cesarean section and/or other
unforeseen items $_____

If your bottom line is less than $2,000, try again, because you have missed some major expenses!

Keep good records and all receipts, because any profits are taxable income and you may need to hire an accountant to file your income tax.

Plan advertising in advance of the breeding, because some advertising may take as much as two months to set in motion. A national all-breed magazine such as *Dog World* is your best prospect. Local papers have minimal results unless there are no other breeders in your area. Breed-oriented magazines rarely are effective, because you are telling people who already may have too many Bouviers that you are in the same boat. Have your advertising planned and ready to insert as soon as you know that your female is pregnant.

In the Beginning

Your female is finally in heat, and the exciting prospect of breeding is at hand. Check with the first-choice stud dog owner to see if the timing is mutually convenient and that the stud dog is not ill or being shown. Be prepared to tell them the exact date when the heat cycle started. At this time, you can refer to your mapping book to also tell them of your bitch's previous heat patterns. You can then set the best time for your arrival.

If you travel out of town with the bitch, it may put her heat cycle on hold for a day or two unless she is used to traveling. Some get so upset that they even go out of heat! When you do get to the stud dog owner's home, take some time to let the bitch relax, relieve herself, and feel comfortable before being introduced to the stud dog. A relaxed female is more

receptive. Continue mapping as reference for future breedings.

All stud dog owners have their own way of managing the stud and the breeding. Some will insist that you muzzle and hold your bitch to prevent her from biting anyone. Some just put the two dogs in a run together and watch. While it is important to be sure that your female is being bred to the dog for which you are paying, you must depend upon the experience of the stud dog owner, who will know his or her own dog's needs, to dictate the actual breeding procedure. Hopefully you are working with someone in whom you have confidence.

It is generally preferred to breed every other day during the bitch's receptive period until two or three breedings have taken place.

Countdown: Nine Weeks to Puppies

After the breedings have taken place and you return home, monitor your female carefully. She may still be receptive, so don't assume that she will not be willing to breed with another dog. She may go out of heat immediately or may have a greatly shortened heat cycle. When she does go out of heat, her vulva may not return to its original size but may stay somewhat swollen. Try to keep her food intake steady for the first four or five weeks.

Week Four

At twenty-eight days after the first breeding, plan to take your bitch to an experienced vet who will palpate (feel) her abdomen for puppies. They will be about the size of a walnut by that time. Don't try to do this yourself! Only someone who is experienced can do it and not hurt the puppies or the bitch. This is not an infallible procedure but can be a helpful guide to pregnancy. You also may ask your veterinarian about a blood test to check on pregnancy. Keep careful track of any discharge from the vulva that is unusual, creamy, pussy, bloody, brown, or bad smelling. When in doubt, consult your vet. It is always better to be safe than sorry.

Many bitches get morning sickness at about four weeks into their pregnancy. Vomiting, diarrhea, and generally feeling sorry for themselves are not unusual but rarely last more than a week. If you feel that the problem is something more serious, take her temperature. You should be taking her temperature to get a benchmark on her normal temperature at least once

Figure 10-1

WHELPING CHART

Date bred (January)	Date due to whelp (March)	Date bred (February)	Date due to whelp (April)	Date bred (March)	Date due to whelp (May)	Date bred (April)	Date due to whelp (June)	Date bred (May)	Date due to whelp (July)	Date bred (June)	Date due to whelp (August)	Date bred (July)	Date due to whelp (September)	Date bred (August)	Date due to whelp (October)	Date bred (September)	Date due to whelp (November)	Date bred (October)	Date due to whelp (December)	Date bred (November)	Date due to whelp (January)	Date bred (December)	Date due to whelp (February)
1	5	1	5	1	3	1	3	1	3	1	3	1	2	1	3	1	3	1	3	1	3	1	2
2	6	2	6	2	4	2	4	2	4	2	4	2	3	2	4	2	4	2	4	2	4	2	3
3	7	3	7	3	5	3	5	3	5	3	5	3	4	3	5	3	5	3	5	3	5	3	4
4	8	4	8	4	6	4	6	4	6	4	6	4	5	4	6	4	6	4	6	4	6	4	5
5	9	5	9	5	7	5	7	5	7	5	7	5	6	5	7	5	7	5	7	5	7	5	6
6	10	6	10	6	8	6	8	6	8	6	8	6	7	6	8	6	8	6	8	6	8	6	7
7	11	7	11	7	9	7	9	7	9	7	9	7	8	7	9	7	9	7	9	7	9	7	8
8	12	8	12	8	10	8	10	8	10	8	10	8	9	8	10	8	10	8	10	8	10	8	9
9	13	9	13	9	11	9	11	9	11	9	11	9	10	9	11	9	11	9	11	9	11	9	10
10	14	10	14	10	12	10	12	10	12	10	12	10	11	10	12	10	12	10	12	10	12	10	11
11	15	11	15	11	13	11	13	11	13	11	13	11	12	11	13	11	13	11	13	11	13	11	12
12	16	12	16	12	14	12	14	12	14	12	14	12	13	12	14	12	14	12	14	12	14	12	13
13	17	13	17	13	15	13	15	13	15	13	15	13	14	13	15	13	15	13	15	13	15	13	14
14	18	14	18	14	16	14	16	14	16	14	16	14	15	14	16	14	16	14	16	14	16	14	15
15	19	15	19	15	17	15	17	15	17	15	17	15	16	15	17	15	17	15	17	15	17	15	16
16	20	16	20	16	18	16	18	16	18	16	18	16	17	16	18	16	18	16	18	16	18	16	17
17	21	17	21	17	19	17	19	17	19	17	19	17	18	17	19	17	19	17	19	17	19	17	18
18	22	18	22	18	20	18	20	18	20	18	20	18	19	18	20	18	20	18	20	18	20	18	19
19	23	19	23	19	21	19	21	19	21	19	21	19	20	19	21	19	21	19	21	19	21	19	20
20	24	20	24	20	22	20	22	20	22	20	22	20	21	20	22	20	22	20	22	20	22	20	21
21	25	21	25	21	23	21	23	21	23	21	23	21	22	21	23	21	23	21	23	21	23	21	22
22	26	22	26	22	24	22	24	22	24	22	24	22	23	22	24	22	24	22	24	22	24	22	23
23	27	23	27	23	25	23	25	23	25	23	25	23	24	23	25	23	25	23	25	23	25	23	24
24	28	24	28	24	26	24	26	24	26	24	26	24	25	24	26	24	26	24	26	24	26	24	25
25	29	25	29	25	27	25	27	25	27	25	27	25	26	25	27	25	27	25	27	25	27	25	26
26	30	26	30	26	28	26	28	26	28	26	28	26	27	26	28	26	28	26	28	26	28	26	27
27	31	27	May 1	27	29	27	29	27	29	27	29	27	28	27	29	27	29	27	29	27	29	27	28
28	Apr. 1	28	2	28	30	28	30	28	30	28	30	28	29	28	30	28	30	28	Dec. 30	28	30	28	Mar. 1
29	2			29	31	29	July 1	29	31	29	31	29	30	29	31	29	Dec. 1	29	31	29	Feb. 31	29	2
30	3			30	June 1	30	2	30	Aug. 1	30	Sep. 1	30	Oct. 1	30	Nov. 1	30	2	30	2	30	Jan. 1	30	3
31	4			31	2			31	2			31	2	31	2			31	2			31	4

Courtesy of Gaines.

a week now anyway. Take it rectally with a rectal thermometer. Try to get her used to having it done while lying on her side. If you don't know how to take her temperature, ask your veterinarian to demonstrate.

Be sure that your female gets adequate exercise. When we had our first litter of Bouviers, we had leased an experienced brood bitch from a major kennel. I informed myself as completely as possible by working hand-in-hand with the bitch's owners, talking to other dog breeders, and reading everything available on the subject. I felt confident going into whelping, only to have the bitch stop at seven puppies, even though she obviously had more inside. We ended up with a cesarean section because she had uterine inertia and lost all of the remaining puppies.

After the fact, we learned that we had made a major mistake. When we had tried to take April for a walk as the pregnancy progressed, she would lie on her back and put her feet in the air because she didn't want to walk. We had all laughed about how cute it was. After all, she was an experienced mother. She should know if she felt good enough to walk. She became a couch potato. I learned my lesson the hard way. We had two more litters out of April, and each day she would be taken for a two-mile walk. She absolutely resisted walking, so instead of dragging her, on went the pinch collar and off we went. After a few days, she gave up the act and walked willingly. The next two litters were born quickly and with no complications. During the final week, we broke up the exercise sessions into several shorter sessions but still insisted on covering as much distance as possible.

Week Five

Around the fifth week of pregnancy, increase your bitch's food intake gradually with high-quality food. Introduce dry puppy food into the diet at this time and gradually replace her normal kibble with that, increasing quantity as well. Supplement with dry milk powder or plain yogurt, which can be made easily at home with dry milk powder. As time passes and puppies crowd her abdomen, you will need to plan on more frequent but smaller meals. Overall quantity of food will continue to increase. Continuously check her rib and hip area to make certain that she is not becoming grossly obese. The food should be going to puppies, not to excessive fat.

If your bitch is carrying a large litter, you may need to work extra treats into her diet to make it more palatable. You may also need to boost her protein intake. An additional chem-screen done at seven weeks will provide you with her blood-protein level,

giving you a good idea of any deficiency. After the puppies are born, her food intake will gradually increase the first ten days of nursing. Some bitches are easy keepers, while others have insatiable appetites, eating twenty-five cups of food and two pounds of meat daily and still end up extremely thin when the pups are weaned. Monitor the bitch's weight carefully and be prepared to provide all that is needed for her.

Full-term canine pregnancy is supposed to last sixty-three days. Always count from the first breeding. Be prepraed two weeks in advance so that your bitch can become used to the whelping box and whatever area you have selected for the delivery room. Most bitches whelp between the sixtieth and sixty-third day. We had one whelp as early as the fifty-seventh day, and another as late as the sixty-fifth day. Do not wait any longer than sixty-five days before you check with the vet to see if intervention may be necessary.

Seven Weeks — Some Important Preparations

Some important considerations in choosing whelping locations would include the ability to keep the room warm, draft-free, quiet, and private, and to keep it clean easily. Whelping and its aftermatch are messy. If you plan to have whelping occur in a room with carpeting, you are going to have a big problem. Puppies are noisy, messy, and smelly.

The homemade whelping box that we use is four feet square and is made of wood. The sides are twenty-four inches high, but one side has a removable panel so that the box is only twelve inches high when first assembled to allow the mother to get in and out more easily. The floor is painted with a lead-free enamel for ease in cleaning, and the wooden sides are oiled with boiled linseed oil so that they clean fairly well. This will contain the puppies for the first four or five weeks unless the litter is very large. Plan to stockpile newspapers — you will be changing the lining very frequently.

Set up the whelping box in a quiet, draft-free area and introduce the bitch to it two weeks ahead of time. Put some papers in the bottom so that as time progresses she will have something to paw at and dig in as part of the nest-making process.

You will also need some safe, fireproof method of raising the room temperature for the first seven to ten days after the puppies are born, because they are unable to control their body temperature for the first ten days. If chilled, they die easily. We previously had a very small whelping room only a few feet larger than the box itself and had satisfactory temperature

These five-week-old puppies will soon be ready to leave this homemade whelping box. Note that the front panel is lower than the sides and back. *Photo by Cheryl Calm.*

control by using two light fixtures with incandescent bulbs of 100 and 150 watts. This room was in the house, so its basic temperature was in the sixty- to seventy-degree F. range. The lights were able to boost it to around eighty degrees F. for the first seven to ten days. We then let it drop back to a more normal temperature as time progressed.

Our current whelping room is in the basement, which is ideal. It is quiet, isolated, and easy to keep at any desired temperature. We use a brooder or infrared light in a special ceramic fixture hung about thirty to thirty-six inches off-center over the whelping box. When you use an infrared light, hold your hand under it at newspaper level for several minutes to assure a gentle warmth. You want to warm the puppies, not cook them. Infrared lights can be dangerous, so read all instructions to make certain that you are using yours properly. If you use a space heater instead, be aware of fire danger and try to set yours in an area where it will be tip-proof and safe. Also remember that your floor can be very cold, especially if it is cement or in a basement. Never put your whelping box directly on the floor. Always place something suitable between the box and the floor as insulation. It is preferable to put the whelping box in a corner so that only two sides are open to the room.

As a regular routine, we have a chem-screen (also known as a blood chemistry profile) and a CBC (complete blood count) done on all of our bitches at seven weeks into the pregnancy. Your veterinarian may discourage this practice; however, it has revealed developing problems in our own breeding program often enough to make it worth the minimal expense.

Also at seven weeks into the pregnancy, start taking your bitch's temperature twice daily, morning and night. Always take it when she is relaxed so that you will get consistent readings. In about 80 percent of pregnancies, the bitch's temperature drops below 100 degrees twelve to twenty-four hours before she is going to whelp. In some females, the temperature fluctuates between 99 and 100 degrees several times and then drops below 99 degrees before whelping. The last ten days to a week, try to take her temperature four times daily so that you have a good idea of what is going on. Keep this information in your mapping book so that you will know what to expect next time. Most bitches are consistent in their breeding and whelping patterns.

At least ten days ahead of the due date, assemble everything that you might need for the whelping. Some suggestions include the following:

- two pair forceps
- waxed thread or dental floss (for tying cords)
- betadine disinfectant
- scissors
- lots of towels — old or cheap ones, because they may become stained
- heating pad
- cardboard box, larger than the heating pad
- lots and lots of newspapers
- prepared puppy formula — recommend Havaloc®
- puppy nursing equipment
- scale to weigh pups accurately to the ounce, weight up to ten pounds
- vet's phone number

Try to find someone dependable to help you in the whole process — preferably someone experienced with the whelping of any breed of dog.

Week Eight — Preliminary Haircut

Hair loss is common during late pregnancy and after whelping. It is one of the few times that the Bouvier does real shedding. Be prepared to brush out your bitch's coat thoroughly every other day for the last two weeks of pregnancy and the first two weeks after whelping.

It is also advisable to do some trimming just prior to whelping. With a ten blade on your clipper, shave around and between the nipples, going two to three inches up the sides. Overall, take the coat down to two or three inches by your favorite method — stripping, plucking, or with a plastic blade over your clipper blade.

Some bitches lose very little coat during pregnancy and whelping, while others lose so much hair that they have bald patches as large as the palm of your hand. Being extra careful with their diet can help limit hair loss but by no means eliminates it. It is wise to plan on nine months for a bitch to fully recover her looks from the whelping process. Serious roadwork may also be necessary to restore her topline.

Week Nine — You're Having Puppies Where?

Now that your whelping room is set up, you need to convince the bitch to use it rather than your bedroom closet. Encourage her to spend time in it each day. Have some newspapers in the bottom of the whelping box for her to paw and tear. That is a normal part of the nesting process that precedes actual whelping. Some females will take to your arrangements right away. Others will try to choose their own den, which is often someplace dark and hard to reach. Be careful, because they may try to squeeze or dig themselves under stairs, under your porch or house, or in some other unsuitable place. The closer they get to whelping, the more persistent this den-making instinct becomes. Watch your female closely.

You need to persist in order to have the bitch accept your choice of whelping location. Have her in there at frequent intervals. Keep the lights low and a radio playing softly, which will drown out some of the background sounds that might upset her.

The last ten days of her pregnancy, she may try to clear the house of other animals in her desire and need to be alone for the birth process. Even an otherwise gentle and submissive bitch may become very aggressive in her desire to drive out other animals, especially female dogs.

Birth Symptoms

Other signs can now be monitored that may help to indicate when birth is imminent. The whites of the female's eyes may begin to get bloodshot three to five days before birth. You may see a clear or white mucous discharge from the vulva a week or less before birth. The vulva will swell greatly as delivery time nears, becoming larger than during the heat cycle and very soft and flabby. Your bitch may be restless and may pant and scratch at the flooring. Some females do this only while in labor, while others carry on the last two weeks to ten days.

In Bouviers, it is common for the bitches to carry some puppies up underneath their ribs where they cannot be palpated. As the pregnancy progresses, they may have slight, invisible contractions that move everything farther down into the abdomen. Most bitches show much greater abdominal distention the last ten days of their pregnancy. Just before labor, they may also exhibit restlessness, panting, and scratching.

As whelping time nears, your bitch may refuse food. Make sure that water is available at all times, but not in the whelping box itself. The mother may be restless and not settle down. In a maiden bitch, this may continue over a couple of days. Be prepared to have someone with her at this time. When she does start having large contractions, write down the times. If at any time she has unproductive straining for a long time (more than half an hour), check with your vet.

It is extremely important that someone attend the bitch during her first whelping, because she will not understand what is going on. She will be frightened and confused.

As birth becomes imminent, make final preparations. Have your cardboard box lined with extra papers, heating pad, and toweling ready to keep puppies warm. Boil your forceps and scissors in water with a tiny bit of disinfectant; keep them covered and allow them to cool. Have plenty of towels available.

Puppies At Last!

When the bitch starts to have strong contractions, give her praise, "Good Girl." Stroke her sides and let her know that everything is all right. When the first puppy begins to emerge from the vulva, your bitch may be in pain and be frightened. She may snap at her rear or at you. Usually she will be so full of puppies that she will not be physically able to reach her rear to aid the birth process. Once again, encourage her with her contractions. The puppy will probably slip out with the sac intact. Many bitches take one look at the resulting mess and leave the whelping box. Their attitude is, "Don't blame me for that mess!"

Be prepared to open the sac immediately. Clear the puppy's face so that he can breathe. Clamp off the cord in two places, one very close to the puppy's abdomen, and cut with the scissors. Tie the cord close to the abdomen with the waxed threat or dental floss. Then remove the forcep. Be sure to cut the thread close to the knot. As soon as the pup is freed from the sac and placenta, place him in a head-down position on your lap and rub him briskly with a towel until he cries.

If the puppy seems full of fluid, hold him in both hands, completely supporting his entire body. The puppy shold be facing away from you. With arms raised to shoulder level, do a brisk downward swing toward your knees, with the puppy's head at a lower level than the rest of his body. If repeated several times, this procedure forces fluid out of the puppy's lungs and nostrils.

Rub again briskly with dry towels. The tongue should be bright pink or red, and the puppy should be crying. Now offer him to the bitch to lick. Many maiden bitches still refuse to pay any attention to the puppy, nor do they eat the afterbirth. Sometimes it takes the birth of three or four puppies before they begin tentatively to lick or to sniff. In the meantime, have your heating pad turned on and placed on top of several layers of newspapers in the cardboard box. Top it with one or two layers of light-colored toweling. Place your hand on the toweling frequently to make sure that it is warm and not hot. You can keep pups in there while they wait for the dam to show interest in them or while the next pup is being born.

If necessary, the puppy can survive without nursing for several hours as long as he is kept warm and dry. Puppies will be fine in the warming box for a little while, but continue to monitor the temperature regularly. Continually change the papers in the whelping box so that it stays clean and dry. If the bitch calms down, offer her the puppy to lick, or see if you can put the puppy on a nipple to nurse. Be ready to remove the puppy to the warming box as needed. Be persistent in placing the puppies on her nipples and giving them to her to lick until she accepts them.

Closely monitor the umbilical cords where you have cut them. Make certain that the string used to tie each one off is cut short. If not, the bitch will worry about it later. If you haven't tied the cord tight enough, it

may bleed. The pups cannot afford to lose any blood, so tie it again if necessary.

Make certain that you keep count of the afterbirths. If you do not get one for each puppy born, make a note of it so that you can tell your vet at the after-whelping physical.

Birth Weights

Keep accurate records of the birth weight and physical description of each puppy, including sex, color, and markings. As you become more experienced, you will be able to tell a great deal about structure by examining the newborn. As the pup's hair dries, you will also be able to predict whether the future coat will be straight, wavy, or curly.

Birth weight of the first few puppies can be an indicator of the overall size of the litter. Normally, the smaller the litter, the larger the individual puppy. When whelping begins and the first three puppies weigh in the ten- to twelve-ounce range, be prepared for a large litter (unless the female has been undernourished or is immature). A nice-size puppy will weigh one pound. If he is significantly more than one pound, delivery will be difficult. If he is significantly less than one pound, survival is less likely. We have had puppies as large as one and three-quarters pounds and surviving puppies as small as four ounces. The later took a tremendous amount of outside intervention to keep alive but did grow to normal adulthood. He was one of a litter of fifteen, all of which survived. While we supplemented the first ten days, the mother took over all nursing duties after that and would keep the puppies sorted into two groups. One group lay between her front paws while the other nursed.

Extra-large puppies can be difficult to deliver. Often in these cases the sac has already broken and you will be presented with the head or a couple of feet. Since the puppies are wet and slippery, be prepared to grasp them with a towel or washcloth. Apply gentle but firm downward pressure so that the puppy is pulled toward the bitch's feet. Work with the contractions if you can. Be very careful that no undue pressure is put on the area of the umbilical cord, because you could cause an umbilical hernia or actually tear out the puppy's abdomen if you are too rough. Puppies are fragile. Take it easy. If you get upset, you will only upset your bitch.

One of the most common problems of birth is having the puppy born while the bitch still retains the placenta so tht the puppy is effectively tied to his mother. Any roughness here can injure both pup and bitch. Clear the puppy's face so that he can breathe

A litter of very large two-and-one-half-week-old puppies. In Europe a litter is called a "nest." *Photo by Linda Schneider.*

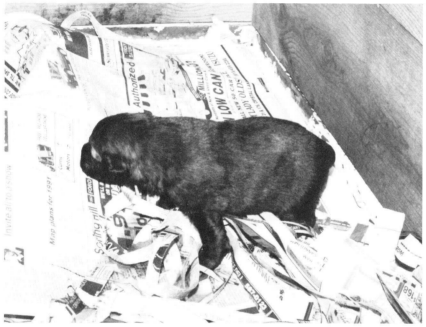

This large two-and-one-half-week-old puppy is just starting to get up on its feet. *Photo by Linda Schneider.*

right away. Then wait a few moments to see if the afterbirth will be expelled. If not, you can try to slide the lips of the vulva back far enough to apply a forceps, clamp the cord, and cut it to free the pup. When it is an extra-tight squeeze, I have reached into the vulva with my fingers and pinched off and broken the cord with my fingernails. You have to clamp the cord tightly with your fingertips *immediately* before you move your hand or the pup will bleed from the navel before you can get the cord tied. This is another good reason to have two persons present. An extra sest of hands to control the bitch while all of this is going on is invaluable.

As your female deflates, allowing her to reach her rear, let her participate in the birth process as much as good sense dictates. She should eat the afterbirths if she so chooses. If the birth process is long and tiring, be prepared to offer her high-energy food in small quantities every two hours. You may try a cup of cottage cheese and some honey to keep up energy levels. Also, give her free access to water outside the whelping box.

Offer to take the bitch out to relieve herself as needed, but take a towel with you in case you get a surprise delivery while outside.

Expect the bitch to rest and go without contractions for regular intervals during the birth process. Often, they whelp two puppies over a twenty-minute period, then rest for half an hour to an hour before they start having contractions again. Every bitch is different. We have had thirteen puppies in as little as two and one-half hours (that kept three people busy cutting, wiping, tying, and rubbing), and nine pups over twenty-eight hours. There is no accurate guideline. However, bitches that are physically fit definitely have puppies more quickly and with less effort and fewer complications.

You should have already discussed with your vet the circumstances under which he or she would want to be consulted on an emergency basis. Be sure that you have an appropriate after-hours phone number!

If a cesarean section becomes necessary, insist upon after-surgery antibiotics that are compatible with nursing puppies. This was another lesson that I learned the hard way. The bitch went from the cesarean section into metritis (a serious uterine infection), because no antibiotics had been prescribed. The metritis took such strong antibiotics to clear up that the bitch could no longer nurse the puppies. This meant that I had an orphan litter to raise. Feeding seven puppies every two and one-half hours around the clock for three weeks is an experience never to be forgotten.

If you should be faced with orphaned puppies, I strongly suggest that you have your vet teach you how to tube-feed them. With tube-feeding, the formula is in a syringe, a tube is passed into the puppy's stomach, and the formula is gently inserted. This is a tricky procedure but can make the feeding go more quickly and efficiently. Tube-feeding should also be backed up with periodic bottle-feeding, because the puppies do really need to nurse.

When you believe that the birth process is complete, make an appointment with the veterinarian for a hormone shot (pop shot) that will help to expel any afterbirths. The mother will also need to be examined for retained puppies. This should be done as soon as possible. She should receive the shot even if you believe that all afterbirths have been expelled.

Bring the puppies with you for a brief physical at this time. They can travel in their heating-pad box. The vet will look for any obvious birth defects and will listen to their hearts. Have the vet check to make sure that each puppy has a complete anus. Any defective puppies should be put to sleep. Also, you may consider culling puppies that are of incorrect color (pale cream, white, or washed out). If you have a very large litter (more than eight puppies), you may wish to cull extremely small puppies.

Puppies that are less than 50 percent of the birth weight of the average litter size have a small chance for survival. For instance, if the average weight of the large puppies in the litter is sixteen ounces, and you have a puppy weighing eight ounces, he is a poor prospect for survival. If a puppy has a poor chance of surviving, it is emotionally easier to have him humanely put to sleep than to find him dead or dying in the whelping box.

Your bitch will continue to have a bloody discharge for three or four weeks after delivery. For the first few days after delivery, she may have black stools or diarrhea from eating the afterbirths. This is normal. Her temperature will be elevated for a few days after delivery; however, if it exceeds 103 degrees, contact your vet. The vet may also recommend after-whelping antibiotics. Some breeders use them regularly and believe that they prevent metritis (a uterine infection) or mastitis (a breast infection). If antibiotics are used, be very careful that they are of a type that will not harm the nursing puppies or give them diarrhea.

Puppy Dog Tails

Plan to have the puppies' tails and rear dewclaws, if any, removed between three and five days of age. If the puppies are large at birth (one pound or heavier), try to get the tails done at three days. If small, have them done at five days. Having the front dewclaws done is optional.

The puppies' tails should be cut one-half inch long and "cut to stand." For ease in measuring, suggest tht the vet draw a line one-half inch in on an index card. Then the outside edge of the index card is placed underneath the tail, firmly against the puppy's body. The vet then cuts on the line. Two sutures are recommended for puppies weighing one pound or more, while one suture usually will suffice for those weighing less than one pound. These are usually absorbable sutures and do not need to be removed later. They will dissolve by themselves. If your female is thorough in licking, be careful that the stitches are not prematurely licked out. Also watch for tail-stub infections. Check the puppies' rears every day to make sure that the dam is keeping them adequately clean by licking and that the tail is healing normally.

Some unenthusiastic mothers do not lick their puppies' stomachs and rears enough. This is necessary to stimulate digestion and defecation. If she won't do it, you will have to with a clean washcloth dipped in warm water. Do this at least four or five times a day for the first two weeks, after which time the puppies are better able to go on their own.

We treat tail-stub infections with betadine. If the problem occurs, ask for your vet's choice of treatment. Before you leave the office after tail docking, ask for a styptic powder in case the tails or dewclaws bleed when you get home. Some lines seem more inclined to bleed than others. Keeping the puppies on light-colored toweling in the heating-pad box and on clean papers in the whelping box will help you to monitor this. Have the tails done at a time of day when you can be around to check on the puppies for at least twelve hours afterward. It doesn't take much blood loss to kill a tiny pup.

Your Daily Checkup

You now need to check the puppies frequently. Go over each one thoroughly at least once a day. Check his weight to make sure that he is getting enough to eat. Gently pinch the skin at the back of his neck to make certain that he is not dehydrating. The puppy's skin should quickly go back into place. If it stays pinched together for a few seconds, he is dehydrated, and you will need to get more liquid into the puppy immediately. That puppy will have to be supplemented and watched more closely. If a puppy is seriously dehydrated, he is very difficult to rehydrate. Consult your veterinarian, because a subcutaneous injection of appropriate fluids can be injected if advisable.

Sometime you may find a puppy off in a corner by himself. If he has gotten chilled, do not try to feed him until you have gradually warmed him in your heating-pad box. Once he is back to normal, try keeping him separated from his littermates and feeding him as if orphaned for twenty-four hours before returning him to the litter. Occasionally, you may see the dam push a puppy into a corner by himself, or keep one between her front paws, not encouraging him to nurse. Keep a close eye on this pup. When a puppy has an internal problem, sometimes the dam seems aware of it. We have always assumed that the puppy smelled differently. Even with your best care, you probably will not be able to save such a pup.

Expect all of the puppies' weights to double between ten days to two weeks of age. As long as you keep good records by daily weigh-ins, you will be aware of any potential problem puppies. Be prepared to supplement as needed.

At about ten days of age, puppy noses may be running slightly with a clear liquid. This is normal. In a day or two you will notice the puppies' eyes and ears begin to open. While the eyes are going through the opening process, keep the pups out of bright light. At first you may notice that the puppies will have

One-week-old puppy being bottlefed by Sandra Calm. *Photo by Cheryl Calm.*

blue eyes. Don't worry — they will darken up later. This is perfectly normal.

At ten to fourteen days, you will notice the puppies pulling themselves around by their front legs. They will probably be very active. Be prepared to put the other panel on the whelping box so that they cannot escape by crawling over mother and then over the top. After you insert the extra panel, monitor the dam carefully to make sure that she will jump over the side of the whelping box to feed the puppies. You may have to help her the first few times. Soon she will learn to look over the sides to see where the puppies are so that she will have a clear landing spot. It is often helpful to have a half-height panel to add, because some bitches refuse to jump over the full height. Or you may be able to fashion a set of steps that she can use.

Toenails on puppies can grow very quickly and will need to be trimmed every few days to prevent the mother's stomach from becoming scraped and raw.

The puppies will be up on their feet at about three weeks, or a little less if they aren't very plump. Fat puppies are a little slower to walk.

Weaning

Once the puppies are on their feet, it is time to get serious about weaning. They will also start getting their teeth at this time. Between teeth and toenails, mother will be glad to see that you are weaning them.

Make any changes in the puppy's diet gradually. We usually begin weaning with one meal a day consisting of a high-quality puppy food mixed with hot water to soften. The food will have to sit for fifteen minutes or so depending on how hot your water is and on the brand of puppy food that you use. Please check the label on the food to be sure that there are no soy products in it. If there are, choose a better food. I avoid dog food with soy because I strongly believe that soy is not metabolized as a complete protein by the dog, at least as it is prepared by most dog food manufacturers.

Once the food has softened, add enough more warm water to make it the consistency of very soft oatmeal. If the food won't soften thoroughly, and to make sure that there are no lumps, you may wish to run it through a food processor or blender. A small blender designed for drinks and crushed ice works the best. Test the temperature of the food on the inside of your wrist to make certain that it is just warm, not hot. To this, add two heaping tablespoons of *plain* yogurt with a live culture. The live yogurt culture will help the bacteria in the puppy's intestines deal with the new diet.

Offer the food in a very low pan to the puppies once a day, after mother has been out of the whelping box at least one hour. You may have to dip your finger in the food and then put it in each puppy's mouth to get them started.

After the puppies have been eating one meal for four or five days, expand it to two meals. Obviously they would be allowed to nurse freely the rest of the day, after they have been offered a meal.

When the puppies have successfully eaten two solid meals a day for four days, start on three meals a day. At the same time, keep the bitch away from the puppies for longer periods of time. When the puppies are eating three meals a day, you may wish to keep the bitch away from them most of the time, letting her in with them two or three times a day. At this time, also begin cutting down on the bitch's food. Gradually start getting her back to a more normal diet.

After another four or five days, move the puppies to four feedings a day and begin to strictly limit the bitch's visits to twice a day for a few days, then once a day for a few days. After that, they should be kept apart until her milk dries up. In some bitches this may require a shot from the veterinarian. At this point, return the bitch to her diet prior to pregnancy both in content and amount.

There are several important considerations to weaning. If you do it too abruptly, you can cause severe stomach upsets in the puppies, leading to bloody diarrhea and death. You can also cause mastitus — a severe inflammation of one or more sections of the bitch's udders. As long as weaning is handled gradually, you should be trouble-free. Have some rice baby cereal on hand to incorporate into the puppy food if the stools seem a little soft. And be certain to check your bitch's udders daily throughout the nurs-

These three-week-olds can easily eat out of this low-sided pan.
Photo by Linda Schneider.

ing process for hard or hot areas. These might indicate mastitis. If there is a problem, check with your vet immediately. You ought to be good friends with him or her by this time.

Constantly monitor the puppies' stools for color, consistency, and any strange odor. Check with your vet for a worming schedule. We are on a regular worming program established by our vet that takes care of roundworms and hookworms. Watch out for mucus in the stools, for loose stools, or for stools that are lighter than normal in color. If you have puppies that don't gain weight well, take a stool sample into the veterinarian immediately. There are other parasites that can seriously affect or even kill your puppies. Both giardia and coccidia are parasites that can cause serious problems. It's a good idea to have the stools checked several times at regular intervals beginning at three weeks of age.

If you have a sensitive nose, you will be able to notice a different odor if something is wrong with the puppies' stools. You can even become sensitive enough to smell the blood in a slightly bloody stool when you walk into the whelping room. This takes considerable experience from more than one litter. If you do see a bloody stool, consult the vet immediately. Varieties of bacterial enteritis can take a whole litter down in twenty-four to thirty-six hours. Since we quit trying to rush weaning, we have had fewer stomach upsets in the pups.

Plan an inoculation schedule with your vet. This will be a series of shots at two- to three-week intervals, beginning at six weeks of age. Have your vet recommend what type and brand you should use. If the vet is cooperative, he or she may show you how to give these shots yourself. You can buy the syringes and the ingredients for the shots from many large dog-supply catalogs and save yourself a fortune if you have a large litter. Make sure to keep the vials refrigerated when not in use. We plan on shots every other week from the sixth through the sixteenth weeks.

Socialization

Once the pups are weaned, the socialization process begins. Play the radio for several hours during the day so that the pups get used to noise. At about two weeks after the birth, carefully selected visitors are acceptable. Be aware that the bitch may not accept strangers at this time, and you may have to put her in a separate room when people come to call.

While excessive handling of the pups is a bad idea, it is a good idea to get even very young puppies used to being handled. If they cry, sit near the whelping box with a pup on a towel in your lap, gently stroking

him until he settles down. Then put him back and get out another pup. It is never too early to get them used to the human touch as long as you don't overhandle them.

Don't isolate young pups from usual household noises. Use your vacuum, drop metal pans, and slam doors. Don't tiptoe around. Their ears will open up at about two weeks of age, and it is a good idea for them to get used to normal sounds after that time.

As the puppies get older, drag all guests to see them, to hold them, and to pet them. Human contact is good for them, as long as the humans are careful and considerate. No unsupervised play with children should be allowed unless you trust the children completely. A bad experience at this tender age can ruin a puppy for life.

Between six and seven weeks of age, we usually begin physical and temperament evaluations of the puppies. I once attended a seminar about puppy temperament evaluation suggesting that it be done only on the forty-ninth day of age, by a stranger, in a

These three-week-old puppies are getting carefully supervised attention from their friend Miss Libby Massa. *Photo by Linda Schneider.*

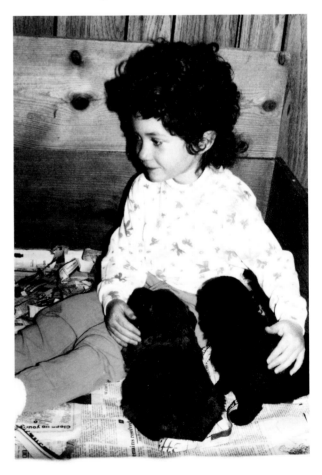

strange location. A long set of subtests followed. It was an effective test, but there were several problems with it. Between six and seven weeks of age is the time our vet most prefers to crop the ears of the puppies, which means that the evaluation would come at a time when the pup would not be feeling his best.

Even if you are not into formal testing, a number of worthwhile observations can be made. Most temperament variations are not easily detectable until the pups are at least six to seven weeks of age, or slightly older. Don't evaluate puppies that are ill, have just had ears done, or have just been fed. If pups are sleepy or sick, they will not act normally and will throw off your evaluation.

We also test for sound sensitivity. We feed our dogs in metal pans. Once the pups are old enough not to be traumatized, I occasionally drop a pan on the hard floor in their vicinity, first twenty feet away, then closer. Have someone help you observe the pups. How do they react? Jumping or wincing is normal. We are interested in recovery. You want pups to be interested — to come and investigate. If a pup goes off in the corner and hides, watch out for that puppy. Retest again in a few days. If the pup continues to have a problem, be careful where you place that pup. I consider this a serious fault that would eliminate that pup as a breeding prospect. Please note that fear of electrical storms and sound sensitivity are *not* related.

We also like to see which puppies are natural retrievers, or which ones like to chase an old towel on a string. This sort of activity helps us to sort out working prospects. We test one puppy at a time. We might roll a ball or a wadded-up piece of paper, very low, just in front of the pup's face, and see if he will go after it. Some will chase it and then ignore it, while some will grab it and run away. Others will get it and, with your encouragement, will bring it back to you. The latter would receive the highest score. Bouviers that do not automatically retrieve can be taught to retrieve when they are older. Don't eliminate a nonretriever from breeding or from a working program.

When we drag an old towel on a string, we do it slowly, teasingly, and temptingly for one puppy at a time. For the working prospect, the ideal puppy would grab the towel and carry it in his mouth. He might also growl or shake the towel. This test is not infallible but can indicate a tendency for "prey drive" (a highly desirable working characteristic).

One of your biggest concerns should be the shy puppy. We have seen some "touch-me-not" litters as early as three days after birth. These pups will squeal or cry out if you touch them. If you have such a litter, make it a habit to handle each puppy daily. Lay him in your lap and stroke him until he is quiet. Later on, be observant of all of the puppies when you have company in to see them.

Encourage people to come in and see your puppies. While the puppies have company, evaluate their reactions. Is one puppy always hanging back? Does one stay in the corner or even shake in fear? If a puppy consistently has such a problem, please have the courage to put him to sleep. Even out of the best of parents, physical or emotional problems may occur. That shy puppy could easily turn into a fear biter, a potentially dangerous dog. Such animals are very rare. Most puppies are friendly and outgoing. That is the way they all should be.

The puppy may also be shy due to physical causes. One pup showed a persistent unwillingness to form human bonds in spite of special efforts at socialization and unusual personal attention. We were mystified until, at some four months of age, we noticed something odd about her expression. When examined, one eye was distended and white. She was taken to the vet, who discovered juvenile cataracts. One had slipped internally over the normal eye drainage tube, causing glaucoma and destroying the sight in one eye. She was, of course, immediately euthanized. The point is that you must always search for an underlying physical cause for what may appear to be a character flaw.

Ear Cropping

Ear cropping is usually done at six to seven weeks of age. Long before his services are needed, you should have lined up a veterinarian experienced in doing ears. Bouvier ear crops are similar to Schnauzer ears, as a point of reference. The most effective method is to obtain a large head study of a Bouvier with the ear-crop style that you prefer so that your vet can study it. Variations are endless. Sometimes even the most carefully cropped ears cease to grow after cropping so that they come out much too small. Or they may grow excessively after cropping and may look more appropriate on a Great Dane. A really talented vet is an artist when it comes to suiting the ear crop to the puppy's head size and ear set. This is an intuitive process, and no directions that I would be able to write would help. Make sure that you go to an experienced person! Some breeders are so particular that they fly in vets from out of their area to be assured that the ears will be done to their taste.

It is common to fast puppies from food and water six to twelve hours prior to surgery. Also, some vets have minimum age or weight limits for cropping. Find out such requirements ahead of time.

When you do get the puppies' ears cropped, remember that some lines of Bouviers are very anesthetic-sensitive. Our vet keeps each pup on a heart-lung monitor while operating and has indicated that some puppies take the amount of anesthetic that would be given to a two-pound kitten. These are puppies that usually weigh in excess of ten pounds. Advise your vet to proceed with caution. We have lost several puppies even with these precautions. After the ear crops, the vet gives me the opinion of the anesthetic sensitivity of that litter, both as a whole and if there were any particularly sensitive individuals. I then share that information with puppy purchasers.

Inform yourself of ear after-care. This must be determined between you and your veterinarian, because each vet has his or her own method. Stitches may need to be removed later. You will wish to return to the vet for stitch removal, at least with your first litter. If tape is a part of the ear support in the after-care, be aware that some lines of Bouviers have severe tape allergies. I have heard of ears falling off when tape was removed. I would not tape ears any longer than three or four days at a time without removal of the tape. This way, you can be certain that no reaction will occur. Some tapes cause more problems than others. Athletic adhesive tapes that have small holes and that allow the skin to breathe work better than others. In some instances, masking tape works well because it is more inclined to stick to itself than to the fur.

We don't usually tape ears but do put in liners made with Dr. Scholls' Molefoam®, cut in a teardrop shape. The paper liner is removed from the Molefoam®, and the sticky surface is coated with human surgical adhesive. I prefer colostomy adhesive, which comes in a can with a brush applicator on top. These liners are placed in the ears even before the stitches are removed. They are cut so that the edges are rounded and the bottom end can be inserted deep into the ear. Each application usually lasts about a week. If the ears aren't too oily, it may last a little longer. When the liners begin to loosen up, they are taken out, and the ears are allowed to rest for forty-eight hours before being wiped out with alcohol or peroxide. New liners are inserted as necessary. Occasionally, one ring of tape is placed around the base of the ear to help it to cup.

Photo Diary of an Ear Cropping

The following photo series depicts only one of a number of methods used to crop ears. The puppy has been anesthetized with an IV anesthetic. You will be able to see the IV tube and syringe next to the puppy's right front leg in some photos.

Once the puppy has been anesthetized, the skull is shaved with a #15 blade in the same pattern as is done for an adult. The ears are shaved with a #40 blade. A tuft of longer hair is left just below the point for gluing later.

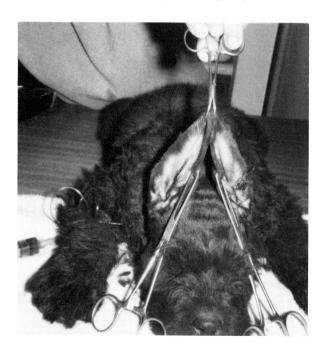

In this photo, the ears are centered over the head. The point of the cut is marked on both ears. Great care is taken to make certain that the ears are cut identically.

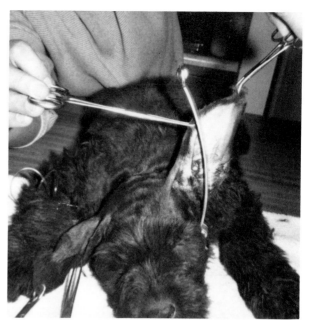

Special ear clamps are used. The clamps shown are slightly curved. The clamps have the ear inserted in them from the point marked in the previous picture. The bottom of the clamp is placed close to the skull.

Another view of the clamped ears. The clamps are tightened down firmly to reduce blood loss.

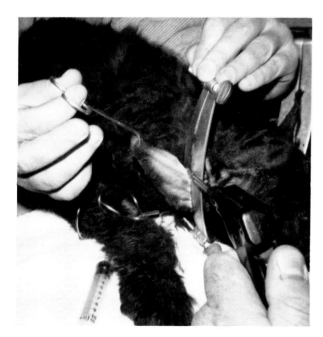

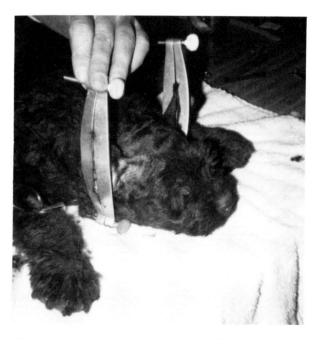

The ear is being cut with a surgical cautery. Its high temperature burns through the flesh. The cautery is slowly passed along the edge of the outside of the clamp. Because the electric cautery seals blood vessels as it passes through the flesh, there is very little blood loss. No stitches are needed.

This photo provides a clear view of the cauterized edge. If any of the blood vessels continue to bleed, they can be lightly touched with the cautery to seal them.

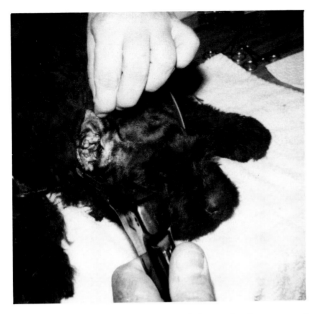

There is an extra tab of flesh left at the bottom of the ear that may need to be removed. It can be scis-red off, then lightly touched with the cautery to stop bleeding.

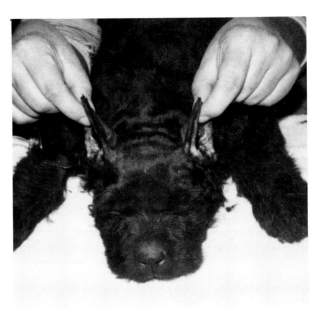

The finished product beautifully fits this puppy's head.

Above: The completed ear crop from another angle.

Right: The cut portions of the ears are of identical size.

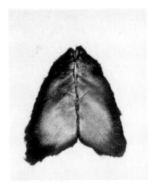

A rubber-type adhesive is used to glue the ears together. This is why extra hair is left below the cut point on the back of the ear.

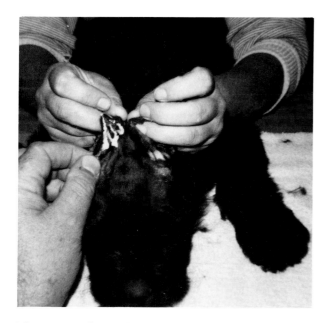

The ears are then pulled together on top of the head.

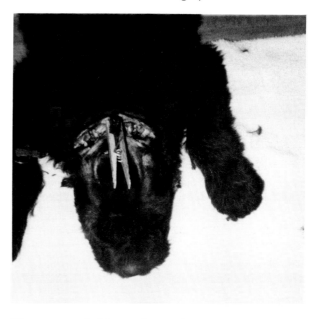

The ears are held together with one or two wooden spring clothespins. The clothespins are removed after ten minutes once the glue is set.

Aftercare of the ears with this method consists of allowing the cut edges of the ears to form crusts for about five or six days. After that time, an antibiotic or soothing cream is applied to the cut edges several times per day to prevent the ears from contracting while they heal. At ten days, the glued portions of the ears are separated by shaving the hair with the clipper. Remember that the hair was left a little longer at this point from the original clipping. A #10 or #15 blade should even things out nicely. A majority of puppies cropped this way will need no further ear supports.

Photo series courtesy of Dr. Erik Houttin, Flanders Field Kennels.

Puppy Selection

There is no foolproof way to pick the best puppy, because many faults and characteristics won't be visible for months or even years. The following is a list of some long-delayed variables, which, of course, vary considerably line by line. If you don't know your puppies' genetic background in depth, you are bound to get additional surprises.

Bites — in some lines, bites are fine until after seven months of age and then go out.

Heads — in many lines, the head doesn't really come in until between two and three years of age. The "pin head" could really be beautiful later.

Color — that black puppy could turn pale gray after ten months of age. And that lovely fawn could easily go white or cream. Many Bouviers change color slightly each year. They usually grow slightly darker with age, although this is not so with creams.

Rears — many Bouviers have narrow rears until after two years of age, when they can become more narrow, stay the same, or get considerably wider.

Height — while some Bouviers get nearly their full height before one year of age, a number of others grow an inch or more between two and three years of age.

Missing Teeth — won't show up until all the teeth are in — after six months of age.

Topline — some lines have strong toplines, while others have weak toplines that sag and weaken with age, sometimes even in spite of extensive roadwork.

Hips — preliminary X-rays only give you a peek at what may come. Hips can improve slightly but more likely will get worse. You can OFA-certify suitable hips after two years of age.

Width, Bone, and Substance — nearly all lines of Bouviers coarsen with age. If you have a large puppy that is heavy-boned and wide at a year, it will be a cow at six. Bouviers grow wide and fill out until they are six years old.

Monorchidism — males that have only one testicle are sometimes readily picked out. In other instances, the male starts out with two testicles, but one must

cript pets turn into remarkable attractive individuals. In other litters, extremely attractive puppies fall apart later. This is one reason why no importance should be placed on Bouviers that finish their championships as puppies. While these individuals have gone through an extremely attractive stage, as they develop they may literally fall apart. The bite or topline may go, and many other problems may arise. Very few pups that were champions as youngsters develop into significant adults.

Two darling ten-week-old puppies with excellent heads, bone, and substance. *Photo by Cheryl Calm.*

A handsome puppy shown here with molefoam ear liners.

be on a "short cord." It gradually goes up higher and higher until it can no longer be felt. After four months of age or even later, your pick of the litter may turn into a nice pet.

Eye Color — puppies that have dark brown eyes can have eyes that lighten considerably or even turn yellow after six months of age. If I hadn't evaluated the litter under twelve weeks of age, I wouldn't have believed it. Both parents had good, dark eye color.

Floating Teeth — this used to be a common problem. The two middle lower front teeth may start out in perfect alighment. As the dog ages, these two teeth slip lower and lower until their tops may be very close to the gum line. They also often slip forward, throwing off the bite as they slip lower. This often becomes apparent after three years of age.

Some litters that I would have described as nondes-

Companion-quality pups would be those with obvious physical defects. Bad bite, hair or eye color, monorchidism, long backs, long, narrow heads, or narrow fronts or rears are some of the faults that would qualify an otherwise fine puppy as a companion.

Working puppies possess more of an attitude and temperament than physical characteristics, although large, heavy-boned puppies are usually considered to lack agility and are less likely to be placed as working puppies. The working candidate should be bright, active, outgoing, curious, and mischievous. This is the puppy most likely to be classified as a "pain in the butt." He or she is into everything. When tested, this puppy is not sound sensitive and ideally exhibits "prey drive." I also test the pup's nose by hiding tiny bits of liver sausage on the floor close by and see if he shows interest in sniffing for it. This test is repeated

Other Procedures While the Puppy is Anesthetized for Ear Cropping

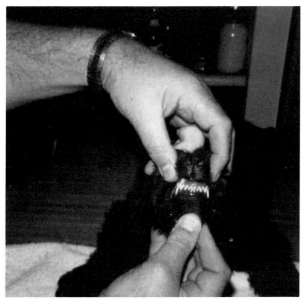

Here the puppy is being evaluated while he is still asleep from the ear-cropping process. This pup has a lovely, wide scissor bite.

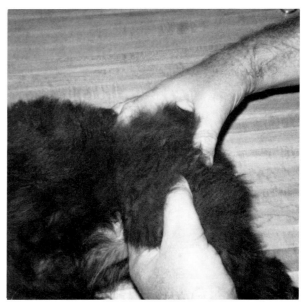

Some veterinarians will be able to palpate the puppy's hips for laxity while the puppy is anesthetized.

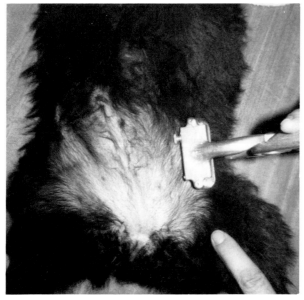

This puppy is also being tattooed while asleep. Interchangeable numbers and letters are inserted in a squeeze-type tattoo clamp. Each letter and number consists of a number of pin holes that are punched into the flank.

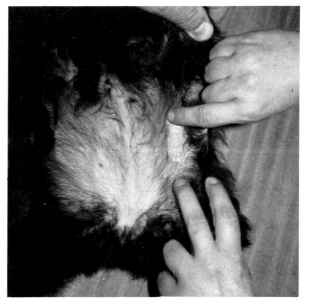

After the holes are punched, a special dye (usually green colored) is rubbed into the holes.

Photo series courtesy of Dr. Erik Houttin, Flanders Field Kennels.

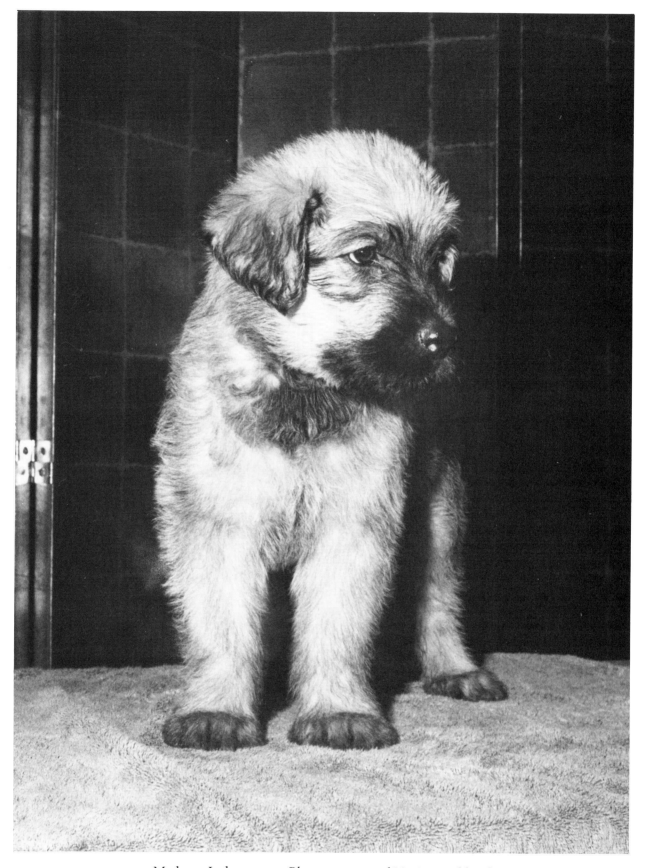

Madrone Ledge puppy. *Photo courtesy of Marion Hubbard.*

three or four times over several weeks to see if he can learn to use his nose to find the treats. I prefer a working candidate to look as good as possible. While some seem to feel that "the uglier the better" when it comes to work, there is no reason why the working dog cannot also be a champion. If you are going to put all that work into the pup, pick out the most attractive candidate with a working attitude that you can find.

When choosing the show candidate try to pick the most physically perfect specimen that you can find. Temperament plays a part here, too. You need an "up" and showy attitude. A beautiful dog that is a deadhead won't get far. You may wish to refer to Chapter 2 on puppy selection.

If you have done your genetic homework and have made a good breeding, so much the better. Most of all, you need a lot of luck. More than one great dog has started out as someone's pet. We were going to sell Leah as a pet, but she didn't match the purchaser's carpeting. So we kept her. She later became a Champion, Group Winning special, Sch H III, CD, TD, OFA, and 1984 North American Working Bouvier Champion. Too bad about the rug!

Evaluating Your Success As A Breeder

We are frequently asked how long you should hold a puppy to be sure that he is a good breeding prospect. The answer surprises most people — four or five years. Your super pup has a lot of growing to do before he proves himself as an individual. His bite has to hold, he has to keep a good topline, he must have all of his adult teeth, and he must have good color and coat texture. He should move fluidly and faultlessly. When he passes preliminary hip X-rays at one year and OFA X-rays at two years, that is only the beginning. The bottom line on the value of the pup is not how good looking, how sweet, or how funny that animal is. Ultimately, the question about a breeding animal is, what will he produce? What good will it do to have that beautiful male with the super coat, great head, and popular temperament if he throws an unacceptable level of serious genetic defects? If he throws bad bites, bad temperaments, unacceptable color, and monorchidism, it doesn't really matter how pretty himself is — he's a genetic time bomb. Don't be so short-sighted as to forgive serious genetic defects in the line in order to produce one show winner.

Edmee Bowles and Jasper du Clos des Cerberes. Informal photo at the American Club Specialty, 1978.

Breston v h Klumpke, shown with his breeder Adrianus Klomp going Best of Breed at the Dutch city of Oss in 1981. **Sire:** D Ch Arkos Anoesca v Dafzicht; **Dam:** Kasandra v h Klumpke.

N° 56. — 15 MARS 1948.

E F Bowles

l'aboi

REVUE CANINE BI-MENSUELLE

LES

BOUVIERS

SOPRANO DE LA THUDINIE
(L.O.S.H. 113156)

Front cover of *L'aboi*, from March 1948. The issue was devoted to the Bouvier.
The dog is Justin Chastel's Soprano de la Thudinie.

European Origins of the Bouvier Des Flandres

The key factor forging the Bouvier des Flandres as we know the breed today is that shortly after the breed emerged in Flanders, it was scattered and then evolved in separate, isolated spheres. The First World War was the immediate cause of this dispersion, but other factors — national borders, regional languages, and cultural barriers — accelerated and maintained it. The political borders between Belgium, Holland, and France are obvious factors. But the predominant force shaping the breed was the cultural and linguistic chasm between the Dutch-speaking Flemish of northeastern Belgium and the French-speaking Walloons of the southwestern region.

The Bouvier has evolved in five basic traditions: the Flemish, the Walloonian, the French, the Dutch police lines, and the Dutch "conventional" lines. Just as the land bridge allowed migrations from Asia to Alaska and closed again, there have been periods of contact and a flow of breeding animals from one sphere to another. But these links have been brief and sporadic, and isolation has been more the norm. It is amazing that all of this has taken place in such a small geographic region.

Superficially, this isolation has diminished in the past three decades. In this era, much Belgian breeding stock has gone to Holland. Combining these dogs with their traditional lines enabled the Dutch to ride a crest of breed popularity to a position of international dominance in terms of bloodlines and show wins. Although this development has been the primary force driving the evolution of the breed for two decades, from a long-term perspective it is just another "land bridge," another migration, rather than a permanent cultural link.

The Homelands

Flandres was from the Middle Ages until relatively recently a quasi-independent state in the Low Country of Europe, adjacent to the North Sea. For many decades, the territory under the domination of the Flemish counts varied according to the fortunes of war and intrigue. Later, the Spanish, the Dutch, the French, and others had a turn at control, although there was usually a large measure of local autonomy. The land commonly perceived as Flemish today makes up a major portion of Belgium, the Dutch province of Zeeland, and French Flandres, now the "department" of Nord. Throughout this area, the indigenous language is Flemish, which is essentially a minor variation of Dutch.

In order to know where the Bouvier evolved, locate on a Belgian map the rivers Leie and Schelde (Lys and Escaut in French) in the provinces West and Oost Vlaanderen, and note where they join in the city of Ghent (Gent in Dutch and Gand in French). One of the difficulties in the study of Bouvier origins is having to deal with both a French and a Dutch name for most geographical features, and sometimes an English version for the more prominent. Locate the cities Kortrijk (Courtrai in French), Ieper (Ypres), and Roeselare (Roulers). It is in this immediate area that the Bouvier des Flandres, which was first registered as the Bouvier des Roulers, evolved.

If you look perhaps 100 kilometers to the east and south, you will find the city of Charleroi and the nearby village of Thuin, where a number of years later many of the most famous French-speaking Bel-

CHENIL DE L'ILE MONSIN

Propriétaire : **M. Edmond MOREAUX**

Rue Alphonse Tilkin, 12

LIEGE

Urraca de l'Ile Monsin
(LOSH 133580)

Tamia de l'Ile Monsin
(LOSH 122318)

Urielle de l'Ile Monsin
(LOSH 133579)

Le chenil comptait parmi ses sujets le premier bouvier des Flandres qui fut champion de travail, à savoir. **Champion Francœur,** de Liège 1929, qui, en plus, remporta plusieurs C.A.C. aux expositions.

Par ses parents **Jane et Danilo de la Lys,** il descendait de Dragon de la Lys, de Draga de la lys, de Champion Nic, etc.

Avec Diana des Farfadets, il a donné **Eline** et **Champion Jim du Bungalow.**

Une nichée de **Eline du Bungalow,** par **Dion de Belgique** qui remporta un C.A.C. et qui, malheureusement mourut à l'âge de 3 ans,

Champion Francœur de Liège 1929
(LOSH 19303)

donna **Gabari du Bungalow,** gagnant de plusieurs C.A.C. en expositions.

Gabari du Bungalow et **Cina du Château de Fays** ont donné **Khédive du Gabari,** qui accouplé avec **Kobra de Beaufays,** donna **Quinto.**

Marquise de l'Ile Monsin, fille de Champion Francœur de Liège 1929, arrière-grand-mère de **Reine du Lac aux Dames,** chienne d'un courant de sang étranger mais de très haute lignée, qui accouplée avec **Quinto,** donna **Tamia de l'Ile Monsin, Urielle de l'Ile Monsin** et **Urraca de l'Ile Monsin,** tous inscrits au L.O.S.H.

Inside front cover of *L'aboi,* from March 1948.

gian breeders would for a time become the center of the Bouvier world. Farther east, almost to Germany, is the city of Liege, where Edmond Moreaux would found his "de l'Ile Monsin" line.

Much of what we know today about the evolution of the Bouvier appeared in a March 15, 1948, article in the Belgian canine magazine *L'Aboi* (literally, *Bark*) written by Louis Huyghebaert. Huyghebaert was a major canine authority of the era who played a principal role in the evolution of the Belgian sheepherding breeds. Huyghebaert explores the linguistic and cultural history of Flandres and reproduces portions of a number of paintings over the past several centuries depicting the dogs in the region, speculating on the role that they played in the evolution of the primitive Bouvier. Even when not cited specifically, this important historical document is the source of much of the information presented in this chapter and, indeed, in every Bouvier book.

The name Felix Verbanck is intertwined with Belgian Bouvier affairs from the early 1920s, when he produced several litters, through the 1970s. He was a leader of the Belgian Club for several decades and a respected counselor and advisor. In his correspondence with Edmee Bowles, Verbanck refers to Huyghebaert as a friend, and there is no doubt that between these two men little remained unknown about the evolution of the Bouvier des Flandres. A great deal is also drawn also from Justin Chastel's book, *The Bouvier de Flandres Today and Yesterday* (1976).

The French word "bouvier" refers to a cattle worker. Thus, the name of the breed describes its function and region of origin. In this sense, the Rottweiler is a German "bouvier." Actually, the term "bouvier," while perhaps used in French-speaking regions, would not have occurred in Flandres where the breed evolved because the language of the people was Flemish, a Dutch dialect. In his homeland, the Bouvier is to this day "de Vlaamse Koehond." Even to this day, some of the Flemish breeders and trainers regard the name "Bouvier des Flandres" as left over from the days when the invading barbarians from France attempted to impose an inferior culture on the Flemish people.

Huyghebaert claims that the Flemish monasteries of the Middle Ages, particularly the Abbey of Duynen at Coxyde, played a major role in the evolution of the indigenous working dogs on the broad, flat plain lying between the river Lys and the North Sea. (Coxyde is near the city of Veurne at the extreme western point of Belgium, just north of Dunkirk.) Some three centuries later, this would be the stock from which the Bouvier would be created. From their founding the the Middle Ages, monasteries were bastions of civilization in Europe. They were large and

A shepherd at the sea.

After the painting of Hermann Leon (Paris, Salon of 1876). The dog lying down is a Briard, the other a Picard, both of cross-breeding.

powerful economic and political units, with many members and vast farmlands. They were complete, independent social entities, with their own water systems, blacksmith shops, breweries, flour mills, and other facilities.

Such was the importance and influence of the monastery of Duynen that King Henry III of England granted the monks permission to build and maintain their own wharfs in the thirteenth century. Clearly, there was significant trade and social interaction between the British and the Flemish over several centuries, providing ample opportunity for the migration of canine breeding stock from Great Britain.

A brief quotation is appropriate here:

It is certainly known by the readers that the monks of St. Hubert, in the Ardennes, developed the bloodhound, and the Cistercians of St. Bernard, in the Alps of Switzerland, developed the St. Bernard, and have given their names to these breeds. If our Bouviers do not have a patron saint it must be because they played such a democratic role. Although on occasion they were used in hunting savage beasts, the wolf principally, their function as guard dog was too ordinary to justify a particular title, especially the name of a saint. This does not preclude, however, that the first breeders of bouviers were pious monks, founders of the last and powerful Abbey of Duynen on the west coast of Flandres near Coxyde.

Huyghebaert presents a careful, detailed argument to substantiate that over several centuries, the monks

"breeders of the bouvier," he is speaking in the generic sense; that is, he is refering to "bouviers" with a small "b." The monks sought suitable breeding stock in order to create, through selective breeding, a race of large, rough-coated guard and chase dogs. They needed such dogs to protect their horses and other livestock, especially in their remote and isolated operations that were distant from the mother house at Duynen. Their specific interest in a rough-coated dog was no doubt enhanced by their proximity to the

Left: A farm dog with cut ears. A fragment of a picture by J.B. Oudry (1686-1785). See the fable, *The Wolf, the Mother, and the Infant. Above:* The "Matins" of Gaston Phoebus. Miniature from a fourteenth-century French manuscript.

imported Scottish Deerhounds and perhaps other rough-coated sighthounds, in sufficient numbers to fundamentally change the overall gene pool of the regional working farm dogs. It is also possible that dogs similar to the Irish Wolfhound were included. Indeed, the rough-coated "greyhounds" of the British Isles were no doubt many and varied in this era, and the distinction between the deerhounds and wolf-hounds may not have been as sharp as it is today.

When Huyghebaert refers to the monks as the first

North Sea, with its cold, damp winds.

Clearly, the monks thought nothing of introducing totally unrelated breeding stock into their program when they felt that it would improve the functionality of their working dogs. In fact, Huyghebaert cites letters from the abbot at St. Hubert to the French King recommending that he use English "greyhounds" in order to maintain his St. Hubert bloodhounds. In that era, the term "greyhound" generally referred to large, gray sighthounds, including those with a rough coat.

Left: Bouvier des Ardennes. Photo by Loesberg, Liege, 1913, reproduced in *L'aboi,* March 1948.

Below, right: A Belgian sheep dog with rough coat. A study from a photo by Gevaert. Circa 1900.

It is perhaps Huyghebaert's most important thesis that the presence of the offspring of these diverse, rough-coated British sighthounds in the Flemish breeding pool provided a major genetic resource for the evolution of the harsh, rough Bouvier coat some three centuries later.

To understand the origins of the Bouvier, it is important to realize that the political boundaries of modern Europe in many instances have little to do with the cultural and linguistic attributes of the human beings populating certain regions. Belgium is a prime example, being contrived in 1835 as a buffer state between France on the south, the Netherlands to the north, and Germany to the east. About half of the population speaks Flemish and resides in the northern provinces, including East and West Flandres. The remainder is French by language and culture. Only about 20 percent of the population is able to speak both major national languages.

From medieval times to the twentieth century, the omnipresent force of Flemish history has been the accident of geography placing it in a transition zone between the French and German spheres of influence. Although this has had positive aspects, perhaps helping to make the region a center of commerce, it has also provided a convenient "neutral" ground on which others have engaged in war and then returned to relatively unscathed homelands. Apparently, much of the Flemish population regarded the invading Germans in the First World War as liberators from the oppressive French, which certainly varies from the version of history that we are taught in school! The point, of course, is that the history of the region, and thus of the Bouvier, is incredibly complex and subject to emotional interpretation.

These contemporary facts of life have had major impact on the evolution of the Bouvier des Flandres. I know a number of people intimately involved in Bouvier affairs who have had the course of their lives altered forever by the heel of the Nazi boot. Twice in the twentieth century, Belgium has been devastated by a major Franco-German clash that placed the fragile emergence of the Bouvier breed in dire jeopardy.

Because of this history, the dogs present on Flandres fields and farms late in the nineteenth century were drawn from many sources, most of which will never be known in detail. An isolated, homogenous land with little trade, peopled by those of common culture and language, undisturbed by outside intercourse for decades or centuries, is perhaps capable of producing totally distinctive animals of purely local evolution, dogs that constitute a centuries-old "breed." Such conditions in no way existed in Flandres, and the Bouvier as a distinct breed is clearly of relatively recent evolution.

This lack of documented, ancient lineage is not relevant and does not render the Bouvier common or less than noble. On the contrary, the tremendously varied qualities of the breed result from a gathering together of diverse canine roots and the consolidation in the crucible of the stockman's work. Many no doubt came, were found wanting, and died out — a mere presence was not enough to ensure a place in the genetic heritage. The unfit were purged. Those that emerged were purified, possessing the essential qualities of the Bouvier des Flandres. One is wiser in the ways of both men and dogs when it is understood that nobility is not to be found in names of ancestors but rather in the quality of the soul.

Something of Value

The appearance of the Flemish cattle dogs — the progenitors of the Bouvier as we know him — at the turn of the century was not uniform. The dog that served a purpose was kept and bred, and the resulting commonality of appearance was related to the dog's ability to do similar work in the prevailing climate and geographical circumstances. Thus, man and nature imposed a joint selection process to produce regional prototypes — dogs that because of common function and informal but persistent selectivity in breeding gradually took on similar physical and character attributes.

This should not be looked upon in an overly romantic light, for the stockman was not especially concerned with the abstract aesthetics aspects of dog breeding. His need for effective working animals provided the opportunity for the Bouvier progenitors to evolve. Some breedings to a desirable stud were perhaps arranged, but others likely took place at the whim of nature. That the dogs were expected to work in exchange for their sustenance was ultimately sufficient. The process, imperfect and haphazard though it was, worked.

The Bouvier breed founders were men who, with common purpose, selected from among the indigenous stock and bred for a specific type. They kept records of descent and eventually drew up a formal written Standard for character and conformation. They were driven by the desire to preserve and enhance a set of native qualities that had stood the test of time for generations in an environment where the nonfunctional animal was purged by economic neces-

Wolf chase with a "Limier" and a Matin. An engraving on wood from the seventeenth century. The "Limier" is some sort of tracking dog.

sity and where survival of the fittest was an elementary facet of life rather than an esoteric academic conception. These working dogs of the stockman were in immediate danger of disappearing due to the rapid social and economic changes overtaking the farming culture in the ancestral regions, largely as a consequence of advancing agricultural technology.

If man is in any way noble, then it is in the striving for more than mere sustenance. The breeding of excellent dogs is an aesthetic enterprise, just as is the creation of a fine piece of furniture or an oil painting. The primitive stock, resident on the farms of the homeland, represented something of value that was in imminent danger of being lost forever. The men and women who in the first three decades of the twentieth century consolidated the Flemish farm dogs into the Bouvier des Flandres as we know him served as creators and guardians of the heritage. If our lives are more fulfilled because of our dogs, then we are in the debt of those creators. Our corresponding obligation is to breed so as to preserve and protect the essential attributes of the Bouvier body and soul and thus pass on what we have received.

Because the purpose of the founders was to preserve existing qualities, there was no reason for the large-scale introduction of the blood of other breeds in order to modify physical or mental attributes. The primitive stock was no doubt drawn from diverse local types, the influence of which persisted for a number of years and is seen even today in the variety in size, substance, and coat among individual Bouviers. This consolidation is in stark contrast to the derivation of breeds such as the Doberman Pinscher that were the result of genetic engineering. To form those breeds, a number of established breeds were mixed and in a very short time produced dogs with specific preconceived characteristics.

There is, of course, no doubt that an occasional dog of a different background was introduced experimentally throughout the early years. The period following World War II also necessitated using questionable, undocumented stock and perhaps even the outright introduction of the blood of dogs obviously not Bouviers. But the derivation from working farm stock is what produced the essential attributes of the Bouvier des Flandres.

For many years, diverse "bouvier" varieties existed according to region and the vision of their proponents. It was a long time before the creation of a single breed was irrevocable. The situation was not finally resolved until the common Franco-Belgian Standard was formulated in the 1960s. The primitive stock could just as easily have been consolidated into several different breeds; in fact, as recently as the late 1940s, men were bitterly opposed to the consolidation in Belgium.

Although "bouvier"-type dogs were shown and efforts were made to establish a breed in the first decade of the twentieth century (and perhaps even earlier), the current stock traces roughly to the 1910–1920 period, although many dogs with unknown ancestry were still being incorporated into the breeding program during the 1920s and even later. Thus, the establishment of the Bouvier as a breed came somewhat later than for some of the other utility breeds. There is about one generation, in human terms, between the time late in the nineteenth century when German Shepherd breeding began in earnest and the early years of this century when the same process began for the Bouvier. In these early years, however, Flandres was devastated by the First World War, further delaying the solidifying of breed type.

Left: Gent (Belgium) police officer in night service and uniform with Bouvier-type police dog, in front of kennel building. Photo circa 1906. *Courtesy K. Vickery. Below:* Border patrol officers and their dogs, about 1900. These dogs are clearly Bouvier progenitors!

Although the Bouvier progenitors were primarily dogs of the cattlemen, the sheepherders of Belgium also developed distinctive kinds of dogs somewhat smaller than the Bouvier according to their own needs. Four breeds were created, differentiated according to coat color, length, and texture. The black Groenendael and the tawny Tervueren are long haired and are similar in appearance except for color. The Groenendael and Tervueren take their names from cities in the province of Brabant, near Brussels, where they originated. The short-coated Malinois is somewhat similar in appearance to a less-angulated, lighter-boned, and more square German Shepherd. Louis Huyghebaert, author of the L'Aboi article from which so much as been drawn, and his brother Frans founded this breed in the 1890s. They lived in the province of Antwerpen, in the city Mechelen (Malines), from which the breed draws its name. Among the Belgian shepherds' dogs, the Malinois is widely regarded as the best working and sport dog. He is prominent and successful in the Dutch Police trials. In the Belgian Ring Sport, he predominates, typically representing as much as 90 percent of the entries.

The Laeken, virtually unknown in America and uncommon in Europe, is similar in appearance to the others, being gray, of wiry coat, and of distinctive body shape. Because of the coat texture and color, there is a superficial resemblance to the Bouvier, although the ears are naturally upright rather than being cropped, and the overall body type is clearly that of the sheepdog rather than the Bouvier. The city of Laeken is just north of Brussels.

In the early years of the twentieth century, two primary types of Bouvier emerged, each with their passionate advocates. The first variety was variously known as the "Bouvier des Roulers," "Bouvier Belge," or "Bouvier Pikhaar." These dogs were also referred to as being of the "type Moerman," after the famous breeder Joseph Moerman. Moerman was active in the city of Roulers until about 1910 and advocated this type of Bouvier. The male was to range up to 27½ inches and his coat color was to be black, brindle, or iron gray. The Societe Royale St. Hubert (S. R. S. H.) in Belgium first formalized this type as a breed in 1912.

The other variety was referred to as the "Bouvier des Flandres" in this era and was associated with the name of the early breeder L. Paret. (Although Paret is discussed extensively in historical documents, I have never been able to find his complete first name.) The coat color ranged from true fawn in all shades to sorrel, charcoal, gray, and brindle. His coat was to be much rougher than that of the Bouvier de Roulers. These dogs were to be relatively small, with the males ranging from 22½ to 24½ inches, tiny by today's

standards. About 1912, a primary advocate of the Paret type was the Frenchman M. F. Fontaine, who was at the time vice-president of the Club St. Hubert of the North (in the north of France).

Chastel quotes extensive passages from various canine magazines in the years before the war, from about 1910 to 1915, supporting either the Paret type or the Moerman (Roulers) type. Since the Roulers was recognized by the Societe Royale St. Hubert (SRSH) and the des Flandres by the Belgian Kennel Club, the conflicts between the two bitterly competing canine organizations added significant fuel to an already healthy fire.

Huyghebaert summarized the situation in the first decade of this century by stating that three basic types of existing native dogs would be used to create the modern Bouvier. These were, ranked according to size:

- The harsh-coated sheepdogs at 21½" to 23⅝"
- The Bouvier des Flandres at 23⅝" to 25½"
- The giant Bouvier de Roulers at 25½" to 27½"

The distinction between the human advocates was actually greater than that in the dogs themselves. The primary points of disagreement had to do with size and coat. As a broad generality, it can be said that through the 1950s the Dutch would prefer the large, dark Roulers type, while the French would prefer the much smaller, more roughly coated Paret type. The Belgians would begin to resolve the question in 1913, when the Society of St. Hubert began to register the Bouvier des Roulers. Although the Paret type no doubt made its contribution, the simple fact of history, available in the breeding records for everyone to verify, is that the Roulers type has come to predominate modern lines. Indeed, the light-colored, twenty-four-inch Paret type would hardly be recognizable as a Bouvier today.

In Flemish Belgium in the 1920s and 1930s these types consolidated into a true breed in the modern sense. The majority of Bouviers throughout the world, including Holland and France, are today derived primarily from this Belgian melding, with its emphasis on the Roulers type. The older-style Dutch breeding, much of which still exists today, was to play an important role in the 1960s and 1970s, when the Dutch blood was heavily mixed with the tightly bred Belgian stock. In my opinion, the Dutch stock, with its more well-preserved Roulers type, was a vital genetic reserve and has been the salvation of the breed over the past two decades. The reality is that there is very little record of French blood in modern lines, and claims of French origin are mostly a matter of myth.

Thus, the seemingly simple question regarding the country in which the Bouvier originated in is in fact

Left: Pick de Boesinghe and Mirza, 1912. *Courtesy Justin Chastel.*
Above: A typical Belgian female from the 1920s: Zora de Zwynaerde LOSH.21513
Sire: Goliath de la Lys LOSH.13021 '22
Dam: Blondina LOSH.15588 '23
Photo courtesy Justin Chastel.

complex. It is true that most of the Bouvier progenitors evolved in lands now included within the boundaries of Belgium, but this process occurred for many generations before European politicians created the Belgian state early in the nineteenth century. Clearly, the question to ask concerns the character of the people among whom the Bouvier evolved; in this narrow context, Belgium is certainly an accurate answer.

France is cited as a country of origin, but this is only indirectly true. The primary Bouvier progenitors clearly arose among the Flemish people, who were culturally Dutch and thus essentially of Germanic background. It is true that part of the region where the Bouvier originated is now, because of relatively recent political manipulation, within the modern state of France. This is, however, weak ground on which to characterize the breed as "French."

On the other hand, many of the breeders, such as Moreaux and Chastel, who took the primitive Flemish stock and molded the breed, were in a cultural and linguistic sense Frenchmen. This development occurred both in France and among the Walloons (the linguistically and culturally French Belgians in the more southern and eastern parts of Belgium). Thus, many of the modern developers and consolidators of the Bouvier were and are in a cultural sense French. This

is a much more convincing argument for French participation in the foundation of the breed.

The written records of the founders, such as Verbanck, are unfortunately confusing and contradictory. It is virtually impossible to definitely establish breed origins prior to the stud records, which begin in 1913 in Belgium. In addition, many dogs of unknown origin were incorporated into the program through the mid-1920s, and a few even later.

The Beginning of the Modern Era

The formal establishment of the various utility breeds began late in the nineteenth century. In Belgium, much of the guidance and encouragement came from a Professor Reul, a veterinary surgeon who authored a book titled *Les Races de Chiens* (*The Breeds of Dogs*), published in 1894. Although Dr. Reul's primary interest was the Belgian Sheepdog, Verbanck indicates that there was a brief article on the "bouvier" (small "b") and quotes: "The cattle dog is for the most part a shepherd dog or a dog that resembles him in general make-up, but who is bigger, fiercer, more aggressive and has a bolder look. He accompanies livestock sellers in their wanderings through villages to fairs and markets and directs the herds along the roads; it's up to him to watch over the cows in the fields. In all the small farms, the cow dog has a guard role to fulfill. At night he becomes a watch dog."

The first recorded efforts to formalize the Bouvier as a breed occurred in the first decade of the twentieth century, when two Flemish breeders in the region of the river Lys — Paret and Moerman — began programs for selective breeding. Their stock was drawn from Sheepdogs, Matins, and various dogs of unknown and mixed ancestry. The name "Matin" is often used in historical discussions. This does not refer to a breed in the modern sense, but rather to a

sion of Belgian registration numbers in the section on pedigrees.)

The natural question is, why were these rustic dogs of the farmer and drover ignored for so long? Why did it take until the first half of this century before they attracted attention for their aesthetic qualities? It must be understood that originally the working dogs were thought of only in the context of their function, that is, as sheepdogs, cattle dogs, or watch dogs with little regard for appearance or background. For centuries, the large-scale landowners and otherwise wealthy upper classes conducted careful breeding programs and kept accurate records for the dogs to which they had an emotional attachment, that is, their

Left: Rex and Nelly and their puppies. Owner: M. Paret. *Right:* Rex and Nelly in 1910.

variety or function, that is, a big protection dog. The Dutch term "Rekel" is apparently almost equivalent. Introduction of the Matin into the Bouvier lines implies that people simply went out and bred their animals to big guard or protection dogs.

The first specific reference to individual dogs intended to be Bouvier prototypes is to a pair called Rex and Nelly owned by Mr. Paret of Ghent. They were exhibited in May 1910 at a Societe Royale St. Hubert show in Brussels. These dogs were designated with "RSH" numbers 1766 and 1892, indicating that although no formal standard existed at the time, the concept of the breed was becoming established. (These registration numbers did not indicate, however, that the Bouvier was recognized as a breed. See the discus-

hunting dogs. The idea of keeping records of descent of the dogs of the peasants and other lower-class workers would never have occurred to them or to anyone else. Therefore, it is no accident that the formalization of the working breeds occurred at a time of political upheaval, when the working and farming people were gaining more political power in proportion to their numbers.

Louis Huyghebaert writes about the Paret family in the *L'Aboi* article cited earlier:

These dogs being considered justly as the founders of the present day Bouviers I will call them the Paret Family. I had the personal pleasure to judge the sire "Rex" (RSH 1766) and the dam "Nelly" (RSH 1892), both shown at the International in Brussels on May 21-23, 1910, at the Cinquante Park, organized by the Societe Royale Saint-Hubert.

After so many years, now that these dogs and their masters have passed away, I like to remember the Paret family surrounded by Rex and Nelly and their five puppies whose names will later appear in the book of origins and pedigrees. At that time, scientific selection was not considered but the family Paret impressed me so deeply that I made notes and took photographs to illustrate my report.

Huyghebaert quotes from his report on the 1910 show as follows:

The Bouviers are only represented by two dogs, — a magnificent couple belonging to Mr. L. Paret of Ghent. I rejoice to see this breed represented by so few. The Bouviers are not show dogs and will not gain by shows when one sees what happens to native breeds. I only hope they will stay away from show benches, diplomas and medals as long as possible.

I still recall the humiliating asterisk (1927) placed next to the variety of Bouviers in the official catalogues, which formerly dishonored our native sheep dog varieties. Nor were these (sheepdogs) later allowed to be registered in the Book of Origins — that Gotha of dogs — because they were not nearly noble enough.

Since then our sheepdogs have found a place and different types are now recognized. Certainly these are fine results but alas, how many "nothings" as to character and temperament have become part of the breed because of favor in the shows! How many terrible dogs have been bred under the pretext of descent from "champions"? And what "champions," my God, and in what classes of pure fantasy did they obtain this distinction?

Let this be a lesson to Bouvier fanciers!

If they are determined to have shows let there be no exaggerations, we must retain the true character and type of the breed.

The temperament is excellent, one need only look at the eye of Rex and his companion Nelly to love these good dogs. Rex is by far the better of the two, for he has more of the bouvier type. Nelly has more of the sheepdog expression.

As I have said at the show in Amsterdam in 1909 and must now repeat: the Bouvier should look gruff and rustic. He should be a block which disdains all elegance . . .

It is perplexing, because although Huyghebaert strongly implies that these Paret dogs are direct ancestors of today's Bouviers, Verbanck is emphatic that this is not so. It is true that there is no mention of Paret in the earliest SRSH breeding records, but it is possible that his dogs were behind the earliest progenitors or that they were registered with the "Kennel Belge." Unfortunately, it seems unlikely that this contradiction will be satisfactorily resolved.

In his report on the 1910 show, Huyghebaert also refers to the exhibition of Bouviers in the Netherlands as early as 1909. This activity has been verified through Raad van Beheer records, which unfortunately are sparse and incomplete. Huyghebaert's activity in Holland at this time is also mentioned in the Dutch book by van Gink-van Es. Her book reproduces a poster for the 1909 show, held on May 23, and the catalog page, complete with a listing of puppies for sale. It also records Rex as being out of Pic and Bella and Nelly's parents as Beer and Sarah. (Since half the rough-coated working dogs in Belgium or Holland were called Pic or Pick, and the females were Bella or Mirza, do not read too much into this.)

Also at this time there was a society of Bouvier breeders in the city of Roulers in West Flandres known as the "Roeselaersche Hondenclub." In August 1912, they held a meeting attended by a number of SRSH officials and judges. Among those present were Mr. Houtart, Mr. Levita, Baron van Zuylen van Nyevelt, Mr. Van Hereweghe, Veterinary Dr. Louis Scharlaken (breeder of the influential stud Pickzwart), and others. Vital Taeymans and a man named Orban served as judges of the dogs present, which served as a model for the Standard. These men drew up the Standard of perfection, which was shortly to become the first official Standard of the breed recognized by the Societe Royale St. Hubert. Dr. Scharlaken was a breeder in Roulers, active from about 1910 or perhaps earlier until at least 1925. He was appaently a protégé of Moerman, as all of his dogs appear to be from the founder's personal lines.

This Standard for the "Chin Bouvier de Roulers" was accepted by St. Hubert in 1912. Starting in 1922, dogs were registered as "Bouvier Belge des Flandres," and it would not be until 1933 that registrations with St. Hubert would take place under the name "Bouvier des Flandres."

In 1913, four male and four female Bouviers were entered into the *Book of Origins*. In 1914, there were three males and two females. Among these thirteen dogs were:

Pickzwart, born in 1912 out of Picka and Mirzette
Marius, born in 1910 out of Pic and Miss
Ch. Zola, born in 1908 out of Pic and Bella

Sarah van hut Kantientje, Belgian female with a Flemish name, whelped in 1943, is important in both Belgian lines, and particularly in Dutch lines through her grandson Rato v d Ouden Dijk. This is most unusual for a dog of this era. Sarah was from lines out of the mainstream of the era, but apparently a valued producer. *Photo courtesy Annie Verheyen.*

Boltom (LOSH.36208), owned by Jules Roryck, was born in 1927. Photo circa 1933.

Sire: Djil du Chateau LOSH.15480 '23
Dam: Florine (F. Van Steenbergen)

Photo courtesy Felix Grulois.

Ch. Bella, born in 1911 out of Baron and Nette
Ch Picard, born in 1910 out of Pic and Bella

It is clear from these early records that much of the foundation breeding was done by Joseph Moerman of Roulers. In a sense, the Bouvier was created by linebreeding to his foundation male "Pic." Marius, Zola, and Picard are listed as bred by Moerman. Zola and Bella were owned by a Mr. Deryckere in Roulers.

The breed was making rapid progress when the war broke out, bringing activity to a standstill. The parts of the country where the Bouvier was largely bred, and where it was becoming more and more popular, were entirely destroyed. The population left the country, and most of the dogs were lost. Many were abandoned and died, and others were acquired by the Germans, perhaps to play a role in the evolution of the Giant Schnauzer. Chastel's book, *The Bouvier des Flandres Today and Yesterday,* has a dramatic and emotional passage where he relates his father's valiant efforts to retain his own personal dog, a well-trained Malinois. Finally, in 1917, he had to sell him for a sack of wheat so that his family could eat.

Ramses de la Dragerie, whelped in 1943, represents French breeding of this era.

Sire: L'Ami de la Boheme LOF.1003
Dam: Pistache de l'Epiniere LOF.881

Among the dogs to survive the war and serve as a foundation for the future were Pickzwart, bred by Dr. Scharlaken; Sultan, owned by Messrs. van der Vennet and Gryson; Picko, owned by Mr. De Poorter; and Bella and Kis de Ramillies, owned by Mr. Mottoulle. The female Cora, bred in 1917 by Alphonse Faes directly out of Moerman's lines, also contributed greatly to the postwar recovery.

In 1920, six adult males, five adult females, and seven pups in a "de Ramillies" litter born in 1919 were registered. (The registration book is always one year behind; that is, 1919 pups are registered in 1920.) Among the adults that are significant in the founding pedigrees are Filou, born in 1910; Sultan, born in 1911; and Cora, born in 1917. In 1921, sixteen adult males (including the immortal Nic), eighteen adult females, and three litters appear. And in 1922, for the first time under the name "chiens de Bouvier Belges des Flandres," registrations were twenty-six males, thirty-one females, and sixteen litters, including the first "de la Lys" litter of Philemon Gryson.

Perhaps the best representation of the foundation lines is found in the pedigree of Francoeur de Liege, born in 1924. He was Edmond Moreaux's immortal champion and Ring competitor.

Figure 11-1

```
              Unknown
          Nic  B Ch; LOSH.10266 '16 (Ownr N.Barbry,Sottegem)
              Unknown
    Danilo de la Lys   LOSH.13275 '22
          Picka   (Delva)
      Pickzwart   LOSH.14959 '12
          Mirzette   (Scharlaeken)
    Draga  B Ch; LOSH.10273 '19 (Owr Gryson,Brd VanAckere)
          Duc   (J.Mottoulle)
      Flandrienne ex Cora  LOSH.11737  '14
          Bella  (Moerman)
B Ch FRANCOEUR DE LIEGE  LOSH.19303 '24 Ownr:Moreaux
          Filou   LOSH.9569 '10 (J.Boone)
      Duduc   LOSH.12872 '13 (Br A.VanderHeeren)
          Lise   (VanderHeeren)
    Moorki   LOSH.13128 Jun'18 A.Roscam/Ow E.Dubron/Br
          Unknown
      Mirza   (Michel deBruyne)
          Unknown
    Janne de la Lys  LOSH.15050
          Unknown
          Nic  B Ch; LOSH.10266 '16 (Ow N.Barbry,Sottegem)
          Unknown
      Wilna  LOSH.14526 Sep'20 Th.Blaton/Br Ph.Gryson/Ow
          Max   (Ch.VanderVenne)
      Mirza   LOSH.11749  '17 (Br Mme.Cambien-Devos)
          Nera  LOSH.10280 '13
```

In the pedigree, "LOSH" is an abbreviation for "Livre Origines Saint-Hubert" and is the official registration number assigned by the Royal Society of Saint Hubert, the Belgian equivalent of the AKC. The Dutch numbers are designed as "NHSB," which is the abbreviation for "Nederlands Hondenstambock," or Netherlands Dog Registration. The dogs without a number, such as Picka, Mirza, and Max, were of undocumented origin but were sought out because they possessed qualities that the founders needed to perpetuate. Note particularly the males Nic, found on a farm during the First World War, and Filou, the most famous son of Moerman's "Pic," born in 1910. These males appear on both sides of this pedigree and, in fact, were in every sense founders of the breed. More will be said about Mr. Moreaux, who became a singularly important individual in the development of the breed in later chapters.

In 1929, there were 15 adult males, 23 females, and 282 pups in 45 litters. Prominent kennel names were "du Pandore," "de la Barriere," "de Maeter," and, of course, "de la Lys." One litter had the kennel name "of Detroit," and the litter did, in fact, whelp in that Michigan city. By 1935, a peak was hit, when 935 Bouviers were registered with the SRSH, a number that would not be exceeded in the twenty years after the Second World War.

It is to be clearly understood that the establishment of the stud book by the SRSH did not establish the Bouvier as a single, unified breed. During the same general period the Kennel Club Belge and Le Societe Centrale de Paris recognized the Bouvier des Flandres (or the Bouvier Francais des Flandres) as a competing type.

The Club National Belge du Bouvier des Flandres was formed in Ghent on January 15, 1922. This group was associated with St. Hubert rather than with Kennel Belge and was an outgrowth of the by then predominant Roulers faction. Starting in the mid-1920s, Chiens de Bouvier Francais des Flandres were also registered with St. Hubert but never more than one or two per year and often with no entries for an entire year.

Chastel indicates in his book that much of the early Bouvier activity in Belgium centered on the Kennel Belge (Belgian Kennel Club). He referred to it as "a dissenting organization not affiliated with the F.C.I." and goes on to comment that it "seems to have had the favor of those interested in working breeds." Reading between the lines, it seems apparent that even

This remarkable photo, probably of the female Lyda bred by Philemon Gryson, was supplied by Annie Verheyen. It is stamped with Gryson's name on the back, and the notes, perhaps in the founder's own hand, are "Lyda de la Lys" and under that "Duduc." Gryson probably thought of her as a "de la Lys" dog, even though she was registered simply as "Lyda," daughter of Duduc.

Pic (Brd: J. Moerman)
Filou LOSH.9569 '10 (Brd: C. Dousy)
Charlotte
Duduc LOSH.12872 '13 (Brd: A. VanderHeeren)
Unknown
Lise (VanderHeeren)
Unknown
Lyda LOSH.10278 '18 (Owner Gryson)
Pic (Brd: J. Moerman)
Filou LOSH.9569 '10 (Brd: C. Dousy)
Charlotte
Tata
Unknown
Mirza (M. deBruyne)
Unknown

then the working and show lines were divided.

Although the evidence is sparse at best, it appears that Kennel Belge had much more difficulty in getting going after the war and more or less failed in its attempt to compete with St. Hubert. I have been unable to find documentaion of Bouviers registered with Kennel Belge that made genetic contributions to the modern Bouvier and must conclude that such lines, which probably amounted to very few dogs, have died out.

In future years, the most influential breeders were to be farther east in Belgium, outside the predominant Flemish region, in France and in the Netherlands.

Representative of the breeding at "de la Lys" is the dog Actif, who after many successful show presentations in 1924 died suddenly. (Offspring of a female littermate do carry down.) This pedigree (see Figure 11-2) and the others in this section are taken from Huyghebaert, with additional information from St. Hubert records.

Goliath de la Lys
LOSH.13021 '22

Sire: Nicolo de la Lys
LOSH.11712 '22
Dam: Flandrienne Ex Cora
LOSH.11737 '14

The Bouviers "de la Lys" and Early Bloodlines

The most prominent and respected of the founding Flemish kennels was that of Philemon Gryson, named after the River Lys that flows through the region of Flandres where the Bouvier evolved. Dragon de la Lys and Goliath de la Lys are among the many well-known and influential products of this kennel. The bitch Flandrienne was one of the original Bouviers acquired. This kennel was located at Saint-Denis Westrem, which is just west of the city of Ghent in East Flandres.

Figure 11-2

```
ACTIF, (LOSH 16357), black, whelped August 8, 1923

          Nic  B Ch; LOSH.10266 '16
       Nicolo de la Lys  LOSH.11712 '21  gray
          Margot
    Goliath de la Lys  LOSH.13021 '22  gray
          Duc  (J.Mottoulle)
       Flandrienne ex Cora  LOSH.11737 '14  gray
          Bella
ACTIF  LOSH.16357 '23
          Unknown
       Nic  B Ch; LOSH.10266 '16    black
          Unknown
    Durca de la Lys  LOSH.13283
          Pickzwart  LOSH.14959 '12 brd
       Draga  B Ch; LOSH.10273 '19 black
          Flandrienne ex Cora  LOSH.11737  '14
```

The male Nic was perhaps the most famous Bouvier in the early years. Mrs. van Gink–van Es indicates that Nic was believed to have been born near the town of Moorslede, about ten kilometers southwest of Roulers in Flandres. She states that he was purchased in 1915 from a farm family fleeing by rail to France, literally at the station, and subsequently came into the hands of Veterinary Captain Barbry of the Belgian Army. This dog was trained for signal corps work and served well for three yers. After the war, he was sent to the kennel Sottegem, owned by the brother of Captain (later Major) Barbry, where he was registered with St. Hubert and then was bred and shown extensively. The literature also indicates that he was later owned by Mr. Gryson at "de la Lys," although his owner at the time of registration was Mr. Barbry.

Champion Nic, 1921 (LOSH.10266), owned by Mr. Grayson, Saint-Denis Westrem.

Nic became one of the earliest Belgian champions. When he was shown in 1920 at the Olympic show in Antwerp, the judge, Charles Huge, commented:

> Nic is the ideal type of the Bouvier. He has a short body, with well developed ribs, short flanks, strong legs, good feet, long and oblique shoulders. His head is of a good shape with somber eyes and an ideal courageous expression. His hair is dry and dark. The tail should not have been cut so short. I hope that this dog will have numberous progeny.

These wishes were realized, because when Nic died in 1926, his immediate descendants formed a major portion of the foundation stock of the Bouvier. Notable examples include Goliath de la Lys (a grandson), Maximilien, Ch. Dragon de la Lys, Mirza de Turnhout, and others. This is all the more remarkable in that virtually all of his progeny were produced in only two years, 1921 and 1922.

Belga de la Gendarmerie, NHSB.7740, imported by J. Wolfs of the Bouvier kennel "van Maarland," became the dam of the first two Dutch-bred Bouviers to become Netherlands Champions, and grand dam of the third and fourth! This granddaughter of the immortal Nic was truly the foundation of not only the kennel van Maarland, but of the entire Dutch Bouvier movement.

Breeder: Ferdinand Nijs, Deinze, Belgium
Owner: J. Wolfs, Kennel van Maarland, Oss, Netherlands
Sire: Dragon de la Lys LOSH.11776 '21
Dam: Lary LOSH.23865 '23 (Owner F. Nijs)
Born: February 15, 1925
Regr.: NHSB.7740 LOSH: 24598

Dam of Dutch Champions Boef Belga van Maarland and Bobby Belga van Maarland.

The brief article published by the Belgian National Club, from which the above is drawn, goes on to comment:

> The breeders must not forget that the Bouvier is first of all a working dog, and although they try to standardize its type, they do not want it to lose the early qualities which first called attention to its desirability. For that reason, in Belgium a Bouvier cannot win the title of Champion unless he has also won a prize in a working competition as a police dog, as a defense dog or as an army dog.

Huyghebaert commented on Actif's pedigree as follows:

> Actif was the product of Champion Nic 1921 on one side and Pikzwart 14959 on the other.
> Though the name Dragon de la Lys does not appear in this pedigree one can see the bloodlines. He is a brother of a previous litter of Durca de la Lys 13283, mother of Actif.
> In the early pedigrees the name Duduc (12872) is often seen. This dog was sought out as stud by the breeders of Courtrai and thus he appears in pedigrees of other breeders. A member of this family is Betty de la Lys (11774), kennel mate of Milton (15936) and one of the best bitches of the time. Her pedigree follows further on; here again Ch. Nic 1921, of unknown origin, has been top producer of quality. One can thus conclude that this dog, though of unknown origin, is the source of the best Bouvier blood lines.
> We are publishing here the photo of Bouboule de Courtrai (23085) owned by Mr. J. Rasschaert of Courtrai (bred by Mr. Gryson). The bouvier in question is better built than he appears in the photo. (His pedigree is detailed in Figure 11-3.)

Note that "Bouboule de Courtrai" was bred by Mr. V. Gryson, who was the brother of Philemon Gryson of "de la Lys" fame. Bouboule is a significant breeding factor, a true foundation of the breed. Also note the male Duc owned by Mr. Mottulle, who was an active breeder just after the war under the kennel name "de Ramillies." Madame Cambien's "du Sellier" kennel was destined to remain active through the late 1930s.

In the following genealogy of Betty de la Lys (Figure 11-4), note particularly the name Filou, who was a product of the Moerman family in the city of Roulers. This male occurs in many pedigrees of this era and was apparently a strong factor in stamping the Moerman type on future generations of the Bouvier de Rou-

Bouboule de Courtrai LOSH.23085.

Figure 11-3

```
                    Filou  LOSH.9569 '10
           Duduc  LOSH.12872 '13
                    Lise  (van der Heeren)
   Jim du Sellier  LOSH.19345 '20
                    Unknown
           Dia  (Mme A. Cambien)
                    Unknown
   Boby du Sellier  LOSH.16547 '22
                    Unknown
           Max  (M. van der Venne)
                    Unknown
   Bella du Sellier  (a Mme A.Cambien)
                    Filou  LOSH.9569 '10
           Nera  LOSH.10280 '13
                    Mirza  (M.deBruyne)
BOUBOULE DE COURTRAI  LOSH.23085 '24
                    Unknown
           Nic  B Ch;  LOSH.10266 '16
                    Unknown

   Arga de la Lys  LOSH.13106
           Picka  (Delva)
   Pickzwart  LOSH.14959 '12 brd Scharlaken
           Mirzette  (Scharlaeken)
   Riga  LOSH.11754 '19
           Duc  (J.Mottoulle)
   Flandrienne ex Cora  LOSH.11737 '14
           Bella
```

Figure 11-4

```
   Unknown
   Nic  B Ch;  LOSH.10266 '16  (Ownr N.Barbry,Sottegem)
   Unknown
BETTY DE LA LYS  LOSH.11774 '21
           Filou  LOSH.9569 '10  (Brdr C.Dousy)
   Duduc  LOSH.12872 '13  (Brdr A.VanderHeeren)
           Lise  (VanderHeeren)
   Lyda  LOSH.10278 '18  (Ownr Gryson)
           Filou  LOSH.9569 '10  (Brdr C.Dousy)
   Tata
           Mirza  (M.deBruyne)
```

---

lers and then on the modern Bouvier des Flandres. Note that Filou was a son of the dog Pic, bred by Moerman about 1908. Although Pic was never registered, he was nevertheless a foundation of the breed.

Another female named Mirza, a granddaughter of the Mirza owned by Mr. deBruyne, also is prominent in early pedigrees. There are other references to Bouviers out of an unregistered Mirza, indicating that probably at least one other female had this name among the foundation stock.

Huyghebaert's commentary continues:

Bouboule was shown in Saint-Denis Westrem in the first special show for Bouviers, organized in 1925 by the "Club National de Bouvier Belge des Flandres."

There were twenty-two entries placed by Judge L. Van Damme. In the class for junior males first place winner was Cesar du Pont-a-Rieu, first place female was Zora de Zwynaerde. In the open classes the places of honor went to Molly, owned by M. Pattyn, and to Bouboule described as follows:

Magnificent type as for the head and expression, good shoulders, well built as to body, legs — also good coat and gait though a little stiff in forelegs . . .

If one compares the photo of Bouboule with that of his grandfather Champion Nic (10266) one sees immediately the common family traits although Nic is bigger and he seems better in certain points, especially the top lines.

To better judge the expression of these two dogs, I am lacking a good head study. To fill in this gap a little bit, I have had recourse to a true masterpiece representing in profile the head of Nickol 17522 born the 27th of August 1923, who received good ratings by the judges Ch. Huge and Taeymans.

As shown in the pedigree (Figure 11-5), Nickol and Bouboule both have the blood of Filou, product of the family Moerman, of Roulers."

Dogs such as Pic, Charlotte, Pico, and Laura go back to the first decade of the twentieth century, when men such as Moerman, Mottoule, Deryckere, Faes, and Scharlaken were creating, on the plain of Flandres in the region of Roulers, the Bouvier breed as we know it today. Many variations in spelling occur among these unregistered dogs, and it is hard to know how often a "Pic," a "Pico," or a "Pick" are the same dog. Where identified, the owners or breeders of these founding dogs are mostly men, such as Dr. Schalaken, known to be close associates of Mr. Moerman of Roulers.

The bitch Zora de Zwynaerde, out of Goliath de la Lys and Blondina (LOSH.15588), is in the background of the French "la Boheme" breeding.

As these commentaries and pedigrees show, it would be virtually impossible to overstate the contribution of Mr. Gryson and his "de la Lys" breeding program to the creation of the Bouvier des Roulers, that is, the Bouvier des Flandres. As late as May 24, 1945, a "de la Lys" litter appears in the "Livre des Origines" (Register of Origins) of the Societe Royale Saint-Hubert with a "M. Ph. Gryson" listed as "producteur." The address is given as "Avenue of the Bouvier, of St-Denis Westrem." It would seem that two otherwise unremarkable females, Tadila and Tavie de la Lys, by Quick Star de la Gendarmerie out of seven-year-old Mascotte de la Lys, were the final products of this founding kennel. It is clear that Mr. Gryson was a man of immense determination and perseverance, not unlike the breed for which he did so much.

To further exemplify the early lines, I have selected a pedigree from the archives of Miss Edmee Bowles, founder of the world-renowned "du Clos des Cerberes" line and pioneer of the breed in America. This dog is a male that she used as stud when she was active as a breeder in Belgium before the Second World War. (Figure 11-6.)

Figure 11-5

```
                Unknown
        Pick  (M. van Damme)
                Unknown
    Picko  LOSH.9570 '18 (Brdr H.Lesage)
                Unknown
        Mira
                Unknown
NICKOL  LOSH.17522 '23
                Unknown
        Max  (Ch.VanderVenne)
                Unknown
    Bellatte  LOSH.11731 '19
                Pic  (Moerman)
        Filou  LOSH.9569 '10 (Brdr C.Dousy)
                Pico
        Charlotte  (Doussy)
                Laura
    Nera  LOSH.10280 '13
        Mirza
```

Figure 11-6

```
        Brick  (R.Vandenbroucke)
    Milton  LOSH.15936 '19
        Lize  (G.Dekeeghel)
Milton de la Barriere  LOSH.18580 '24
        Nic  B Ch; LOSH.10266 '16
    Myarka de Turnhout    LOSH.18292 '20
        Cora  LOSH.9575 '17
POP DU PANDORE  LOSH.72130 '35
        Brick  (R.Vandenbroucke)
    Milton  LOSH.15936 '19
        Lize  (G.Dekeeghel)
Kelly du Pandore  LOSH.35638 '29
        Brutus de la Lys  LOSH.11771 '21
    Alona  LOSH.23024 '25 (Brdr L.Petit)
        Naka de la Lys  LOSH.15594 '23
```

Two of the males upon which the breed was founded, Nic and Milton, appear in Figure 11-6. Indeed, in looking through the Belgian breeding records, four predominant early sires appear to have served as the foundation. One was Pic, bred by Moerman about 1905. Pic was never actually registered but is behind many important breeding animals, most important being the male Filou. (Pic may have died when registrations began in 1913. It is also possible that Mr. Moerman himself had died or become inactive, because no records are available of his activity beyond about 1910.) A second was Pickzwart (LOSH 14959), born in 1912 and bred by Dr. Scharlaken of Roulers. Nic and Milton round out the four males that, though themselves of unknown origin, are truly the cornerstones on which the Bouvier breed has been built.

Although the names of Milton's sire and dam are recorded, they do not have registration numbers and their origins are unknown. Milton was bred in 1919 by G. Dekeeghel of Watou and owned by O. Vincke in Mons. Mr. Vincke went on to become the owner of the very influential and successful Bouvier kennel "du Pandore," which was active into the late 1930s. Miss Bowles used the male Pop du Pandore in her "du Clos des Cerberes" program. According to my computer recores, Milton sired more than thirty offspring that carry forward to today's lines, the latest being a couple of "du Pandore" litters whelped in 1929.

In the course of my research, I obtained the entire set of Belgian (St. Hubert) breeding records from the beginning in 1913, with hundreds of pages listing thousands of dogs. Virtually all modern lines — Dutch, French, and Belgian — can be traced directly back to these founding lines, registered in Belgium first under the name Bouvier des Roulers and then Bouvier Belge des Flandres. It is clear that the Bouvier of today, thoughout the world, is descended primarily from the Bouvier des Roulers, as bred by Moerman, Gryson, Scharlaken, Faes, and the others in the region of this Flemish city. In particular, there is simply no record or evidence of the existence of surviving separate French lines, although farm dogs from Picardie were no doubt present, along with much English and other European stock, in the culturally Dutch region of Flandres where the Bouvier evolved and the breed was created.

Traviata de la Thudinie LOSH.120883.

Sarcus du Clos des Jeunes Plantes
One of the most famous Bouviers out of modern French breeding, Champion of both France and Belgium.

Sire: Oscar du Clos des Jeunes Plantes
Dam: Nilette du Clos des Jeunes Plantes

Postwar Evolution in Europe

The Struggle to Survive

World War II was a difficult time for the Bouvier, especially in France, where the fruit of several long-term breeding programs was to a large extent lost. Because the modern Bouvier largely evolved out of the Belgian reconstruction after the war, and because for a number of years before the war the French breeding was predominantly an offshoot of the Belgian Bouvier des Roulers lines, any trace of possible originating French lines was lost forever. The terrible devastation of the Bouvier breed by the Nazi atrocity is illustrated by the fact that the registration levels in Belgium during the 1930s, approximating a thousand dogs a year, was not approached again until the 1960s.

Although not as much military activity occurred in Holland as in Belgium, the Dutch population nevertheless suffered greatly under the German occupation. I am told by a friend, who was a child in Holland at the time, that one meal was the family cat, although he was not aware of this until later. The consumption of dogs, including Bouviers, occurred in both Belgium and Holland, and no doubt elsewhere.

The Belgian registry book shows perhaps twenty to thirty dogs from 1945 to 1949 listed as "origin unknown." This means that they were dogs obviously of Bouvier ancestry but whose actual history was not known or could not be documented. In general, it seems that while the terrible deprivations under the Nazi occupation brought breeding to a standstill, and good dogs were lost, the majority of lines can still be traced through the war. Apparently, the use of really unknown dogs for breeding was minimal. Indeed, Chastel bred important litters in both 1943 and 1944 while Belgium was still under Hitler's control.

To lend a perspective, in 1950, 292 dogs were registered in Belgium in 53 litters, and 8 as individual (older) dogs, 6 of which were of unknown origin. (Most of these were born in 1949, the record book always being one year behind.)

Soprano de la Thudinie sired about 10 percent of these dogs. Other prominent stud dogs include Servus du Clos des Cerberes from Miss Bowles's prewar breeding and Urmin du Gratte-Saule, who at that time was a primary stud in Moreaux's "de l'Ile Monsin" kennel. Prominent kennel names include "de Belgique," "du Ble' d'Or," and "de la Gendarmerie," in addition to "Thudinie" and "de l'Ile Monsin."

The early 1950s were very hard for the Bouvier everywhere, for in 1952, only ninety-one were registered in Belgium by the Societe Royale Saint-Hubert. The situation did not improve much, for the total was eighty-six in 1953 and hit a low of sixty in 1954. It was 1957 before more than one hundred were registered.

Unfortunately, it is not clear if "Kennel Belge" was active in this era, or how numerous its registrations might have been. French records were so poor that in many instances it was difficult to get an import registered with the AKC. Even today, pedigree information from this era in France is virtually nonexistent. Estimates by a reliable and experienced French breeder indicate that perhaps twenty-five or thirty pups were being registered annually during this period.

In 1954, 207 Bouviers were registered in the Netherlands, although there were likely many unregistered dogs, especially among the police-trained dogs whose owners regarded them as Bouviers. Even to this day, many of the Dutch Police dogs are of mixed or undocumented origin. This should not be construed to mean that their breeding is random, but only that they are of a line maintained by trainers who have little use for the formalities of registration.

Clearly, in the early 1950s, the Bouvier was at low ebb worldwide, and his continued existence stood in the balance. Many of the prewar breeders were too old or unable to continue, economic conditions were difficult, and the canine organizations of France, Belgium, and the Netherlands were in disarray. It is said that even Chastel was deeply discouraged and that only Verbanck was able to encourage him to carry on.

Belgium

The predominant figure in the Bouvier world after the war was Justin Chastel. From his home and kennel just outside the village of Thuin near Charleroi in the Walloon (French-speaking) region of Belgium, he played a pivotal role in the evolution of the breed. It is interesting and instructive to note that Chastel's "de la Thudinie" kennel is within ten miles of the French border. Along with Felix Verbanck, Edmond Moreaux, Felix Grulois, and a handful of others, he created the modern Bouvier as it exists worldwide.

Both Chastel's father and his uncle were dog breeders, one of the Malinois and the other of the Belgian Sheepdog and later the Bouvier. Therefore, it was not unnatural that Justin Chastel's boyhood interest in breeding would become a lifetime preoccupation. Although he dates his kennel from 1932, when he received a dog as a gift from his uncle, the first Thudinie Bouvier in modern pedigrees is a dog called Lucifer, whelped in 1937. This male was the son of Albionne de Biercee, born in 1933, who was Chastel's foundation bitch. Chastel notes in his book that he was able to purchase Albionne for a relatively reasonable price

A group of Bouvier des Flandres de la Thudinie at the Brussels show in 1952. These were the dogs on which Justin Chastel would found the modern Bouvier.

Eliane de la Thudinie, whelped in 1955, was the foundation of Felix Grulois' "du Posty Arlequin" line, and thus of the modern Belgian Bouvier.

Sire: Ch Argus de la Thudinie LOSH.159075 '51
Dam: Canaille de la Thudinie ALSH.2274

Photo courtesy of Felix Grulois.

Justin Chastel with Irca de la Thudinie (on the left) and Felix Grulois with Hackim du Posty Arlequin, winners at Paris in the early 1960s.

because an ear had been damaged in a fight. A littermate, Maria de Biercee, produced a daughter Lariane (in 1937) who was imported into the United States. This bitch appears in the pedigree of Si Jolie du Clos des Cerberes and thus is in the background of many modern American Bouviers. As can be seen from the pedigree (Figure 12-1), these littermates were only three or four generations removed from the dogs of unknown origin taken from Flemish fields.

Figure 12-1

```
                    Kis de Ramillies  LOSH.10263 '17
              Djil du Chateau  LOSH.15480 '23
                    Gyp  LOSH.11744 '21 (Br Alph.Faes)
        Boltom  LOSH.36208 '27
              Unknown
              Florine  (F.Van Steenbergen)
              Unknown
    Foltic du Vi-Blanc  LOSH.45856 '31
                    Dragon de la Barriere  LOSH.21555 '25
              Athos des Champs Clos  LOSH.32665
                    Ruth  LOSH.31467 '24
        Ellia de Saint-Alphonse  LOSH.38362
                    Jim du Sellier  LOSH.19345 '20
              Pila du Sellier  LOSH.17930 '22
                    Dina  LOSH.16871 '17
ALBIONNE DE BIERCEE    LOSH.57019 '33
                    Milton  LOSH.15936 '19
              Top de Bouffioulx  LOSH.22719 '25
                    Betty du Pandore  LOSH.16714 '23
        Boris de Sang-Froid  LOSH.29758 '27
                    Azur  LOSH.16362 '23
              Flora du Genie  LOSH.28827 '25
                    Mordienne du Genie  LOSH.14770 '22
    Dosia  LOSH.36545 '29
                    Sultan  LOSH.9573 '17
              Vif de la Ferme Elisabeth  LOSH.14215 '22
                    Gitane  LOSH.11742 '20 (Br A.Faes)
        Caprice de Prische  LOSH.32707
              Turco  (Hertefeldt)
        Miny  LOSH.15775 '21
              Didi
```

Shortly after Chastel began his program, the Germans began to march, and the dogs were entrusted to a local farmer named Guerriat. Some level of breeding was maintained, because in 1944 the dog was born that would propel Chastel to the first rank of Bouvier breeders. This magnificent animal was Soprano de la Thudinie, and such in his ubiquitous place in the breed that the majority of Bouviers today trace their male line directly to him. Even forty years later, photographs of Soprano show a remarkably handsome Bouvier — bold, stately, masculine. Soprano was a grandson of Lucifer, who had been bred back to his mother to produce Mirette, the dam of Soprano. This genealogy is depicted in Figure 12-2.

Guerriat, the farmer who kept Chastel's dogs, became a small-scale breeder under the name "du Gratte-Saule." Indeed, the region around Charleroi, the larger city near Thuin, was for many years the major center of Bouvier breeding in the French-speaking portion of Belgium, in large part due to Chastel's leadership and influence. The pedigree (Figure 12-3) of the mother of Wanda and Wandru des Coudreaux, U'Ada (born in 1946), illustrates breeding trends of the era just prior to the war and also of Chastel's evolutionary period.

Felix Verbanck was among the pioneering breeders in the 1920s under the kennel "de Royghem". Thereafter, he became inactive in this role but was a pivotal leader for the Bouvier community in Belgium for nearly fifty years. He did much to aid the early American breeders in locating and purchasing breeding stock. Much of his correspondence with Edmee Bowles from the early 1950s until shortly before his death has come into my possession. He was instru-

Figure 12-2

```
                    Athos des Champs Clos  LOSH.32665
              Edu de l'Eau d'Heure  LOSH.38364 '30
                    Caprice de Prische  LOSH.32707
          Gollino  LOSH.75535 '32
                    Triumph de Pont-A-Rieu  LOSH.19905 '24
              Beberte  LOSH.62859 '27
                    Lisotte  LOSH.62858 '25
          Joris du Ble d'Or  LOSH.76351 '35
                    Sultan  LOSH.9573 '17
              Vif de la Ferme Elisabeth  LOSH.14215 '22
                    Gitane  LOSH.11742 '20 (Br A.Faes)
          Eprise du Beryl  LOSH.39705 '30
                    Milton  LOSH.15936 '19
              Erfa du Pandore  LOSH.27918
                    Betty de la Lys  LOSH.11774 '21
Belg Ch SOPRANO DE LA THUDINIE  LOSH.113156 '44
                    Milton  LOSH.15936 '19
              Klaas du Pandore  LOSH.35074 '29
                    Efra du Pandore  LOSH.27917 '27
          Lucifer de la Thudinie  LOSH.88012 '37
                    Foltic du Vi-Blanc  LOSH.45856 '31
              Albionne de Biercee  LOSH.57019 '33
                    Dosia  LOSH.36545 '29
          Mirette de la Thudinie  LOSH.95153 '38
                    Boltom  LOSH.36208 '27
              Foltic du Vi-Blanc  LOSH.45856 '31
                    Ellia de Saint-Alphonse  LOSH.38362
          Albionne de Biercee  LOSH.57019 '33
                    Boris de Sang-Froid  LOSH.29758 '27
              Dosia  LOSH.36545 '29
                    Caprice de Prische  LOSH.32707
```

Figure 12-3

```
                    Bouboule de Courtrai  LOSH.23085 '24
              Gascon du Pont-Royal  LOSH.54406 '32
                    Era du Pont-Royal  LOSH.50088 '30
          Kiou del Roque du Moulin  LOSH.82249 '36
                    Foltic du Vi-Blanc  LOSH.45856 '31
              Hermanie del Roque du Moulin  LOSH.55821
                    Disse du Pont-Royal     LOSH.52182 '29
      Ravachol LOSH.110805 '43
                    Gabylo du Pandore  LOSH.29685
              Econome  LOSH.40620
                    Babelle  LOSH.40613 '27
          Janola  LOSH.72136
                    Dragon de la Barriere  LOSH.21555 '25
              Doris    LOSH.34184
                    Marie  LOSH.28512
Belg Ch U'ADA DU GRATTE-SAULE  LOSH.127972 '46
                    Milton  LOSH.15936 '19
              Klaas du Pandore  LOSH.35074 '29
                    Efra du Pandore  LOSH.27917 '27
          Nick du Ballieux  LOSH.100987 '39
                    Glouglou  LOSH.49869 '32
              Joliette du Ballieux  LOSH.75199
                    Hebe du Beryl  LOSH.57514
          Silane de la Thudinie  LOSH.117337
                    Klaas du Pandore  LOSH.35074 '29
              Lucifer de la Thudinie  LOSH.88012 '37
                    Albionne de Biercee     LOSH.57019 '33
          Mirette de la Thudinie  LOSH.95153 '38
                    Foltic du Vi-Blanc  LOSH.45856 '31
              Albionne de Biercee  LOSH.57019 '33
                    Dosia  LOSH.36545 '29
```

Hakim du Posty Arlequin LOSH.184149

Whelped: October 17, 1958
Breeder: Felix Grulois (Thuin, Belgium)
Sire: Bonzo l'Ideal de Charleroi
Dam: Eliane de la Thudinie

Photo courtesy of Annie Verheyen.

Bing de la Vallee de l'Ecaillon
Winner at Brussels in 1954

Whelped: 1952
Breeder: Fernand Malaquin (France)

Photo courtesy of Annie Verheyen.

mental in Bowles's importation of several bitches, notably Wandru des Coudreaux about 1952 and Remado's Katleen about ten years later, who was bred by Verbanck's nephew Maurice Dauwe.

A large part of Verbanck's effectiveness lay in the fact that he was never a really active breeder himself. This enabled him to lend counsel and to give advice without arousing fears that in so doing he would favor his own breeding line or his personal sense of importance. His moral authority served as a worldwide guiding light for the Bouvier for many years.

Verbanck's brother Florimond was also active in canine affairs and was a prominent Schipperke breeder. In the late 1940s, Florimond was president of the Belgian Bouvier Club and Felix was secretary, a post that he held until his death in the early 1970s.

Another predominant figure in Bouvier history is Edmond Moreaux, who through his "de l'Ile Monsin" line shaped the breed in France, Holland, and Belgium. ("Monsin" is an island in the River Meuse, which flows through the city of Liege where Moreaux lived.) His involvement spanned Bouvier history from the 1920s until his death in the early 1970s. Even today, the name "Moreaux" is legend wherever people love the Bouvier des Flandres.

Moreaux was already a prominent figure in the Bouvier world in the 1920s, when his stud Francoeur de Liege became both a Belgian Conformation Cham-

pion and a Champion of Work in the Belgian Ring. For three years, from 1928 through 1930, the team of Moreaux and Francoeur placed highly in the Bel-

Farouk de la Thudinie, International Champion.

Sire: Demon van het Lampegat LOSH.438654
Dam: Arca de la Thudinie LOSH.372517

Below: Tapin de la Thudinie, Champion International, a prime stud for Justin Chastel in the early 1970s. Compare this dog with Soprano, a quarter century earlier, to see the consistency in type maintained for so many decades by this architect of the Bouvier. *Left:* Tina de la Thudinie, littermate to Tapin.

gian Ring Sport national championships. Francoeur, whelped in 1924, was a son of Danilo de la Lys, and his mother was Janne de la Lys. He was a great-great-grandfather of Miss Bowles's Belco.

Moreaux lived in the city of Liege in eastern Belgium, only about twenty-five miles from the German border and even closer to the Dutch border to the north. He was totally devoted to strong, aggressive dogs and apparently shared many character traits with the dogs that he so loved. It is said that on one occasion he refused to see Verbanck when Verbanck called without an appointment. He had a distaste for Americans, apparently caused to a large extent by the

of this line is Cendrillo de l'Ile Monsin (see Figure 12-4), who was used extensively by Justin Chastel.

Cendrillo was never shown. Moreaux would ignore the show ring for years and then go out and clean up, perhaps as a reminder that he could do it whenever the fancy struck him. Reine du Lac-aux-Dames was a direct descendant of his great champion Francoeur de Liege.

Moreaux was willing to look far beyond his own lines, for even with such a great stud in his kennel, he went to France in the later 1950s to purchase a dog known only as Ely (Figure 12-5) out of Whist du Bois des Saules (a French Champion) and a bitch

Cendrillo de l'Ile Monsin
The legendary stud and working dog of Edmond Moreaux, circa 1955. *Photos courtesy of Annie Verheyen.*

terrible impression made by an obnoxious American handler on a dog-purchasing tour. My impression is that, while he was deeply devoted to his dogs and to his breeding program, he was a distant figure who did not much participate in the social aspects of the "dog game."

Although moderately active as a breeder from the beginning, Edmond Moreaux came into his own after the war. In the mid to late 1940s, he became a predominant international figure, respected and influential in France, the Netherlands, and Belgium. Perhaps the best known and most influential example

Figure 12-4

```
                    Soprano de la Thudinie  LOSH.113156
        Tito  LOSH.119452 '45
                    Rakina de la Thudinie  LOSH.109891
        Urmin du Gratte-Saule  LOSH.132612 '46
                    Nick du Ballieux  LOSH.100987
        Silane de la Thudinie  LOSH.117337
                    Mirette de la Thudinie  LOSH.95153 '38
CENDRILLO DE L'ILE MONSIN  '53
                    Khedive du Gabari  LOSH.80127
        Quinto  LOSH.107791 '42
                    Kobra de Beaufays  LOSH.81280
        Tamla de l'Ile Monsin  LOSH.122318
                    Jarnac des Farfadets  LOSH.73225
        Reine du Lac-aux-Dames  LOSH.112668
                    Ilotanie  LOSH.65726 '34
```

called Wyla. Ely became a Belgian Champion and an influential stud dog. Both Ely and Cendrillo were great-grandfathers of Marc de le Thudinie, and both were also great-grandsons of Soprano.

In the pedigree (Figure 12-5), the "LOF" numbers indicate French registration.

Thus, from the late 1940s until the 1970s, Moreaux was a prolific and productive breeder, and his "de l'Ile Monsin" kennel name is behind most of the best Bouviers throughout the entire world today. Indeed, much of Chastel's success was based on Moreaux's work, and if Chastel was the father of the modern Bouvier, then Moreaux was the godfather, the guardian on the soul. He and his dogs are still spoken of with deep respect in Belgian Ring Sports circles. There are those who believe that the Bouvier would be a better dog today if Moreaux had been as influential a leader as he was a breeder and sport participant. What is certain is that Edmond Moreaux will stand forever as a towering figure in the history of the Bouvier des Flandres.

Sad to say, the Bouvier no longer appears in the Ring Sport, the primary working-dog arena in his homeland. I have a bittersweet memory of standing by the Ring where the Malinois now alone represents Belgium and listening to a sad old man talk wistfully of when Bouviers competed, remembering the era of Moreaux. The last Bouvier to appear in the Belgian Ring championships was the dog Itarzan, whelped in 1961. He competed at the championship level from 1964 to 1967. Itarzan was owned and trained by Eddy ten Grootenhuyzen, who subsequently became a well-known judge, St. Hubert official, and writer on canine affairs. The pedigree of this dog is illustrated in Figure 12-6.

Itarzan was out of a ten-year-old male bred to a Dutch female. Even at birth, he was a throwback to an older and more honest era. Mr. ten Grootenhuyzen wrote to me that upon retiring Itarzan, he searched in vain for a Bouvier up to this standard and finally gave up, concluding that the day of the Bouvier as a

---

Figure 12-5

```
                     Soprano de la Thudinie  LOSH.113156
            U'Felon de la Thudinie  LOSH.137211
                     Albi  LOSH.183982 '39
      Whist du Bois des Saules  F Ch; LOF.1.Bouv.4587
            Kadour de la Romanee
                     Rina de Neubourg  LOF.1.Bouv.1437
                     Jade de la Romanee
Belg.Ch ELY  LOF.1.Bouv.8808 '55
      **
            Utah  LOF.1.Bouv.2264
      **
Wyla  LOF.1.Bouv.5147
      **
      Tosca du Clos des Duizettes LOF.1.Bouv.1437
            **
```

In the later 1950s, Edmond Moreaux of "de l'Ile Monsin" fame purchased Ely from France. He became Belgian Champion and a key stud in Belgian lines.

Ely LOF.8808
Born: 1955
Sire: F Ch Whist du Bois des Saules LOF.4587
Dam: Wyla LOF.5147

Figure 12-6

```
                  Quick Star de la Gendarmerie
         Siam   LOSH.116080
                  Rosalina   LOSH.109798
   Yvan van Waterschei   LOSH.151862 '49
                  Bruk de la Gendarmerie   LOSH.98734
         Sara de la Gendarmerie   LOSH.114760
                  Kina de la Gendarmerie   LOSH.63850
ITARZAN   LOSH.188407 '59
                  Lindos   KNPV NHSB.101932 '46
         Brestonico   NHSB.156987
                  Margo   NHSB.139011
   Sami   NHSB.197935 '57
                  Brestonox   NHSB.137473 '49
         Astraa   NHSB.165113
                  Erna   NHSB.152293 '52
```

serious working dog in Belgium had come to an end. The same is true in France, where none of the serious trainers will consider a Bouvier.

Finally, note in Itarzan's pedigree the kennel "de la Gendarmerie" of Ferdinand Nijs in Deinze, which is perhaps ten kilometers west of St. Denis Westrem, the location of "de la Lys." This kennel was based on a female of unknown origins, born in 1923, known simply as Lary. This bitch was bred to several of the "de la Lys" males to found a line that would flourish for another twenty years.

A bitch of Moreaux's breeding, Irisa de l'Ile Monsin, was bred in 1961 to produce a litter that would shape the breed for years to come. Remado's Kitty became the dam of Marc de la Thudinie. Katleen went to America to become a modern cornerstone of Edmee Bowles's "du Clos des Cerberes" line. Remado's Kandy became a stud for Moreaux, producing Oly, Otsa, and Omsky de l'Ile Monsin, which are particularly prominent in modern Dutch pedigrees. Remado's Keizer appears in the pedigree of several French champions.

As an example of Moreaux's influence, the great Dutch champion Oscy van Dafzicht, whelped in 1972, was a son of Oly de l'Ile Monsin. The other influential stud dog in the Dutch "Belgian renaissance" beginning in the later 1960s, Noup de la Thudinie, was not only a son of Marc but also a grandson of Cendrillo on his mother's side. Similar examples of Moreaux's influence in France can be seen in many modern French pedigrees.

Auguste Franshet, who founded his "Belgique" line in 1923, was for more than forty years a well-known and respected breeder, judge, and treasurer of the Belgian Bouvier Club. His first litters, out of Mirliton (LOSH.18207) and Graciella (LOSH.13721) were whelped in 1923 and 1924. From the 1924 litter, he kept Baron de Belgique, and Baronnesse de Belgique became one of the most productive and influential females of the era. Chastel refers to Franshet as an intimate friend of Verbanck and one of the pillars of

the club. Throughout the years, Franshet is listed as among those present at important meetings and conferences representing the Belgian club. Perhaps the best-known dog of Fraushet's line was Fricko de Belgique, whelped in 1956 and sire of Ike de Belgique, who was to become sire of the fabulous Remado "K" litter, mentioned above, in 1961.

In Ike de Belgique's pedigree (Figure 12-7), note that Wanda des Coudreaux was a littermate to Wandru, who Edmee Bowles brought to America in the early 1950s.

Figure 12-7

```
                  Unbloc   LOSH.130913 '46
         Arian   LOSH.160304
                  Utsa de Groeninghe   LOSH.134381
   Fricko de Belgique   LOSH.175335 '56
                  Whist du Bois des Saules   F Ch
         Donatienne des Coudreaux
                  Wanda des Coudreaux   F Ch; '48
IKE DE BELGIQUE '59
                  Unbloc   LOSH.130913 '46
         Arian   LOSH.160304
                  Utsa de Groeninghe   LOSH.134381
   Erna de Belgique
                  Xoro de la Thudinie   LOSH.144462 '48
         Caroline du Maine Giraud
                  Ucaba   LOSH.128447 '46
```

In addition to Ike, Fricko's illustrious progeny include Karl de l'Ile Monsin, Idole du Posty Arlequin, and Iota du Posty Arlequin. The death of Franshet in 1967 brought to an end the "de Belgique" line after more than forty years, but his contribution is still present in the best of today's Bouviers throughout the world.

February 1963 marked the beginning of a new era in Bouvier history, for on that day a litter of five dogs and two bitches was born, including Marc de la Thudinie. None of the others are prominent in Bouvier pedigrees. In Marc de la Thudinie's genealogical chart (Figure 12-8), note Moreaux's strong influence on both sides.

Figure 12-8

```
                  Cendrillo de l'Ile Monsin '53
         Hion de la Thudinie   Ch; '58
                  Demoiselle de la Thudinie
   Job de la Thudinie   B/A Ch; '60
                  Bonzo l'Ideal de Charleroi '52
         Hulotte de la Thudinie '58
                  Flambee de la Thudinie '56
MARC DE LA THUDINIE '63
                  Fricko de Belgique   LOSH.175335 '56
         Ike de Belgique '59
                  Erna de Belgique
   Remado's Kitty '61
                  Ely   B Ch; '55 LOF.1.Bouv.8808
         Irisa de l'Ile Monsin
                  Balta de l'Ile Monsin   B Ch
```

Several years earlier, Chastel had become concerned about the temperament of his dogs and about the Bouvier in general. On the advice of Verbanck, he had made use of Moreaux's Cendrillo de l'Ile Monsin at stud, which turned out to be a fateful move. Chastel writes that he was drawn to this dog because he could not get close enough to examine the bite and in fact never put a hand on the beast. It is clear what he wanted in the way of improved character! Chastel quotes Moreaux as believing that Cendrillo's extraordinary character was largely due to his dam, Tamia de l'Ile Monsin. This influential bitch also appears on the other side of Marc's pedigree. Marc's progeny include Nolette, Noup, Orsonne, Oula and Olaf de la Thudinie, and Naris du Posty Arlequin. These dogs, whelped in 1964 or 1965, played important roles in the evolution of the modern Bouvier, particularly Olaf.

Marc was to be a heavily used and influential stud dog and a prominent show dog on two continents. But this alone was not enough to herald the advent of a new era. The real significance of the birth of Marc was that Chastel was entering a fifteen- or twenty-year period during which he would almost single-handedly crate the modern Bouvier by breeding very tightly on Marc and a few closely related dogs. Previously, he had incorporated much outside blood into his breeding program, but from this point forward he would turn inward and stay within his own line. At about this time, Verbanck was, because of age, becoming much less active as a leader and adviser. Chastel was emerging as the new leader and, for better or for worse, would embark on a new course.

The other key figure in this scenario was Felix Grulois, who, beginning in the mid-1950s, became through his "du Posty Arlequin" line almost as prominent and influential as Chastel himself. For a number of years, the programs of Chastel and Grulois would be tightly intertwined and would become the most influential and predominant in the world. Chastel and Grulois lived within a mile or two of each other in the Belgian village of Thuin. Sad to say, after a number of years of close cooperation, there was a falling out between these two important breeders.

Much of the driving force behind this Thuin dominance of the Bouvier world was the American money being paid for dogs such as Job, Marc and Noceur de la Thudinie, and Nota and Naris du Posty Arlequin. Chastel's and Grulois' access to American cash had as much or more to do with their power and influence than the inherent quality of their dogs.

Chastel and Grulois were also among the most influential and active judges and took turns putting each other's dogs up. Indeed, at one point in the 1970s, there were ten Bouvier judges in Belgium, with Chastel and his wife and Grulois and his brother accounting for 40 percent of them. This may have discouraged the younger generation from becoming breeders or encouraged them to go into other breeds.

Among the Belgians who have become prominent breeders subsequent to 1960 are Alfons and Annie Verheyen. Their van de Buildrager kennel is located at St.-Job-in-'t-Goor, which is just north of Antwerp and a twenty-minute drive south of the Dutch border. Prominent dogs from this kennel include Xar and Bingo van de Buildrager. Yago van de Buildrager was imported into the United States by Fred Joyner in Maryland and used at stud sparingly, but with significant success, particularly by Marion Hubbard at Madrone Ledge. At Centauri, our second litter was a breeding of April du Clos des Cerberes to Yago, which produced several excellent females that have gone on to make their own contributions to the breed. The Buildrager kennel is very close to the original location of Miss Bowles's du Clos des Cerberes kennel at Schilde.

Probably the largest Bouvier program in Belgium today is Omar Bastelier's "van de Macecliers" kennel, located near Benrzel, twenty kilometers southeast of

Felix Grulois, Belgian Bouvier breeder, world-famous for his "du Posty-Arlequin" line.

Idole du Posty Arlequin, dam of Lais du Posty Arlequin, who became one of the most important stud dogs in Belgium.

Sire: Fricko de Belgique LOSH.175335 '56
Dam: Eliane de la Thudinie LOSH.184569

Photo courtesy of Felix Grulois.

Heros du Posty Arlequin LOSH.184151

Sire: Bonzo l'Ideal de Charleroi
Dam: Eliane de la Thudinie
Whelped: 1958

Quasimodo du Posty Arlequin, successful show winner for Felix Grulois in the early 1970s.

Ayox du Posty Arlequin
LOSH.384335
Representative of modern
Belgian breeding.

Sire: Zais du Posty Arlequin
LOSH.358693
Dam: Vadrouille du Posty
Arlequin LOSH.317588
Born: 1976

Photo courtesy of Felix Grulois.

Antwerp. Adonis van de Macecliers is perhaps the best-known product of this kennel. Hadonis van de Macecliers, out of Clim van de Macecliers and Baba van de Macecliers, is currently one of the better-thought-of males in Belgium today. Claudia v. d. Macecliers was imported into Holland and bred to Hoscy Dukke Bianca fan it Hanenhiem to produce Dayan Claudia v Hagenbeek, winner of the Dutch Specialty and sire of two World Show winners before being brought to America by Erik Houttuin.

Although currently breeding only on a small scale, Rex and Simone Keeman's "van het Lampegat" kennel, located at Leopoldsburg just south of the Dutch border, was in the 1970s a prominent Bouvier establishment. Although Keeman is Dutch and began his breeding operations in Holland, his breeding stock has been drawn entirely from classic Belgian show lines, with heavy emphasis on the Thudinie lines. Picard Generique Tania van het Lampegat, out of Rico de la Thudinie and Generique Tania van het Lampegat, became a Dutch Champion in 1978. Picard is the sire of Henk and Gerda Harmers's Dutch Specialty Winner and Champion of Holland, Gillroy Kelly v d Cerbeushof, who was resident in the United States for a few months. Several other Dutch breeders have made good use of Picard.

An interesting aspect of the worldwide Belgian predominance is that the Bouvier has apparently never been especially numerous there, even considering that Belgium is such a small country. As previously mentioned, about fifty litters a year have been typical from the 1940s to the present. There is also an unknown number of dogs who cannot be registered but whose owners no doubt regard them as Bouviers. In 1977, there were about as many Dobermans as Bouviers registered in Belgium and four times as many German Shepherds.

France

Among the most prominent of postwar French kennels is that of "des Coudreaux" at Leysat near Montfermeil. It was founded by a Monsieur Corbier and was carried on by his daughter Mme. Sorin after his death. Important dogs from this kennel include Ygor, Alymre, and Wanda. A littermate of Wanda, Wandru des Coudreaux, was imported by Miss Bowles in the early 1950s.

The pedigree of Etoile (Figure 12-9), whelped in 1955, illustrates the postwar French breeding trends.

The other French kennel of great significance in this era was that of Fernand Malaquin in the city of Thiant. The foundation was a female named Sapho, who produced many notable winners. When bred to the famous male Quasimodo, she produced Volpi de la Vallee de l'Escaillon, who would become the sire of Argus de la Thudinie. Malaquin was a major show winner in the late 1940s and through the 1950s and produced several notable dogs that would win distinction in the French Ring. Chastel concludes his com-

Figure 12-9

```
            Azor de la Boheme  LOF.119
      Quasimodo  F Ch; LOF.1156 '42
            Meg de la Boheme  LOF.1056
      Voulzzi de la Boheme  LOF.4521
            Quinio du Grand Sauzay  LOF.944
      Uniqueo de la Boheme  LOF.4133
            Raani
  Azor Dit Axoum de Pierre Sereine  LOF.8073
            Sherif des Trois Iles  LOF.1193
      T'Joel des Trois Iles  LOF.1572
            Sonia des Trois Iles  LOF.1285
  Vani de Grandin  LOF.4571
            L'Ami de la Boheme  LOF.1003
      Sirene de Grandin  LOF.3746
            Naja de Mont Glonne      LOF.816
ETOILE DES COUDREAUX '55
            Soprano de la Thudinie  B Ch
      U'Felon de la Thudinie  LOSH.137211
            Albi  LOSH.183982 '39
  Whist du Bois des Saules  F Ch; LOF.4587
            Kadour de la Romanee  LOF.187
      Rina de Neubourg  LOF.1888
            Jade de la Romanee  LOF.57
  Antinea des Coudreaux  LOF.6938
            Jaf du Chateau de Villers  LOF.1104
      Samos des Trois Iles  LOF.1281
            Rita de la Gueulardiere  LOF.1101
  Wanda des Coudreaux  F Ch; LOF.3735 '48
            Ravachol  LOSH.110805 '43
      U'Ada du Gratte-Saule  B Ch; LOSH.127972
            Silane de la Thudinie  LOSH.117337
```

mentary on this kennel in this way: "In 1962, to the great regret of the proprietor, the breeding of the Bouvier des Flandres came to a close at the Vallee de l'Ecaillon . . ."

The general situation in France appears to be about the same as in Belgium, where Bouviers are not especially common. Dr. LeLann, the well-known French judge, stated in a recent article in the French Club journal that about 700 Bouviers per year have been registered in Belgium and France together, which is not very many dogs for nations that would claim custody of the Standard. In Amsterdam, on the other hand, Bouviers on the street are a common sight, and the Bouvier has, in fact, become popular in Holland over the past thirty years.

The French postwar breeding program was heavily dependent on Thudinie blood. A good example is Carol du Maine Giraud, perhaps the most prominent French Champion of the early 1950s, who was a double grandson of Soprano and thus of pure Thudinie breeding. Prominent French kennels of recent years include "de la Buthiere" of Gaston Defarges, "du Val de Rol" of Marie-Claude Niquet, and "de l'Epee" of Laurette Lepage.

Starting in the mid-1950s, one of the leading French breeding programs has been that of Mr. and Mrs. Gerard Gelineau, under their kennel name "du Clos de Jeunes Plantes." Mr. Gelineau is vice-president of the French Club and a Ring (working) judge, while Mrs. Gelineau is a prominent conformation judge.

Their kennel is at le Blanc, in the beautiful French countryside some five hours' drive south of Paris. Perhaps the best-known product of this program is Quarl du Clos des Jeunes Plantes (Figure 12-10), whelped in 1967, who became both a Champion of Beauty and a Champion of Work. Quarl was a French Ring Championship Finalist from 1972 through 1975.

Figure 12-10

```
            Unbloc  LOSH.130913 '46
      Arian  LOSH.160304
            Utsa de Groeninghe  LOSH.134381
  Fricko de Belgique  LOSH.175335 '56
            Whist du Bois des Saules  F Ch
      Donatienne des Coudreaux
            Wanda des Coudreaux      F Ch; '48
  Karl de l'Ile Monsin  LOSH.202914 '61
            Tito  LOSH.119452 '45
      Urmin du Gratte-Saule  LOSH.132612 '46
            Silane de la Thudinie  LOSH.117337
  Florida de l'Ile Monsin  LOSH.176224
            Urmin du Gratte-Saule  LOSH.132612 '46
      Barlette de l'Ile Monsin
            Tamia de l'Ile Monsin  LOSH.122318
F Ch QUARL DU CLOS DES JEUNES PLANTES  LOF.13275-214
            Whist du Bois des Saules  F Ch
      Ely  B Ch; LOF.8808 '55
            Wyla  LOF.5147
  Iraky de l'Ile Monsin
            Urmin du Gratte-Saule  LOSH.132612 '46
      Elma de l'Ile Monsin
            Barlette de l'Ile Monsin
  Ninon des Casseaux  LOF.12235-60 '64
            Carol du Maine Giraud  B Ch; LOF.8031
      Gredin du Maine Giraud  F Ch; '57
            Disse du Maine Giraud
  Jassy du Maine Giraud
            Carol du Maine Giraud  B Ch; LOF.8031
      Dulcinee du Maine Giraud  LOF.8681
            Brunehaut du Maine Giraud  LOF.7810
```

As can be seen from Figure 12-10, this great dog was almost purely of Edmond Moreaux's famous "de l'Ile Monsin" breeding program and thus was of Belgian rather than French background. Therefore, when you look just below the surface, you find that Moreaux is behind most of the best-working Bouviers throughout the world, including Holland, Belgium, and France. The one major exception is the traditional Dutch Police lines.

The Netherlands

Although the earliest Dutch Bouviers were drawn from Flemish stock in the 1920s, the Dutch Bouvier community was almost totally isolated from the Belgian and the French through the war and into the 1960s. The Dutch registration book from the mid-1940s through the mid-1960s indicates that only a

Noup de la Thudinie, Dutch Specialty Winner in 1966, is one of the most important Bouviers in breed history, for he is the key on which Coen Semler founded his revolution, that is, the melding of the Belgian line of Justin Chastel with the traditional Dutch lines to launch the "Dafzicht" dynasty.

Sire: Ch Marc de la Thudinie
LOSH.213476 '63
Dam: Iatte de la Thudinie
LOSH.186491
Brd: Justin Chastel
Owner: Coen Semler

handful of Belgian dogs were used, and these were not particularly influential. This "Old Dutch" breeding was of significant quality and depth and was, in fact, behind the dogs' coming to the United States in the early years, including Miss Bowles's Belco. Such dogs can still be seen on Dutch streets and in the countryside today, and I find these big, black, short-coated dogs especially attractive.

Typical of this breeding is Iwan Floss v d Rakkers (Figure 12-11), a prominent Dutch Champion in the early 1950s. As is the custom among many of the Dutch, Iwan takes his mother's name as a second name.

Figure 12-11

```
              Max Simba v Sappemeer  D Ch'41
         Athos van het Velperholt  NHSB.97295
              Blufka  NHSB.81965 '43
 Jupiter v h Kwartier v Maasland  NHSB.139400 '50
              Max Simba v Sappemeer  D Ch'41
         Giovanna Bianca v h Kwartier v Maaslan
              Bianca Aleida v d Zaanhoeve
IWAN FLOSS V D RAKKERS  Holland Ch.  NHSB.157389 '53
              Kohur  NHSB.62665
         Winston v h Kwartier v Maasland  NHSB.93363 '45
              Asta v d Grauwert  NHSB.85415 '44
 Floss Cilly v d Rakkers  D Ch'52; NHSB.130501 '49
              Always Ready Ivan  NHSB.77181
         Cilly v d Rakkers  D Ch'47; NHSB.87194 '44
              Prodina  NHSB.72547
```

There is no doubt a fascinating story behind a dog called Always Ready Ivan, but I have never been able to find out what it is. The parents of this dog are not included in the Dutch records, and a number of other names from the early war years are missing. A fire at

the Raad van Beheer just after the war may account for the lost records.

Twenty-five years later comes the dog Eros van de Zwikshoek (Figure 12-12), which represents the pinnacle of the original Dutch breeding.

Figure 12-12

```
              Job de la Thudinie  B/A Ch; '60
         Lais du Posty Arlequin  '62
              Idole du Posty Arlequin
  Uran Peggy v d Rakkers  D Ch; NHSB.330869 '64
              Hasano  D Ch'60; NHSB.191586 '57
         Peggy Nancy v d Rakkers  D Ch; NHSB.225193 '59
              Nancy Lucia v d Rakkers  NHSB.196933
EROS V D ZWIKSHOEK   Holland Ch.   NHSB.443813 '68
              Arnoroh  NHSB.201858 '58
         Soprano Peggy v d Rakkers  D Ch'64; NHSB.271686
              Peggy Nancy v d Rakkers  D Ch
  Cilia Alma v d Zwikshoek
              Barry v d Veenhoeve  D Ch '59
         Alma v d Zwikshoek  NHSB.314066 '63
              Magda  NHSB.212552 '58
```

Starting in the early 1960s, a number of Dutch breeders, led by Coen Semler of the Dafzicht kennel in Eindhoven, "went Belgian;" that is, they imported dogs from Chastel, Moreaux, Grulois, and other Belgian breeders and sought to produce a much more heavily coated dog in the Belgian style. Noup de la Thudinie, Rif du Posty Arlequin, and Oly de l'Ile Monsin are typical of the imported dogs, born in the early to mid-1960s, that radically changed the Bouvier in Holland.

Coen Semler is among the key figures in Bouvier history, beginning in the mid-1930s when he became

Coen Semler's Ch Hoscy Kata v Dafzicht, whelped in 1975, was the sire of five Dutch Champions, a foundation of the Dafzicht dynasty. (King v Dafzicht ex. Kata v Dafzicht)

an active police (KNPV) trainer. Over the next twenty-five years, he titled twenty-two Bouviers, an incredible record in this most demanding sport. Then, starting in the 1960s, with his training limited by a serious heart condition, he turned to the conformation ring and founded the fabulous Dafzicht dynasty.

At Dafzicht, the breeding efforts weere intense, and it is said that at times Semler had 100 or more Bouviers. These efforts were rewarded, for in 1975, Oscy van Dafzicht became Champion of Holland, followed by Ringo in 1976, both out of Oly de l'Ile Monsin. In 1977, Aron Vedette became Champion. In 1978, only four Bouviers became Champion of Holland, and each of these dogs was from the Dafzicht kennel. In fact, from 1976 through 1978, every Dutch Champion, six in all, was a Dafzicht Bouvier! The pedigree of Hoscy Kata (Figure 12-13), whose progeny would be heavily present in the Dutch Championship lists for several years, illustrates the Dafzicht program.

Hoscy Kata was of pure Belgian breeding except for Bica, who was Semler's primary stud of Dutch background and one of the most widely used and respected male Bouviers in Europe at the time. Picolette du Posty Arlequin was subsequently imported by Ray and Marion Hubbard for their Madrone Ledge program and became a well-known Amer-

Venlo, the Netherlands, March 20, 1977. Coen Semler with Hoscy Kata van Dafzicht for the last time, for later that day he would die in the ring. This was not the end, but the end of the beginning, for the fabulous Dafzicht Bouviers would go on to make the name "Semler" stand alone as the modern Dutch pillar of the breed. As for Hoscy Kata, he would go on to found a line of Dutch Champions and Specialty Winners the like of which will almost certainly never appear again:

Ch. Hoscy Kata v Dafzicht, sire of
Ch. Hoscy Dukke Bianca fan it Hanenhiem, sire of
Ch. Dayan Claudia van Hagenbeek, sire of
Ch. Darwin Grenda v h Grendarcohof, sire of
Ch. Falco Darwin van het Grendarcohof

Figure 12-13

```
            Oecles du Posty Arlequin
      Rif du Posty Arlequin      HD+-  '68
            Picolette du Posty Arlequin Ch
   King v Dafzicht  NHSB.602588 HD-
            Milord ten Roobos  '63
      Rocca ten Roobos  HD-
            Mina ten Roobos
D Ch HOSCY KATA V DAFZICHT  NHSB.812460 '75 HD.Tc.
            Hoss v d Horzeldijk HD-  NHSB.396369
      Bica v d Rozenheerd  NHSB.512062 HD-
            Basca Tamara v d Woestendijk
   Kata v Dafzicht  HD+- NHSB.635688 '72
            Noup de la Thudinie HD-  '64
      Astra Noup v Dafzicht      NHSB.520835
            Rocca ten Roobos  HD-
```

Coen Semler with Bucko van Dafzicht, circa 1970. In the next decade, Semler would redefine the Bouvier in the Netherlands.

Dutch Ch Oscy van Dafzicht, HD + − NHSB.634357

Breeder: Coen Semler
Born: 1972
Sire: Oly de l'Ile Monsin
Dam: Sylvia Reverie v h Witte Dorp

Lurando Noup v Dafzicht NHSB.577145

Sire: Noup de la Thudinie HD − NHSB.393735
Dam: Yulca v Dafzicht NHSB.414077
Born: November 3, 1971

Duc, owned by H. Olders, KNPV (Dutch Police) Certificate with 302 pt.; NHSB.503104.

Sire: Duc v Sevenheym NHSB.425814 '67
Dam: Astrid v h Kloosterzicht NHSB.379706 '66

Coen Semler's "Loef", 1936 KNPV National Champion (Holland)

"Rudy, owned by H. Olders and holder of Dutch Police Certificate.

KNPV m.lof '66 NHSB.338001
Born: April 28, 1964
Sire: Wiboo KNPV '61 NHSB.191502 '57
Dam: Margooh NHSB.269612

Bucko van Dafzicht. This male is typical of Coen Semler's police breeding.

Breeder: Coen Semler, Geldrop, the Netherlands
Born: January 15, 1967
Sire: Borinus KNPV m.lof'66 NHSB.307660 '63
Dam: Marana NHSB.362985

Although the lighter coloring is not desirable, Robby van Donckerhof combines excellent structure and a Dutch Police Certificate to make him an attractive stud. Imported by Dr. Erik Houttuin.

KNPV m.lof NHSB.1122166
Whelped: 1980
Sire: Breno NHSB.869184
Dam: Debby v d Boerenhof NHSB.893884

Ton Peeters' "Iwan" holds KNPV Police Certificates Police Dog I, Police Dog II, and Object Protection Dog, each "met lof," that is, "with honors." This dog has also rated "Excellent" in the Dutch conformation ring.

KNPV met. lof NHSB.128250
Owned and trained by Ton Peeters
Sire: Arno KNPV NHSB.968380
Dam: Xandra v Zonnetij NHSB.1092861
Brd: C. Xhofleer

ican Champion. King, nearly white in color, was one of the few Dafzicht studs of this era that did not become Champion of Holland. (This is significant in that only one or two Bouviers typically become a new Holland Champion in any year.)

Hoscy Kata was a productive stud, as this listing of some of his more notable progeny indicates:

Hoscy Dukke Bianca fan it Hanenhiem
    Champion of Holland '79

Beauprince Amber van Rovika
    Champion of Holland
Bijou Amber van Rovika
    Champion of Holland
Grando Jannette van de Rozenheerd
    Champion of Holland '77

Granda Jannette van de Rozenheerd
Cisca Flandrienen v Dafzicht

In this brief listing, there are four Dutch Champions, an astounding record of production. On the negative side, Hoscy Kata's sire King was a white dog, and light color has continued to plague the Dutch show lines for the past decade.

Coen Semler clearly altered the course of the Bouvier in the Netherlands and made Dafzicht for a time the most predominant and respected kennel in modern Dutch history. At the Venlo show on March 20, 1977, when Semler stepped into the ring to take the lead of Aron Vedette van Dafzicht, Semler collapsed and died. The Dafzicht tradition has been carried on by his daughter Annie Krah-Semler and her husband Heinz.

In recent years, the offspring of the great Dafzicht Bouviers have predominated in the Dutch Championship lists, especially in dogs such as Ch. Hoscy Dukke Bianca fan it Hanenheim (a son of Hoscy Kata van Dafzicht), who was, until his untimely death, perhaps the most prominent and productive stud dog in the Netherlands. The several "van Rovika" champions, such as Beauprince, are for all practical purposes a continuation of the Dafzicht line.

The revolution led by Semler and his cohorts was apparent in the streets of the Netherlands as well as in the show ring. The more heavily coated, Belgian-style dog that they introduced became much more popular among the populace as home companions and pets than the older-style Dutch Bouviers ever had been, and the Bouvier became more popular in the Netherlands than he had ever been in Belgium or

Left: Caya Krijnse Locker's "Peggy" is one of the few Bouviers to hold both an IPO or Schutzhund title and a KNPV certificate. KNPV m. lof IPO I HD-NHSB.1090431. **Sire:** Wilson v d Boerenhof KNPV m. lof. **Dam:** Sonja v d Veldmolen.
Below: Breston NHSB.590069 KNPV met.lof. **Sire:** Duc v Sevenheym. **Dam:** Astrid v h Kloosterzicht. **Born:** 1972. Typical of old-style Dutch Police lines.

France. Whether this is good or bad is, of course, a matter for debate, because rapid increases in popularity have in many instances not been beneficial for the overall quality of a breed. This has been seen many times in America, but the same process can occur in Europe or elsewhere.

To see this trend numerically, consider that although annual registrations were only a couple of hundred in the early 1950s and about 500 in 1965, they reached about 3,500 by 1973. By the early 1980s, the Bouvier had become the most popular breed in the Netherlands, representing about 15 percent of all purebred dogs. Recent annual registration figures are as follows:

Year	1981	1982	1983	1984	1985
Bouvier des Flandres	6844	7085	8993	10200	9320
German Shepherd	5330	5047	5657	6205	5373
Golden Retriever	1649	2337	3106	3695	4604

Fairly typical of modern Dutch Bouviers is Ria Klep's Bram Pasja (Figure 12-14), born in 1983 and winner of the 1988 North American Working Championship in Manassis, Virginia. Halvar Bretta is among the most striking Bouviers to ever enter the show ring and was a widely used stud. In addition to

Figure 12-14

```
                    Ardan Zerna van het Vonderke
          Halvar Bretta v d Boevers Garden  Int Ch; Sch III
                    Bretta v Hoeve Bouvier  SchH I
    Bonaparte Zierce v d Cerberushof   NHSB.1073603 '79 HD+-
                    Xoro ten Roobos
                Zierce ten Roobos
                    Vivie ten Roobos
BRAM PASJA LE JARDIN DU MOULIN  IPO III NHSB.1314647
                Barrie  NHSB.616808 '72
          Donar  SchH III,FH,Dutch Ch. of Work, NAWC '82
                Tusor van de Overheide  NHSB.964040
      Pasja   SchH I NHSB.1210045
              Tazan  NHSB.1009858
          Kanjer  SchH III
              Wanda  NHSB.953324
```

winning the Dutch National Specialty in 1982, he became International Champion and Schutzhund III. He is a massive, powerfully built dark-gray dog with an incredibly broad skull. The breeder and owner, Theo de Wagenaar, has also produced another outstanding Champion of Holland, Spencer van de Boevers Garden, out of the ubiquitous Hoscy Dukke and Jordina Bretta v d Boevers Garden, littermate to Halvar.

Bonaparte Zierce v d Cerberushof (see Figure 12-14) has been a primary stud for Henk and Gerda

Bart Krist of the Netherlands with "Tubo", sire of many KNPV dogs and prominent in German working lines.

Sire: Borisio NHSB.569963 '71
Dam: Brendah v Pleinzicht NHSB.662665
Born: 1977

Mondy Bjorka van de Klein Bosch Hoeve NHSB.1344442, whelped in 1984. Mondy was imported by Dr. Erik Houttuin and was a most productive brood bitch here.

Sire: D Ch Darwin Grenda v h Grendarcohof
Dam: Bjorka Flair van de Klein Boschhoeve
Brd: Kees and Hanneke Hagenbeek

Pjer Diana v d Overstort, born in 1983, is a foundation of Mr. Pater's "de Overstort" line, successor to "Dafzicht" as the predominant conformation kennel in the Netherlands.

NHSB.1311017
Sire: D Ch Picard Generique v h Lampegat
Dam: Bette Diana v d Overstort
Brd: Joop Pater

Harmers at Cerberushof. These successful breeders saw Halvar's potential when he was very young, before he became well-known. The breeding of a top Dutch stud to a Belgian female, as in the mating of Halvar and Zierce, has been typical of the most successful Dutch conformation breeding the past ten to twenty years. On the mother's side, Donar was, of course, Ria Klepp's own great working champion.

Coen Semler totally redefined the Bouvier in Holland from 1960 to 1980, replacing the existing Dutch show lines with his own line, based mostly on the traditional Belgian conformation lines from kennels such as de l'Ile Monsin, de la Thudinie, and du Posty Arlequin. His prominence was clearly resented by many of the other breeders. Semler was a championship-level police-dog trainer for some thirty-five years.

To compete at this level so successfully and for so long, a person must be driven — literally obsessed. Such a person could never accept the Bouvier as only a "show dog." It was not my good fortune to know Semler, but those who did, such as Bart Krist at van Pleinzicht, testify to his ideals. George Kroesin, the Dutchman who did so much to start the current trend of importing top Dutch lines to America and a notable breeder in his own right, quoted Semler as comparing his ideal Bouvier to "that American product, 3-in-1 Oil." This ideal dog, he explained, was winning show dog, a capable police-trial competitor, and a family companion.

I believe that, by his own lofty vision, Semler could never accept two Bouvier types in Holland — the show dog and the working dog. In order for Semler's

Spinks Centy v d Overstort
Dutch Champion

NHSB.1446027
Born: 1986
Sire: Pjer Diana v d Overstort NHSB.1311017
Dam: Centy Tama v h Kurverke NHSB.1135738
Brd: Joop Pater

dream to come true, the Dutch Championship must be purified by a meaningful working requirement, and trainers must be drawn back into the Bouvier community. There is a trace of irony in the fact that Semler, the quintessential trainer, had so much to do with the popularization of the Bouvier as a show dog in the Netherlands, thus endangering the working soul to which he had devoted most of a lifetime. Chastel and Semler are in many ways twin pillars of the breed, remarkable for both their similarities and their differences, yet both understanding the need to maintain the working character.

Europe Today

In contrast to the popularity of the Bouvier in Holland, in Belgium in recent years, about four German Shepherds and a Doberman have been registered for every Bouvier. There is no question that in the 1980s, there was a changing of the guard. Holland became the center of the Bouvier world in terms of numbers, quality, and international influence. At a 1984 Belgian show in Meerhout, where the bitches were judged by Chastel, the Dutch kennels and the Dutch stud dogs

Juno Elza v h Witteveenseven

NHSB.1404505 HD-
Sire: D Ch Hoscy Dukke Bianca fan it Hanenhiem
Dam: Elza Cassandra v h Witteveenseven
Brd: Sien en Harry Lescher

Soray Alexis v d Overstort

NHSB.1513911
Sire: Barry Diana v d Overstort
Dam: Alexis Kristy v d Overstort
Brd: Joop Pater
Owner: Albert de Zwaan

Koran Pjer v d Overstort

NHSB.1554306
Sire: Pjer Diana v d Overstort
NHSB.1311017
Dam: Goya Christie v d
Overstort   NHSB.142468
Brd: Joop Pater

predominated, although these dogs were, of course, to a major extent drawn from Belgian lines introduced into Holland by Semler.

The linguistically and culturally French Belgians and the French on the whole regard themselves as the custodians of the Bouvier. Chastel, for example, entirely ignores a fifty-year Dutch breeding tradition in his book. The French constantly remind us that the Standard is the Franco-Belgian Standard and that, according to FCI regulations, it can only be altered by their mutual consent. However, this is mostly a matter of politics. Also, the Bouvier is and always has

been less numerous in France, in both relative and absolute terms, than it now is in the United States. French registrations have never been more than a few hundred in a nation of some 50 million people. The Dutch and the North Americans, on the other hand, produce several thousand yearly. Large numbers, of course, do not necessarily denote quality, but the Dutch have become increasingly dominant in international competition, such as the World Show.

The Americans and the Dutch are remarkably similar. Both nations have a large and enthusiastic Bouvier community and no discernible overall direction. The

Dutch Specialty winners and champions in recent years have been remarkable dogs but distressingly divergent in type. Both the Dutch and the Americans seem particularly susceptible to fads and to the fashion of the moment, and both countries have a long history of ignoring character or selecting soft dogs in the belief that such dogs are easier to sell. The German-style Schutzhund training, which, while simple and quick enough to serve the breeder as a selection test, is also demanding enough (with a sufficiently correct judge) to maintain correct character. Hopefully, this development will flourish and lead to a more integrated, and thus stronger, Dutch Bouvier community. If current lack of interest in the Bouvier in Belgium and France persists, the future of the breed, for better or worse, would appear to be largely in the hands of the Dutch.

Justin Chastel with his Bouviers de la Thudinie, circa 1988.

Family group of Bouviers, owned by Lucille Gill. These dogs are typical of Jack van Vliet's "du Plateau" breeding in the 1970s. Ch. Chien d'Argent du Plateau (in the cart), Jonathan Mokum Tughs (in harness), and Noelle du Plateau.

The Bouvier des Flandres in America

The creators of the working breeds of central Europe were by and large working-class people themselves. The men and women who brought these breeds to North America were, on the other hand, relatively affluent. This is not surprising, because importing breeding stock has always been expensive, and working people simply lack the time or funds to tour Europe looking for a new hobby. One consequence is that the dogs were selected and promoted for exhibition rather than for work as envisioned by the breed founders.

The Bouvier has been somewhat fortunate in that a few of the people involved in bringing the breed to the United States and Canada, such as Edmee Bowles and, much later, Paul DeRycke, were of European origin themselves and thus had a firsthand understanding of the working-dog heritage. Overt support for the breeding of very soft dogs, which has been the norm in some other breeds, has not occurred with the Bouvier, at least until recently. This is because the Bouvier has not by and large been perceived as a police dog by the general public. The reduction in intensity in American Bouvier lines has been due more to benign neglect than to conscious decision.

Atlantic Passage

It seems likely that over the years, Dutch, Belgian, and French immigrants on occasion brought a Bouvier-type dog with them to America as a reminder — a physical link with the homeland. However, few records remain of such dogs, and they have made no recorded contribution to the modern gene pool.

The first North American Bouvier breeder of whom I am aware was a Mrs. C. Jaecques, who lived on Mack Avenue in Detroit in the 1920s. In March 1927, she produced a litter out of Filou du Sellier and Mirzette du Sellier that included Panto of Detroit, King of Detroit, and Dia of Detroit. These dogs were registered with St. Hubert in Belgium, because the Bouvier was not recognized by the AKC at the time. A second litter was produced in February 1928, and at least one litter from the offspring was produced. Although there are references to this breeding in the notes of Miss Bowles, I am not aware of any additional activity.

In 1937, two Bouviers bred by a man named Vanhaelewijn in Tillsonburg, Ontario, were entered into St. Hubert records, but again, this appears to have been isolated activity with no long-term consequences.

The Bouvier became recognized by the AKC in the late 1920s. Why this step was taken at that time is a bit mysterious in that it would be the late 1930s before more than one or two dogs would be registered here, and the late 1940s before a serious breeding program would commence. An AKC parent club would not come into existence until the early 1970s.

The first two Bouviers in AKC records were Belgian imports that appeared in 1931. These dogs were the bitch Diane de Montreuil and a dog of the same breeding called Hardix, born on November 20, 1926. The sire was Lutin de Mouscron and the dam was Zette du Roy d'Espagne. In 1935 a third Bouvier was registered. No traces of this blood appear in current lines. (There may also have been French imports during this era that could not be AKC registered.)

In 1936, George W. Young, Jr. of Connecticut imported from the Netherlands a male and a female to which many current North American Bouviers may be traced. Bojar van Westergoo was to become a prominent stud and the first AKC Champion of Record. Coba uit het Zuiderlicht was bred in Holland to Eddy Bea van Maarland and whelped what was the first litter (six in number) to appear in AKC records, on August 31, 1936. These dogs, registered in 1937, were called Tory Hollow Bijou, Flandres, Juliana, Paul Revere, Peter, and Riga. Three Belgian dogs, of which no genetic trace remains, were also imported in 1936 or 1937.

In September 1937, Coba produced out of Bojar what was apparently the first American-bred litter to be AKC registered. These seven pups and a lone Belgian import were the only Bouviers registered in 1938. One female, Lisa, was bred to her sire Bojar and produced a litter, two of which were the only registrations in 1939. Lisa was destined to become the first female AKC Champion. Also registered in 1938 was a Belgian female named Lumina, imported by Virginia

of Edmee Bowles. Miss Bowles had bred the Bouvier for some ten years at her family estate near the Belgian city of Schilde when she was driven from her home by the German invasion. She is without question the founder of the breed in America and is recognized as one of the founders of the breed by Chastel, Verbanck, and the general European Bouvier community.

Miss Bowles was born in Antwerp, Belgium, on June 22, 1899. Except for fairly lengthy periods in England while attending school, she spent the first forty years of her life on the family estate near Schilde,

Official registration certificate of the kennel suffix "du Clos des Cerberes" in Belgium.

de Rochemont. Lumina would produce a litter in 1939 that would be registered in 1940.

The year 1940 was, relatively speaking, very busy, with eleven registrations. Bojar van Westergoo produced two litters, one out of Lumina and one out of the female Lariane. Lariane had been imported from Belgium by Julius Bliss, an early enthusiast living in New York City. The lone import that year was Czardas van het Bunderbosch from the Netherlands, registered by Louis de Rochemont. In 1941 and 1942 there were seventeen registrations, mostly pups out of the above lines and one or two insignificant imports. Young, Bliss, and de Rochemont were the leading figures in the prewar era.

In many ways, the story of the Bouvier des Flandres in America really began in May 1942 with the arrival

located a few kilometers east of Antwerp. Although her mother was from an old and influential Belgian family, her father was British.

She mentions having a Bouvier as a child in the early years of the twentieth century. Later, being unable to find another, she had a couple of rough-coated Sheepdogs that would be called Laekens today. When she began serious breeding efforts, she established her "du Clos des Cerberes" line in 1932. This name is taken from Cerberus, the three-headed dog that in Greek mythology guards the gates of hell. In French, "Clos" means a sanctuary or shelter; therefore, the Bowles line is of "the sanctuary of Cerberus." It is a proud name, and for more than fifty years she has produced a line of Bouviers worthy to carry it, making it her life's work.

Ch Marius du Clos des Cerberes, from Miss Bowles' first litter in America. One of the most famous and important dogs of the era.

Whelped: 1943
Sire: Belco NHSB.45565 '35
Dam: Lisa Ch '37
Brd: Edmee Bowles

Ch Aurega du Clos des Cerberes, Best Female at the 1967 American Specialty in Philadelphia. This exceptional bitch, bred and owned by Miss Bowles, was the dam of Altair du Clos des Cerberes, one of the best Bouviers that I have ever had the privilege to see.

Rostan du Close des Cerberes Ch; '58
Telstar du Clos des Cerberes Ch; '62
Remado's Katleen Ch; LOSH.198474 '61
Ch Aurega du Clos des Cerberes '65
Hardy l'Ideal de Charleroi
Deewal Marzie's Lamb '62
Deewal Katona Ch; '57

She was just coming into her own when the German invasion devastated her world, and the world of the Bouvier, for the second time in a generation. Due to her participation in the resistance, she was forced to flee to America, abandoning most of her Bouviers. However, her early efforts were not entirely in vain, for in spite of the terrible ravages of war, some of her Bouviers appear in the Belgian registry in the later 1940s.

The story of Bowles's participation in the resistance and her precarious exit from Europe is one of extreme hardship. She, her mother, and seven-year-old Belco spent many months working their way across France, one step behind an open seaport and half a step ahead of the Germans. Finally, months later, they boarded a liner for America in Portugal. She never learned the fate of many of her other Bouviers. Upon arriving in America in 1942, she spent the remaining war years participating in the Dogs for Defense* program, striking back in some small way at the Germans — for at

---

* The Dogs for Defense program during the Second World War provided a method by which dogs could be donated and trained for military service. Many of the dogs and much of the training was provided by breeders and amateur trainers.

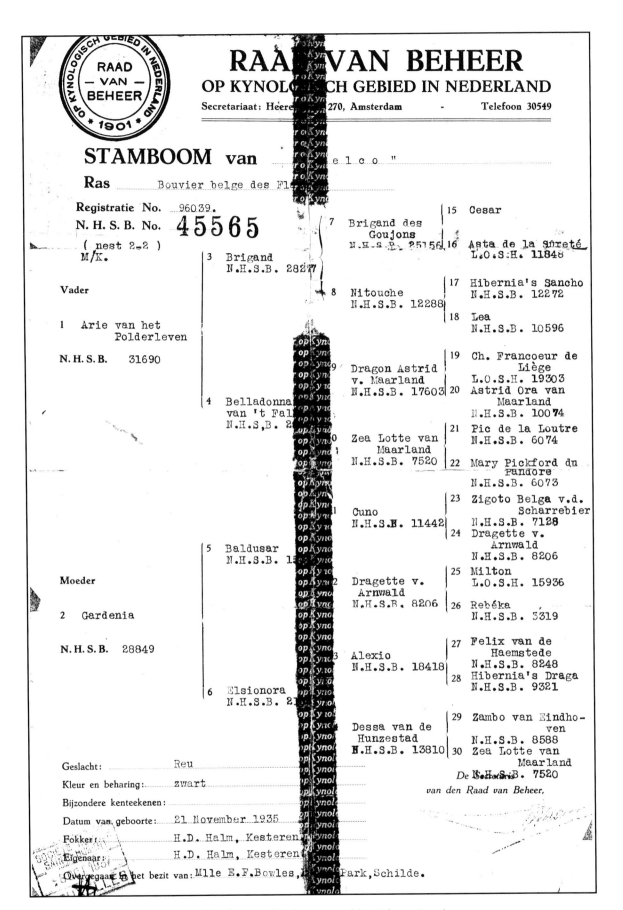

STAMBOOM van " ... elco "

Ras Bouvier belge des Fl...

Registratie No. 960.39.

N. H. S. B. No. **45565**

(nest 2-2)
M/K.

Vader

1 Arie van het
Polderleven

N. H. S. B. 31690

3 Brigand
N.H.S.B. 2827

7 Brigand des
Goujons
N.H.S.B. 25156

15 Cesar

16 Asta de la sûreté
L.O.S.H. 11848

8 Nitouche
N.H.S.B. 12288

17 Hibernia's Sancho
N.H.S.B. 12272

18 Lea
N.H.S.B. 10596

4 Belladonna
van 't Fal...
N.H.S.B. 2...

9 Dragon Astrid
v. Maarland
N.H.S.B. 17603

19 Ch. Francoeur de
Liège
L.O.S.H. 19303

20 Astrid Ora van
Maarland
N.H.S.B. 10074

10 Zea Lotte van
Maarland
N.H.S.B. 7520

21 Pic de la Loutre
N.H.S.B. 6074

22 Mary Pickford du
Pandore
N.H.S.B. 6073

Moeder

2 Gardenia

N. H. S. B. 28849

5 Baldusar
N.H.S.B. 1...

11 Cuno
N.H.S.B. 11442

23 Zigoto Belga v.d.
Scharrebier
N.H.S.B. 7128

24 Dragette v.
Arnwald
N.H.S.B. 8206

12 Dragette v.
Arnwald
N.H.S.B. 8206

25 Milton
L.O.S.H. 15936

26 Rebéka
N.H.S.B. 5319

6 Elsionora
N.H.S.B. 2...

13 Alexio
N.H.S.B. 18418

27 Felix van de
Haemstede
N.H.S.B. 8248

28 Hibernia's Draga
N.H.S.B. 9321

14 Dessa van de
Hunzestad
N.H.S.B. 13810

29 Zambo van Eindho-
ven
N.H.S.B. 8588

30 Zea Lotte van
Maarland
N.H.S.B. 7520

Geslacht: Reu

Kleur en beharing: zwart

Bijzondere kenteekenen:

Datum van geboorte: 21 November 1935

Fokker: H.D. Halm, Kesteren

Eigenaar: H.D. Halm, Kesteren

Overgegaan in het bezit van: Mlle E.F. Bowles, ...Park, Schilde.

De Secretaris
van den Raad van Beheer,

Original pedigree of Belco, owned by Edmee Bowles.

least one of her Bouviers was lost in action on the shores of Europe.

On September 13, 1943, the first American-born "du Clos des Cerberes" litter was produced by Belco out of George Young's female Lisa, yielding Marius, who would become the first "du Clos des Cerberes" American champion. Lisa was a daughter of Ch. Bojar van Westergoo. Jan du Clos des Cerberes, brother to Marius, served with Dogs for Defense and was returned to Bowles after the war. During this period, Bowles was living in Chestnut Hills, Pennsylvania.

Among the earliest advocates of the Bouvier in America was Julius Bliss, who worked with Bowles during the war. The genealogy of the dog Dombey, bred by Bliss and whelped February 16, 1945, illustrates the early bloodlines (Figure 13-1).

Lariane, born in 1937, was a daughter of Maria de Biercee, who was a littermate of Albionne de Biercee, Chastel's foundation bitch and the dam of the first de la Thudinie Bouvier. She was imported by Julius Bliss and bred to George Young's Bojar van Westergoo to produce Inga.

Inga was one of the first Bliss litter of four, whelped April 21, 1940. Unfortunately, Bliss died in the late 1940s, and Dombey went to Miss Bowles. The passing of Julius Bliss was a great loss for the Bouvier in America, because he was one of the breed's most selfless advocates. For Bowles in particular it was a heavy blow, for Bliss had given her support and encouragement. It was several years before she began to really get her breeding program established.

In October 1946, Bowles acquired a rustic old farm near Collegeville, Pennsylvania, outside Philadelphia. The character of this ancient house was a perfect match for that of the woman herself — both were rugged survivors. Belco, the last direct link with her European program, died, apparently as preparations to move were underway, and the place has been known as Belco Farm to this day. The farm is the very essence of the Bouvier, inhabited by the ghosts of Marius, Jasper, and Altair. Pencil sketches at Belco of Dombey and Marius by Miss Bowles have always represented the spirit of this era.

Figure 13-1

```
                  Arie van het Polderleven   NHSB.31690
         Belco  NHSB.45565 '35
                  Gardenia  NHSB.28849
Jan du Clos des Cerberes
                  Ch. Bojar van Westergoo  NHSB.43317 '36
         Ch. Lisa  '37
                  Coba uit het Zuiderlicht
DOMBEY '45
                  Kamboro  D Ch'36; NHSB.24563
         Ch. Bojar van Westergoo  NHSB.43317 '36
                  Alexandrina Olga v Marberg  NHSB.30628
         Inga '40
                  Koller des Champs Clos  LOSH.76690
         Lariane  LOSH.90217 '37 (imp Julius Bliss)
                  Maria de Biercee  LOSH.57021
```

Ch Giaconda du Clos des Cerberes, Best of Opposite Sex at the American Club's first Specialty show in Philadelphia in 1965. Bred by Miss Edmee Bowles at Belco Farm, whelped in 1962. Shown with owner Carl May, well-known Bouvier Specialty judge.

Ch Zorina du Clos des Cerberes, owned by Gladys May, bred by Edmee Bowles. The sire, Ch Chef de Truffe, was pure Thudinie. The dam, Remado's Katleen, was a littermate to Kitty, dam of Marc de la Thudinie.

Bruce Jacobsohn shown here finishing Ch Ishtar du Clos des Cerberes under Vance Evans. Ishtar by Ch Jasper du Clos des Cerberes out of Tania du Posty Arlequin.

Ch Ola du Clos des Cerberes, going Best of Winners for five points at the 1970 American Specialty. Bred by Miss Bowles, shown with George Edge. Ola was out of Marc de la Thudinie and Eliane du Clos des Cerberes. *Photo courtesy of Justin Chastel.*

All in all, the late 1940s and early 1950s were incredibly difficult. Entire litters were put down because no one would buy this almost-unknown breed. From 1943 through 1948, only eighteen Bouviers were registered in the United States, an average of only three a year! Miss Bowles built a grooming and boarding business (and bred Poodles — also successful in the show ring) to support her then-fragile Bouvier breeding program.

Louis de Rochemont was another early enthusiast. He imported several dogs in the late 1930s, including Czardas van het Bunderbosch (whelped in 1938) from Holland. In the words of Ray Hubbard, by way of private communication:

> Louis de Rochemont, a pioneering producer of film documentaries, and producer of "The March of Time" and "The House on 92nd Street," was an early Bouvier owner. In the late 1920s, the de Rochemont's son developed diabetes. The giving of insulin in those days was new and somewhat uncertain and the boy used to go into insulin shock. The de Rochemonts researched various breeds of dogs, using guide dogs for the blind, then a new concept, as a basis of comparison. They finally settled on the

Bouvier because they heard that it was especially sensitive to humans and their condition. The dogs were being used at that time in Europe as guide dogs and were working quite well. They imported a Bouvier and it was trained to follow the boy around and if he went into shock, the

Above, right: Ch Krepsie de la Thudinie, bred by Justin Chastel in 1961, imported by the Hubbards. B/A Ch Job de la Thudinie x Iatte de la Thudinie.

Right: Ch Caliphe du Clos des Cerberes, called "Danny", owned by Louise McCann, bred by E. F. Bowles and B. Jacobsohn, whelped in 1978. Influential stud in Southern California in the early 1980s and one of the best sons of French import Lutteur du Val de Rol.

<pre>
               Vulcain du Clos des Cytises Ch
          Lutteur du Val de Rol Ch; OFA '75
               Tamise du Val de Rol LOF.13986 '70
Ch Caliphe du Clos de Cerberes OFA '78
               Jasper du Clos des Cerberes Ch; '70
          Circee' du Clos des Cerberes Ch
               Radegund du Clos des Cerberes Ch; '72
</pre>

dog got help. Mrs. de Rochemont, who told this story to Marion Hubbard, claimed that the dog saved her son's life a number of times.

Mr. and Mrs. de Rochemont bred one or perhaps two litters in this era but then became inactive. Several of the de Rochemont dogs went to the Walsh family, who would eventually become active and establish the Deewal Kennel in the mid-1950s. A good example is the female Yhelot, bred by Virginia de Rochemont in 1950 and sold to Fred Walsh (Figure 13-2).

Ch Deewal Flagg, shown by Charlie McLean. Ch Deewal Charger x Ch Nelly du Clos des Jeunes Plantes.

Figure 13-2

```
                    Arie van het Polderleven  NHSB.31690
          Belco   NHSB.45565 '35
                    Gardenia  NHSB.28849
   Marius du Clos des Cerberes  Ch; '43
                    Bojar van Westergoo    NHSB.43317 '36
          Lisa  Ch; '37
                    Coba uit het Zuiderlicht
YHELOT
                    Czardas v h Bunderbosch  NHSB.65833
          Polax  '42
                    Coba
   Wallonne  '48
                    Bart Aleida van de Zaanhoeve
          Beeta van Wakershof  NHSB.93941 '44
                    Ransa  NHSB.46936
```

In addition to the dogs, Fred and Dorthy Walsh received a lot of enthusiasm from the de Rochemonts and became increasingly active in the breed during the 1950s. By the end of the decade, they were importing significant Belgian Bouviers such as Hion de la Thudinie and his son Job. The Deewal line of the Walshes and Miss Bowles's "du Clos des Cerberes" line were predominant and the East Coast through the 1950s.

On the West Coast, Evert van de Pol was the orig-

Notable Bouvier personalities from three nations. From the left: Dr. Andre Le Lann of France, noted judge and trainer; Justin Chastel of Belgium, modern architect of the breed; Edmee Bowles, founding breeder in Belgium and America; and Bruce Jacobsohn, latter-years associate of Miss Bowles at Belco Farm. Photo taken in Thuin, Belgium, in 1975.

Ch Vulcain du Clos des Cytises LOF.14872 OFA
This exceptional French stud was imported by the McLeans at Deewal and served as one of their most important breeding resources for a number of years.

Brd: Simone Jousse, Villiers-sur-Marne, France

Quiar de la Thudinie Ch; LOSH.247130
Ringo de la Thudinie LOF.14296-256 LOSH.264359
Nolette de la Thudinie LOSH.225616
Ch Vulcain du Clos des Cytises LOF.14872 '72 OFA
Navarro de la Thudinie LOSH.224290
Roxane du Clos des Cytises LOF.13336-278
Nathalie du Clos des Cytises

Evert van de Pol, standing with Yago van de Buildrager, 1980. To the right, Fred Joyner with unknown dog. *Photo courtesy Marion and Ray Hubbard.*

inal enthusiast. Ray Hubbard's biographical sketch of van de Pol, obtained as a private communication, is as follows:

Evert van de Pol was one of the first breeders of the Bouvier in the United States. Van was a native of the Netherlands and was a baker by trade. After the invasion of the lowlands by the Nazis, he spent the four years of World War II plying the dangerous waters of the North Atlantic as a baker on Merchant Marine ships carrying vital supplies to England. In 1946, upon the end of the war, he decided to emigrate to the United States, bringing his dogs with him. He first went to work for Edmee Bowles at Belco Farm as her kennel manager. Miss Bowles bred several of her bitches to Van's dogs. After a few months he decided to move to the West Coast and settled in San Francisco where he went back to baking to support himself and his dogs and a new wife. Van's new employer was United Air Lines, just beginning to establish flight kitchens. From United, Van took his kennel name — "van de Mainliner." He continued to import animals from Holland and bred regularly in San Francisco. All during these years — approximately 1947 to 1960 — Van was the sole breeder of Bouviers on the West Coast.

One of his biggest dogs — 30 inches at the shoulder and weighing 140 pounds — Ch. Ciscoldo, better known as Champion Calo Sr., was bought by the Calo Dog Food Company and was used as an educational/promotion animal, touring schools and giving children rides in his cart in supermarket parking lots. He also performed with his cart at dog shows.

One of Van's bitches, Silta, lived to the age of 15 and became a familiar sight, walking the hills of Marin County, accompanied by Van in his wooden shoes.

spring of two Dutch Champions, Iwan Floss v d Rakkers and the female Astrien, and had two litters in Holland, descendants of which show up in modern Dutch pedigrees, before she came to the United States. In 1960, she had a litter of 9 puppies sired by Duke. The Sterns kept one bitch puppy from the litter, named Murphy.

In the early 1950s, van de Pol started a Bouvier des Flandres Club of America in an attempt to popularize the breed. Other pioneers of the era, such as the de Rochemont's in New Hampshire and Miss Bowles, helped in the effort but there was not sufficient interest. It would be ten years before another attempt would be made.

Most of the early stock, such as Belco and

Ch Ciscoldo, known as "Calo, Sr.", when he made promotional appearances for Calo dog food.

Owner: Don McNeilly
Brd: Evert van de Pol
Sire: Dutch Ch Basco Aleida v d
    Zaanhoeve
Dam: Silta
Whelped: 1947

Photo courtesy of Judy Higgins.

Doris Stern and her husband, J. D. Stern, bought a son of Ch. Ciscoldo, Duke von Young, from Evert van de Pol in 1956. The dog was then a year and a half old and weighed 80 pounds. Duke was sent to school for special training as a watch dog and went to work as a guard on the Stern estate in San Rafael, California. At that time, there were only 35 Bouviers in the entire western half of the United States.

In 1960, because there were so few Bouviers and those were too closely related to breed, the Sterns imported a Dutch bitch, Arendine van der Vlashoek, who was born in 1956. Arendine, known as Ansje, worked on a farm where she was responsible for herding the ducks and getting them to and from the pond, where she protected them during the day. She was the off-

Bonaparte van Darling-Astrid, was Dutch, although in the late 1940s, Miss Bowles apparently did obtain one or two French bitches that she was not able to register. Bonaparte, born on April 23, 1950, was imported by Evert van de Pol and was later sold to Fred Walsh.

Over the years, Bowles imported a number of significant bitches, the first being four-year-old Wandru des Coudreaux, who came to the United States in February 1953. Wandru was an exceptional animal from a predominant French kennel, a major step forward for the Bouvier in America. One of her chief attractions was that she was a proven brood bitch. Her daughters in Europe included Almyre des Coudreaux, a well-known French Champion used by Miss Bowles as a model for her famous profile head sketch. This likenesss is the emblem of the American club

Ch Woodbine Lone Star Jezebel, owned and bred by Judy Odom. Shown going Winners Bitch and Best of Opposite under Belgian Judge Annie Verheyen at the California Specialty in 1987.

Sire: Ch Gamma du Noveau Monde
Dam: Ch Rombo Halley's Comet

Ch Halston au Dela des Mers, bred by Judy Higgins.

Owners: Judy Higgins and Judy Odom.
Sire: Geant du Noveau Monde
Dam: Raphia du Val de Rol (French import)

and is no doubt the most widely used depiction in the history of the breed. Wandru's sister Wanda also had a significant place in French pedigrees of the era.

The sale of Wandru was arranged by Felix Verbanck after extensive correspondence, much of which provided considerable insight into the history of this era on both sides of the Atlantic. Wandru was bred before leaving Europe but apparently failed to conceive or lost her litter during the nineteen-day Atlantic passage. Perhaps the most notable of her offspring was Si Jolie du Clos des Cerberes, whelped in 1954, who would become the dam of Rostan. Rostan was a big dog with excellent type. His pedigree is in many ways a summary of American Bouvier history to that point in time (Figure 13-3).

Jan du Clos des Cerberes served in the Dogs for Defense program and was returned after the war. He was a littermate to Marius. Lisa was handled by Miss Bowles to become the first champion bitch in America. Ellyrdia was one of a litter of eight born on September 27, 1947, out of a bitch named Silta, who had been imported in whelp from Holland by Evert van de Pol. Silta lived to be some fourteen years old. Two litter-

Figure 13-3

```
                    Arie van het Polderleven  NHSB.31690
          Belco  NHSB.45565 '35
                    Gardenia  NHSB.28849
      Marius du Clos des Cerberes  Ch; '43
                    Bojar van Westergoo    '36  NHSB.43317
          Lisa  Ch; '37
                    Coba uit het Zuiderlicht
  Bel Ami du Clos des Cerberes '52
                    Athos Allette de Teugenaar   D Ch'40
          Basko Aleida v d Zaanhoeve   D Ch'43; NHSB.72632
                    Aleida Santa v d Zaanhoeve  NHSB.60337
      Ellyrdia  Ch; NHSB.117114 '47
                    Dormento  NHSB.58856
          Silta    '45 NHSB.94880
                    Arina Ivana v Lexmonde   NHSB.79622 '42
Ch ROSTAN DU CLOS DES CERBERES '58
                    Belco  NHSB.45565 '35
          Jan du Clos des Cerberes
                    Lisa  Ch; '37
      Dombey
                    Bojar van Westergoo    '36  NHSB.43317
          Inga
                    Lariane  LOSH.90217 '37
  Si Jolie du Clos des Cerberes '54
                    Jaf du Chateau de Villers   LOF1104
          Samos des Trois Iles  LOF1281
                    Rita de la Gueulardiere
      Wandru des Coudreaux '48 LOF3736
                    Ravachol  LOSH.110805
          Uada du Gratte-Saule  B Ch; LOSH.127972
                    Silane de la Thudinie  LOSH.117337
```

Ch Bibarcy's Soldat de Plomb, bred by Art and Mary Pederson in 1969. Ch Deewal Homer x Bibarcy's Job's Daughter.

Ch Bo Peep des Ours, first American-bred bitch to go Best in Show, which she did four times during her fabulous show career. Daughter "Etoile" was the second American-bred Best in Show female, just to keep it all in the family! One of the best-moving Bouviers that I have ever seen. Bred and owned by Tim Wray.

mates, Ciskoldo and Riasta, finished their championships on the West Coast, and Miss Bowles went on to show Ellyrdia to her championship. This litter is included in the Dutch breeding records, with van de Pol listed as breeder of record.

Felix Verbanck, in his letters to Bowles, expressed great concern that van de Pol was introducing the "wrong type of Bouvier" into America, and at least part of the motivation for his efforts to secure top-rate Belgian dogs for people such as Bowles, the Hubbards, and the Walshes was his desire to see the Belgian rather than the Dutch concept of the "true Bouvier" predominate. My opinion is that he was correct, that the most desirable Bouvier type is that exemplified by dogs such as the Belgian Champion Soprano de la Thudinie, that is, powerful, square, agile dogs of moderate size, short in back and not excessive in angulation.

Certain Dutch dogs in this era, such as Roland van Domburg, also exhibited many of these qualities. In retrospect I think it is fair to say that the Dutch show lines, while evolving in a way similar to the Belgians, were behind and were not sending as many of their best dogs here. It was to a great extent Verbanck's attention to the American fancy and his help in sending so many good Belgian dogs here that turned the tide in favor of Belgian influence in the 1950s and 1960s.

About 1962, Remado's Katleen was brought in from Belgium with the assistance of Verbanck, whose nephew, Maurice Dauwe, was the breeder. This young bitch, five months old when imported, was from a litter destined to be pivotal for the Bouvier in Europe as well as a cornerstone of the Bowles line. Katleen's sister Kitty was to yield Marc de la Thudinie, a key element in the Chastel program. A male, Remado's Kandy, was a significant stud dog for Edmond Moreaux, and his get are particularly prominent in modern Dutch pedigrees.

Katleen was bred to Rostan to produce Telstar du

Ch Maijeune's Destinee with Gladys May. This beautiful bitch was Best of Opposite at the American Club Specialty in Detroit in 1982. Bred and owned by Gladys and Carl May.

Sire: Ch Ulfio de la Thudinie
Dam: Ch Maijenue's Alouette
Born: February 26, 1976

Ch Maijeune's Babiliard. Although the Mays have bred and shown many notable Bouviers, "Laird" was among their favorites.

Brd and Owners: Gladys and Carl May
Whelped: 1974
Out of Ch Uris Bras de Fer and Ch Madrone Ledge Venus

Clos des Cerberes, and to Chef de Truffe to produce Schandor. Out of a grandson of littermate Kitty (a son of Marc himself), Katleen produced Brabo, who was to become the sire of several notable Bouviers, including Jasper du Clos des Cerberes.

Bowles, in her seventies and less active due to health reasons, had been written off by many when Jasper emerged from the classes to win the 1971 American Bouvier des Flandres National Specialty at the Westchester Kennel Club. His pedigree (Figure 13-4) is a summary of the Bowles program of the 1960s. Miss Bowles never had the financial resources to "special" her best dogs or to use professional handlers extensively. She nevertheless placed her own dogs in the group and held her own in the American show ring against several generations of top Belgian imports in the hands of professional handlers.

Figure 13-4

```
                    Job de la Thudinie  B/A Ch; '60
            Marc de la Thudinie  Ch; '63
                    Remado's Kitty  '61
        Picard des Preux Vuilbaards  Ch
                    Lais du Posty Arlequin  '62
            Nota du Posty Arlequin  Ch
                    Lolo du Posty Arlequin
    Brabo du Clos des Cerberes  '68
                    Fricko de Belgique    LOSH.175335
            Ike de Belgique  '59
                    Erna de Belgique
        Remado's Katleen  Ch; '61
                    Ely      B Ch; LOF.1.Bouv.8808  '55
            Irisa de l'Ile Monsin
                    Balta de l'Ile Monsin  B Ch
Ch JASPER DU CLOS DES CERBERES  '70
                    Coquin de la Thudinie  Ch
            Chef de Truffe  Ch; '58
                    Draga de la Thudinie  Ch
        Schandor du Clos des Cerberes  Ch; '65
                    Ike de Belgique  '59
            Remado's Katleen  Ch; '61
                    Irisa de l'Ile Monsin
    Altair du Clos des Cerberes  Ch; '68
                    Rostan du Clos des Cerberes        Ch
            Tetstar du Clos des Cerberes  Ch; '62
                    Remado's Katleen  Ch; '61
        Aurega du Clos des Cerberes  Ch; '65
                    Hardy l'Ideal de Charleroi
            Deewal Marzie's Lamb  '62
                    Deewal Katona  Ch; '57
```

Chef de Truffe was a beautiful male purchased by Miss Bowles from Robert and Joan Butts in Springfield, Illinois. Chef became one of her important stud dogs. Mr. and Mrs. Butts had in the middle and late 1950s taken a great interest in the Bouvier, traveling in Europe and importing Coquin de la Thudinie and Draga de la Thudinie, who produced Chef. Sadly, Mr. Butts died suddenly in the early 1960s, cutting short what could have been an important Bouvier story in its own right.

Although I did not see Altair until she was more than ten years old, she was still a magnificent bitch — short-coupled with an exquisite topline and incred-

ible movement. Her dam, Aurega, was received in lieu of a stud fee and was subsequently sold to the Blanford Kennel in Michigan, where she produced a a couple of notable dogs.

Jasper marked a resurgence for Bowles, because during the same period she imported Tania du Posty Arlequin, in whelp to Sim de Bronchain, and later exchanged a pup out of Jasper with Chastel for Xurie de la Thudinie. It is interesting that Miss Bowles never imported a stud dog, believing the bitches to be the foundation of a long-term breeding program and using to good advantage the dogs imported by others. The pup that went to Chastel became Xiran du Clos des Cerberes, a male that produced several Thudinie litters and that was also used by at least one other Belgian breeder.

Through Bouviers such as Jasper, Altair, and Aurega, the Bowles line became justly famous in the 1960s and 1970s, especially for exceptional toplines, short-coupling, and excellent movement. These attributes, and their predominance in the progeny, have had a strong and beneficial effect on the overall quality of American Bouviers. Although the early "du Clos des Cerberes" lines no longer predominate in American Bouviers as they did through the 1950s, the line that began again with Belco is still a vital bulwark of the American Bouvier today. In addition, Bowles paved the way for the imports of others in the late 1950s and early 1960s, particularly those of Fred and Dorthy Walsh and Bob Abady. Thus, while Chastel and others in Belgium were creating the modern Bouvier, Bowles in America was preparing the way for the fruit of their labor, playing a major role in establishing the comparable American heritage.

For more than thirty years, the first rank of American Bouvier breeders has included Ray and Marion Hubbard. Their Madrone Ledge Kennel derives its names from the magnificent Madrone trees that forested their original homesite in California. Their first Bouvier was acquired in 1954 from Evert van de Pol in San Francisco. Their strongest memory of the occasion was the barred door from behind which snarls erupted. This pup, given the simple name Cerbere, was out of pure Dutch stock and developed into a marvelous family pet and guard dog. However, he was not up to breeding standards in conformation.

About 1957, business interests took the Hubbards to Massachusetts, affording them the opportunity of evaluating firsthand the Bouviers in the East. Their impressions from that era are as follows:

> The breed was quite diverse in appearance and conformation at that time. Dutch and Belgian lines were being cross-bred as more dogs were imported from Europe and the results were quite unfortunate. The dogs were actually struc-

Ch Madrone Ledge Woodbine Drumer, shown with owner Judy Odom.

Sire: Ivan D'An Naoned CD
Dam: Madrone Ledge Cassis Ch; '78

Ch Madrone Ledge Druide OFA, bred and owned by Marion Hubbard. Handler in photo is Judy Higgins.

Sire: Ivan d'An Naoned Ch; CD, OFA '73
Dam: Madrone Ledge Cassis Ch; '78

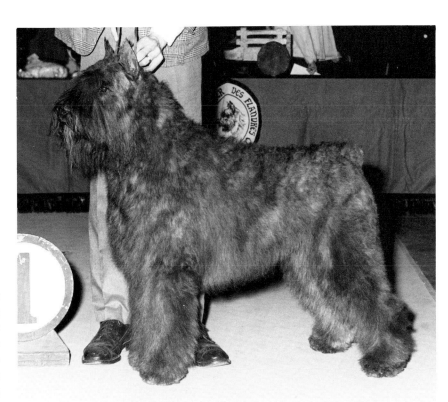

Ch Madrone Ledge Socrate became in 1969 the first American-bred Best in Show Bouvier and National Specialty winner. Bred and owned by Ray and Marion Hubbard. Ch Naris du Posty Arlequin out of Ch Pepita du Posty Arlequin.

turally different. Parti-colored dogs carrying at once short, harsh coats and longer, softer coats gave the impression of a mixed breed. There were also great discrepancies in head type. Long skulls and muzzles were combined with shorter skulls and muzzles resulting in many very overshot and undershot jaws, since it is possible to inherit the various parts of the muzzle separately.

A dog that made a strong impression on the Hubbards, directing their attention to the Belgian and French breeding of the era, was the French male, Etoile des Coudreaux, owned by the Dukes in New Hampshire. This dog, with an excellent double coat of correct texture, was structurally sound. He was described as being a ruddy fawn in color. Apparently, Verbanck commented to Mrs. Hubbard years later that the true fawn was an interesting balance color from which might be obtained, in the offspring, black dogs as well as every shade of gray.

During the mid-1950s, Janet Mack, a Canadian expatriate living in Manhattan, became an important Bouvier enthusiast and promoter. She contacted Felix Verbanck in Belgium and imported the magnificent

Ch. Erlo de la Thudinie and a number of puppies for various clients. Through Mack and Verbanck, the Hubbards, back in California, imported Krespie de la Thudinie in 1961, who went on to become the first West Coast Bouvier Champion in fifteen years.

Marion Hubbard comments:

In 1962, most Bouviers in the United States were still of the black, harsh, short-coated variety with longer skulls and muzzles, hare-footed, not well let down in the hocks — old style Bouviers. Krespie was a revelation — setting a new standard for type and the Belgian style Bouvier. She carried a full double coat, was a spectacular silver-blue-gray in color, and on a fog shrouded day at the Del Monte show, or in the gloomy recesses of the Cow Palace in San Francisco, she shone as if illuminated from within. She had a very typey head, a 3-to-2 skull and muzzle proportion, a cobby body and was well let down in the hocks.

As recently as 1958, only eighteen Bouviers were registered with the American Kennel Club, and only 277 had been registered since the breed was first recognized in the 1930s. Prior to this date, the typical

Ch Gamma du Nouveau Monde, known as "RB", owned by Judy Odom. Winner of the California Specialty in both 1984 and 1985.

Brd: Paul and Rosemary Vautrin
Sire: Ch Caliphe du Clos des Cerberes
Dam: Ch Pria du Val de Rol

year saw only one or two litters, with Bowles responsible for many of them. Since there had been virtually no Canadian activity at this point, the Bouvier has been a numerically significant member of the North American canine community for only the past twenty years or so.

As Bouvier popularity began to increase about 1960, the North American scene became much more active and complex. It is helpful to think of the Bouvier evolution as occurring primarily in three regions, as listed in Figure 13-5.

Figure 13-5

Region	Founding Breeders	Starting
East Coast U.S.	Bowles, Bliss, Walsh, Mack	Mid-1940s
West Coast U.S.	van de Pol, Hubbard	Early 1950s
Michigan/Ontario	Prinsen, McDonald, Westra	Early 1960s

There has, of course, been activity elsewhere, such as the flurry in Alberta starting in the 1970s. These regions are still primary centers of Bouvier interest.

Modern United States Breeding

From the beginning, European trends have shaped American Bouvier evolution. Starting in the mid-1950s, the Belgian dogs of Justin Chastel became heavily predominant among North American imports. By the late 1960s, Chastel was strongly influencing the Dutch gene pool as well. His influence on the French program was to the point where most recent French Champions are predominantly of Thudinie blood. Thus, the mid-1950s marked the advent of a long period of universal Belgian dominance, or, more specifically, a period during which Chastel would be the prime mover worldwide. Animals not coming directly from his kennel came from among the closely related stock of his fellow countrymen, especially the du Posty Arlequin Bouviers of neighbor Felix Grulois.

The Walshes at Deewal and Janet Mack in New York were the most responsible for the surge of Belgian imports in the late 1950s and early 1960s. Shortly thereafter, in the mid-1960s, the Hubbards, having moved back to Long Island, became very active importers of the Belgian lines. They began with littermates Pebbles and Pepita du Posty Arlequin, who came in as pups in 1966.

Marion Hubbard, fluent in written and spoken French, had corresponded with Verbanck, Chastel, and Grulois for many years. Her comments on her first visit in 1967 are interesting:

> The Charleroi Dog Show was an interesting lesson in terms of both the approved character and conformation of the Bouvier. Strength, agility, and strong character were the determining factors. Too large and too light in coat color Bouviers were dismissed. A judge's dinner followed the show and we were guests of Mons. Verbanck. After several glasses of wine had been served, Justin Chastel approached us to inquire whether it was true that Americans spent a quarter of their incomes on dogs!
>
> An excellent spirit of cooperation existed between Grulois and Chastel at that time. They bred to each other's dogs and both kennels were producing the best specimens in Belgium. But there was an obvious difference in the conformation of the dogs that each selected from their litters. Grulois' dogs carried more coat, had more angulation, and were shorter on their leg. Chastel chose the taller, leaner dogs with coarser coats.

The Hubbards had gone to Europe intending to acquire a bitch from Chastel, but he was unable to provide one. Instead, he suggested that they approach Felix Grulois. This time they were successful, and they took home Odelette du Posty Arlequin, destined to become the first female to win an American National Specialty — owner-handled to boot! She also became a valuable breeding resource, producing three important litters.

On the same trip, Grulois offered the spectacular male, Naris du Posty Arlequin. Although they did not immediately accept this offer, Mrs. Hubbard did subsequently purchase Naris for Chet Collier, who was beginning his show career by exhibiting Madrone Ledge Blazen. Ch. Madrone Ledge Socrate, out of Pepita and Naris du Posty Arlequin, became, in 1969, the first American-bred Bouvier to be selected Best in Show and went on to win the National Specialty the following week.

In the late 1960s, perhaps the most prominent figure on the American Bouvier scene was Bob Abady, whose flamboyant antics drew immense publicity to himself as well as to the Bouvier. Abady, the Walshes, and the Hubbards were in major part responsible for importing the Chastel and Grulois stock that has done so much to shape the Bouvier in North American.

Abady was the first Bouvier breeder to emphasize the working character and particularly the guard applications of the Bouvier. This culminated in an incredible *Sports Illustrated* article (1971) in which he is quoted as saying: "A Bouvier bite is a studied thing.

Ch Odelette du Posty Arlequin, bred by Felix Grulois in Belgium in 1965. Imported by Ray and Marion Hubbard. Moka de la Thudinie x Liska du Posty Arlequin.

Ch Picolette du Posty Arlequin produced Rif du Posty Arlequin, prominent in modern Dutch pedigrees for Felix Grulois before being imported by Ray and Marion Hubbard at Madrone Ledge. Ch Naris du Posty Arlequin x Ch Odelette du Posty Arlequin.

It really doesn't matter where he bites you. If he got you on the big toe, you'd probably lose consciousness. Shepherds and Dobermans are slashers: they have a longer jaw, so instinctively they want to let go. They do not have the same jaw structure as the Bouvier."

Abady's most active period began in the mid-1960s, when he was able to purchase Marc de la Thudinie and several exceptional du Posty Arlequin bitches. In the same *Sports Illustrated* article, he implied that his silver tongue (and a significant amount of cash) enabled him to pry Marc away from a reluctant Chastel. It seems more plausible that the Belgian breeder was a willing victim and knew exactly what he was doing. Chastel was perhaps not all that reluctant to dispense with Marc, for he had used him extensively for about two years and was counting on Olaf (who was to become a Belgian Champion, an honor that eluded Marc) and half-brother Lais du Posty Arlequin.

In America, Marc's notable get included Ola du Clos des Cerberes for Bowles, and Prudhon and Picard des Preux Vuilbaards for Abady. On the whole, Marc's production here is not as impressive as might be expected. In Europe, there were a number of exceptional, closely related dogs (such as Lais) to share the paternal duties, yet Marc was predominant. Whether he was not sufficiently available to outsiders here, not used enough, or simply not made good use of, is not known, but a major opportunity seems to have been taken advantage of relatively little.

In summary, Abady brought over a number of exceptional European Bouviers that made contributions to the gene pool. As a result of an unfortunate incident in which he allegedly struck an older woman handling another dog in the show ring, Abady was banned for life by the American Kennel Club. Although through litigation he was able to reestablish the privilege of registering dogs, his influence was diminished significantly. His own breeding efforts were not especially productive beyond the first generation, and the "des Preux Vuilbaard" line came to an end in the late 1970s. The most significant influence of this enterprise comes down through Prudhon and Picard des Preux Vuilbaards, littermates out of Marc de la Thudinie and Nota du Posty Arlequin. Both were sold as pups and went on to distinction in the hands of others.

The early 1970s were a time of transition when some of the founders became less active and new breeding programs began to take shape. Bruce and Rose Ellen Jacobsohn became partners with Miss Bowles at Belco Farm as new directions in breeding began to emerge there. Fred and Dorothy Walsh passed away, and the Deewal name went to Mrs. Walsh's niece Claire McLean and her husband Charlie. Jack Van Vliet, who had been kennel manager for many years at Deewal, retained the breeding stock, which

became the foundation of his Plateau Kennels in New Jersey. Ray and Marion Hubbard were producing and importing winning Bouviers at their Madrone Ledge Kennel in Maryland. Dr. and Mrs. Bodarky were becoming active at their Hanover Farm Kennel in Pennsylvania, based largely on the "du Clos des Cerberes" lines. Bob Abady was in his period of peak activity in Stormville, New York. The center of North American Bouvier activity remained concentrated in the Middle Atlantic states — Pennsylvania, New Jersey, New York, and Maryland.

Much of this activity was based on European imports, especially the modern Belgian lines of Chastel and Grulois. Therefore, the importation of European breeding and show stock has always readily influenced the overall character of the Bouviers here. The relative affluence of the United States has enabled this country to obtain much of the best of the European stock. Although this has produced some exceptional individuals, sound long-term breeding programs are the exception rather than the rule. There are many importers, exhibitionists, puppy sellers, and hangers on, but relatively few real breeders.

From the mid-1950s until well into the 1970s, the imports were predominantly Belgian. Starting in the mid-1970s, the pendulum began to swing as the Belgian influence waned and the French and the Dutch began to take up the slack. Moreaux and Verbanck were dead, and Chastel and Grulois had become less active. New Belgian stars had by and large failed to emerge. Chastel's wife, always an active partner, was in poor health.

To some extent, the change was more apparent than real, because the dogs coming in from Holland and France were often substantially of Belgian kennels only two or three generations back, mostly out of transplanted Thudinie Bouviers rather than the stock indigenous to the respective homelands.

Many imports represented a fortuitous blending of Thudinie blood and the native stock. Lutteur du Val de Rol, owned by Bowles and Jacobsohn at Belco Farm, is a pertinent example on the French side. Most of the recent Dutch Champions and thus their progeny coming over here are of such breeding. Lutteur's background is illustrated in Figure 13-6.

Lutteur was among the best Bouviers to come to America. He had a magnificent head, a beautiful broad bite, short coupling, and textbook-perfect movement. I would have preferred a darker coat and better texture. Lutteur had more real long-term French breeding, represented in kennel names such as "de l'Epee" (the sword), Chateau Morocain, and du Maine Giraud, than any prominent import since Wandru des Coudreaux some two decades earlier. Naris, Marc, Quair, and Vulcain were also imported and subsequently became American Champions.

Figure 13-6

```
                    Naris du Posty Arlequin  Ch
        Quiar de la Thudinie  Ch
                    Naia de la Thudinie
    Ringo de la Thudinie  '68
                    Marc de la Thudinie  Ch; '63
        Nolette de la Thudinie
                    Kania de la Thudinie
    Vulcain du Clos des Cytises  Ch; OFA
                    Lais du Posty Arlequin   '62
        Navarro de la Thudinie
                    Ketty de la Thudinie
    Roxane du Clos des Cytises
                    Gringoire de l'Epee   '57
        Nathalie du Clos des Cytises
                    Jade du Maine Giraud
Ch LUTTEUR DU VAL DE ROL  OFA '75
                    Jal du Chateau Marocain
        Kaid de l'Epee
                    Gueline de l'Epee   '57
    Orlando du Clos des Cytises
                    Gredin du Maine Giraud  F Ch
        Jade du Maine Giraud
                    Dulcinee du Maine Giraud
    Tamise du Val de Rol
                    Naris du Posty Arlequin   Ch
        Pax du Posty Arlequin
                    Naia de la Thudinie
    Rika du Clos du Petit Neuf Pres      B.Sel
                    King l'Ideal de Charleroi
        Minouche du Clos du Petit Neuf Pres
                    Janet du Clos Broquet
```

In the late 1970s, a number of successful kennels became active, including our own Centauri line. A particularly good example is the Rombo program of Rick and Diane Gschwender in the Detroit area, which for several years was dominant there. Best known of this line was Ch. Rombo Flaming Star ("Cricket"), who was winners bitch at the 1982 American Specialty, Best of Opposite in 1985, and Best of Breed at the 1985 Canadian Specialty. Ch. Rombo High Mighty and Proud was the youngest Bouvier to ever win an American Specialty, which he did in Wisconsin in 1985. (Thus, the Gschwenders won both the American and the Canadian Specialties in 1985!)

Sadly, Diane Gschwender passed away in 1986, and the breeding of the Rombo Bouviers came to an untimely end. Her contributions to the Bouvier world went far beyond the Rombo breeding, for she was an active leader in club affairs. Although not involved in training, she was a strong behind-the-scenes supporter of the 1984 Working Championships. In fact, they might not have been possible without her participation.

Ch Hyatt au Dela des Mers
Brd: Judy Higgins and Paul Vautrin
Owner: Judy Higgins
Sire: Ch Nack du Clos des Cytises
Dam: Ch Praia du Val de Rol

The 1980s saw increasing predominance of Dutch lines in America. This trend was in large measure initiated by George Kroesin in Illinois, who brought in many quality Dutch dogs, such as Dona Quibi van Dafzicht, for his Olympus Kennel. His Amon Astrid van Dafzicht was, I believe, the first Dutch Champion to set foot on North American soil. At Centauri, Kroesin's Ch. Abbas van de Boevers Garden is the sire of one of our foundation males, Ch. Centauri's Hanter, co-owned with Sarah Dowling.

By the end of the 1980s, the changing tide had become a Dutch flood as the immense popularity of the breed in Holland and the strong programs of many Dutch kennels had made the Dutch import the primary driving force for the Bouvier in America.

Bouvier Clubs

Bouvier enthusiasts were slow to organize on a national level. In the early 1950s, an attempt failed to begin a club. Finally, in 1962, a second attempt succeeded. Initial leadership was provided by Carl May and John Elliot. Other members of the original committee were Edmee Bowles, Edith Sturges O'Connor, and Fred Walsh. In fall 1963, the AKC accepted the new club's application for membership. The American Bouvier Des Flandres Club finally became a member club of the American Kennel Club on September 14, 1971. This meant that the Bouvier club was entitled to designate a single voting delegate to the AKC and to hold specialty shows.

In the beginning, the well-established breeders and active enthusiasts were primarily on the East Coast, especially in Pennsylvania, New York, and New Jersey. For the first ten years, club affairs and membership centered in this region, and board of governors meetings were mid-Atlantic affairs until well into the 1980s.

One of the factors slowing the growth of the American club was the strength and vigor of the Southern California regional club, which over much of its history has been larger, more active, and better supported than the national club. At times in the late 1980s, the American club was only the third largest American Bouvier organization, ranking after the North American Working Bouvier Association and the California club in terms of membership. Club membership peaked at about six hundred in the late 1970s and early 1980s. Since that time, membership has fallen off significantly.

The primary activities of the parent club have been to run a national specialty show and to put out a bulletin or magazine. The specialty is a conformation show open to a single breed. Only one national spec-

ialty show is held each year, and it often has the largest entry for the particular breed. In addition to the conformation show, the specialty weekend usually features an annual meeting, a banquet, and other social, competitive, and educational events.

The first Bouvier specialty was held in 1965 at the Kennel Club of Philadelphia. Best of Breed was the import Konard du Rotiane. Best of Opposite Sex was American-bred — Miss Bowles's Giaconda du Clos des Cerberes, owned by Carl May.

Through 1973, the specialties were in Pennsylvania, New Jersey, or New York, and the first five were held at the Kennel Club of Philadelphia. In 1974, the club took on a more national flavor and held its specialty in Detroit. In 1978, the West Coast was reached with a specialty in Pasadena.

There are strong, long-term regional clubs in Michigan and Southern California. More recently, clubs have become active in northern Illinois and the Washington, D.C. area. None of these are AKC member clubs. The California, Michigan, and Illinois clubs have on the whole been active, open-minded, and progressive. They, and the Canadian Club, led the way by sponsoring the working championships before the formulation of NAWBA, encouraging diverse activities and bringing over European judges.

The Tanq of Pal-Mar became the first Bouvier in America to hold a Schutzhund title in 1975, going on to SchH II in 1976. Owned and trained by Greg and Candy Filek in Southern California, who worked with Jean-Claude Balu. An unfortunate injury ended Tanq's career short of the III.

Hollandia Evil, Canadian and American Champion, two-time American Specialty winner, top conformation Bouvier in the United States in 1977, and many other show records. Evil, bred by David Westra and owned by Carlo Vander Muren, was truly a great and influential dog.

The Bouvier in Michigan and Canada

In view of the immense popularity of the Bouvier in Canada, it is notable that this interest is relatively recent. The first Canadian Bouvier litter was registered in 1960, more than twenty years after the tentative beginnings in America. This litter, naturally, was out of the Bowles line. The sire was Samson du Clos des Cerberes, and the dam was Rosida du Clos des Cerberes, C.D. The breeder is listed as Jacobur Koekman of Ancaster, Ontario, who was never heard from again. The first Champions were Hertha du Clos des Cerberes in 1960 and Deewal Argusuno in 1961.

In 1962, Frisia's Astrid became the first Canadian-bred Champion, followed the next year by Frisia's Bravo Stephanus, Frisia's Fannie, and Paragon Boefje. Andy Prinsen's Frisia Kennels and the closely associated Paragon Kennels of Bay Meyers can justly claim the honor of being the founding Canadian kennels. Shortly thereafter, David Wetra's Hollandia program and the Roxanne breeding commenced.

Andy Prinsen was a Dutchman who came to Canada after the Second World War and settled in Windsor, across the river from Detroit. His breeding and publicity efforts were the driving forces behind the early popularity of the Bouvier in Michigan, which remains a primary center of activity to this day. He favored the old-style dogs, short of coat and long on aggression, and founded a North American Bouvier des Flandres Working Dog Association. Although that particular entity ceased to exist, the concepts and passion behind it never did quite flicker out.

Andy's first Bouvier was Sabena of Deewal, who when bred to Deewal Argusuno produced Frisia's Peggy. Peggy is behind many of the early Ontario Bouviers with the Roxanne and Bronville Kennel names.

Frisia's Tarzan was a major show winner and influential stud for Prinsen and did much to popularize the Bouvier in Canada and the United States. Many Frisia Bouviers were being imported into the United States during this era. Tarzan's pedigree (Figure 14-1) illustrates the early derivations from the Bowles and Walsh (Deewal) stock. Over the next decade, the Frisia program was strongly influenced by the melding of imported Dutch stock with the original American blood. Frisia's Black Prince, owned by Judy Allen, nicely illustrates these developments (Figure 14-2).

Prinsen was a dynamic, influential figure whose detractors were almost as passionate as his advocates. In polite canine society, his name and kennel became a code word for old-fashioned, aggressive Bouviers — and it was not meant to be a compliment.

In later years, the Frisia program became much less influential. Although Bouvier breeding continued until about 1980, Prinsen apparently took much less interest. He became active in the ministry and at one point had a Detroit-area television show.

In 1968, the "Chenil de Bolshoy" of Paul and Pauline DeRycke at Oxford Station, Ontario, began what was to become one of the strongest and most influential Canadian programs. Their first litter produced Arlon de Bolshoy, out of a French male called Quito and Roxanne's Peanuts. Arlon went to Thea Bossart, achieved the C.D., and began what was to

---

Figure 14-1

```
              Argus de la Thudinie  Ch; '51
         Deewal Argusuno  Ch; '59
              Faussette l'Ideal de Charleroi
    Frisia's Thunder
              Deewal Argusuno  Ch; '59
         Frisia's Bubbles
              Zanda du Clos des Cerberes
FRISIA'S TARZAN  '64
              Marius du Clos des Cerberes  Ch; '43
         Bel Ami du Clos des Cerberes  '52
              Ellyrdia  Ch; NHSB.117114 '47
    Zanda du Clos des Cerberes
              Dombey  '45
         Si Jolie du Clos des Cerberes '54
              Wandru des Coudreaux  LOF.1.Bouv.3736
```

Paul De Rycke, founding North American breeder, initiator of the working Bouvier movement, and known internationally for his famous Bolshoy Bouviers des Flandres. Shown here with thirteen-year-old American and Canadian Champion Hobo de Bolshoy.

Pauline DeRycke with Max de Bolshoy and Gravine de Bolshoy, both Canadian Champions.

Figure 14-2

```
                     Frisia's Thunder
          Frisia's Tarzan  '64
                     Zanda du Clos des Cerberes
     Villandria's Mussolini
                     Arnoroh  NHSB.201858 '58
          Iris  NHSB.356972 '65
                     Betha  NHSB.307662
Frisia's Bello
                     Phynx of Parce  CKC.524805
          Bruno v d Veen Hoeve  CKC.605553 '64
                     Carin v h Spanjarsveld  NHSB.221267 '59
     Frisia's Gidget
                     Bel Ami du Clos des Cerberes  '52
          Zanda du Clos des Cerberes
                     Si Jolie du Clos des Cerberes  '54
C Ch FRISIA'S BLACK PRINCE '73
                     Abdoelhamid v d Ouden Dijk  NHSB.225183
          Ronald  '65
                     Lidamia  LOSH.92065
     Frisia's Hector
                     Frisia's Thunder
          Frisia's Hertha II  '64
                     Zanda du Clos des Cerberes
Frisia's Geeske
                     Phynx of Parce  CKC.524805
          Bruno v d Veen Hoeve  CKC.605553 '64
                     Carin v h Spanjarsveld  NHSB.221267 '59
     Frisia's Gidget
                     Bel Ami du Clos des Cerberes  '52
          Zanda du Clos des Cerberes
                     Si Jolie du Clos des Cerberes  '54
```

become a distinguished career in working competition for Thea. In 1971, Dirk de Bolshoy became the first Canadian-bred to win Best in Show, at the Club Canin in Quebec City. In 1972, Sigurd de la Thudinie also achieved a Best in Show and became top Canadian Show Bouvier.

The significance of these wins, beyond putting the Bolshoy name on the map, was the introduction of modern Belgian lines, especially those of Justin Chastel, into the Canadian Bouvier scene. Dim de Bolshoy (Figure 14-3) is typical of this era. Much of the Bolshoy breeding went into Quebec and was combined with the French lines there.

From the beginning, the Bolshoy program involved much more than beautiful show dogs. The DeRyckes began obedience and protection training on the Bolshoy grounds, which became a center for Bouvier activity. Ch. Sigurd de la Thudinie was among those trained. He and his son, Ch. Hobo de Bolshoy, participated in many demonstrations staged to show the public and Bouvier enthusiasts that properly trained protection dogs are not "savage, half-mad attack

C/A Ch Sigurd de la Thudinie OFA, whelped in 1969, was imported by Paul DeRycke. He became one of the earliest Canadian Best in Show Bouviers and an important stud. He was out of Belgium Ch Rico de la Thudinie and Quelly de la Thudinie.

Figure 14-3

Noceur de la Thudinie B Ch
    Picolo de la Thudinie
        Nolette de la Thudinie
    Cambo's Taipan de la Thudinie
        Bruno v d Veen Hoeve CKC.605553 '64
    Reno of Cambo
        Frisia's Ducky
  Max de Bolshoy
        Ringo de la Thudinie '68
    Tapeur de la Thudinie
        Nina de la Thudinie
    Upolu de la Thudinie
        Rino de la Thudinie '68
    Sheila de la Thudinie
        Oula de la Thudinie B Ch; LOSH.237408
A/C Ch DIM DE BOLSHOY '74
        Rico de la Thudinie B Ch; '68
    Sigurd de la Thudinie C/A Ch; OFA '69
        Quelly de la Thudinie
  Giant of Flanderfield
        Ralf de la Thudinie C Ch
    Fina de Bolshoy C Ch; '70
        Razzia des Herbages Normands C Ch
  Angela of Abercorn
        Troll van de Woolderwei
    Aldo   CD TD (Canadian)
        Villandria's Argena
  Constance of Abercorn

Euro's Heidi

dogs." In 1978, a male out of Max de Bolshoy and Olah de Bolshoy named Quechtor became the first Canadian Bouvier to achieve Schutzhund I. This dog, also known as Toro, was owned and trained by Ann Wachsmuth.

The DeRycke's are held in great esteem by the North American community, as indicated by the fact that the North American Working Bouvier Association has given life membership to only two of the founders — Edmee Bowles and Paul DeRycke.

Hank Hagen's Bronville Kennel at Cookstown, Ontario, shows up in much of the early breeding. A good example is Bronville's Darren (Figure 14-4), owned by Dr. Erik Houttuin at Flandersfield. Flandersfield was active for a number of years at Mississauga, Ontario, before moving to Missouri in the late 1970s.

Blanford was a well-known Detroit-area kennel whose lines, along with the Bolshoy lines, pop up in California, among other places. Penny the Pooh was bred by Joseph McDonald. Boris and Lexoh were Dutch imports. Darren is the sire of Ch. Flandersfield

Canadian Ch Ralf de la Thudinie, whelped in 1968, was imported by Paul De Rycke. Shown here (at left) with daughter Contesse de Bolshoy in 1970. In this era, DeRycke was introducing Belgian breeding on a major scale into Canada. Ralf out of Licou de la Thudinie x Pia de la Thidinie.

Figure 14-4

```
                Iwan Floss v d Rakkers  D Ch
        Arnoroh  NHSB.201858  '58
                Kimanda Juno v d Zaanhoeve
    Boris v d Ouden Dijk  Ch; NHSB.361244 '65
                Donaldor v d Ouden Dijk
        Hertha Carla v d Ouden Dijk  NHSB.313026  '63
                Carla v d Ouden Dijk  NHSB.247592 '60
 Blandford's Basko  C/A Ch; OFA
                Argus de la Thudinie  Ch; '51
        Deewal Argusuno  Ch; '59
                Faussette l'Ideal de Charleroi
    Penny the Pooh
                Deewal Argusuno  Ch; '59
        Frisia's Anne  '63
                Zanda du Clos des Cerberes
C/A Ch BRONVILLE'S DARREN '72
                Emiel  NHSB.177257
        Lexoh  NHSB.200878 '58
                Astrah  NHSB.162305
    Roxanne's Bret
                Deewal Argusuno  Ch; '59
        Frisia's Peggy
                Sabena of Deewal  '56
 Bronville's Bonnie  C CD
                Roxanne's Bret
        Roxanne's Charlie Brown
                Zena
    Beau of Bronville
                Frisia's Tarzan  '64
        Roxanne's Snoopy
                Frisia's Peggy
```

Bully and a number of other important and well-respected dogs.

Closely asociated with the Bolshoy and Bronville lines is the Highsierra line of Marjory Fraser in Caledonia, Ontario. Highsierra's Arius de Bolshoy, whelped in 1975, was, for example, the sire of a male called Dohn, who did considerable winning in the early 1980s in the eastern United States. Bernie Blair's Nobleair Kennel is essentially a continuation of the Bolshoy lines.

Beginning in 1967, or perhaps even earlier, a big, outgoing Irishman named Joseph A. McDonald became active in the Detroit area. He bought dogs, such as Frisia's Anne, from Andy Prinsen. He toured Europe seeking breeding stock, such as Nefga de l'Ile Monsin from Moreaux, and Picolo and Oursonne de la Thudinie. He sometimes combined his Cambo Kennel name improperly with others, such as in the male of his breeding, Cambo's Thornton de la Thudinie. This dog was the most important foundation of Ontario breeding in the late 1970s and early 1980s, but he should not have had "Thudinie" appended to his name, because he was not a product of that European kennel.

Left and Below: Highsierra's Chauvinist James, Canadian Champion bred and owned by Marjory Fraser in Caledonia, Ontario.

Sire: C Ch Highsierra's Bachelor Boy
Dam: C Ch Witch of Highsierra

Ch Je Thor du Clos des Cerberes, prominent in East Coast show rings during the mid-1980s. Owned by P. Andrews.
Brd: E. F. Bowles and B. Jacobsohn
Sire: Ch Centauri's Griffe d'Cerberes
Dam: Ch Europa du Clos des Cerberes

McDonald imported from France (Quitte de la Vallee du Lay and Rustique des Herbages Normands) as well as from Belgium. He bred a lot, with no discernible rhyme or reason, but, to my knowledge, never entered a dog in a show. He bred his old-fashioned Dutch and Fresia stock with his expensive Belgian imports. He apparently had more than fifty Bouviers when he was killed in an automobile accident in the early 1970s.

A prime example of McDonald's influence is Hollandia Evil, bred by David Westra. Evil was only one of the pivotal offspring of Cambo's Thorton de la Thudinie. Evil already had a distinguished show career when he went on to twice win the American Bouvier Club Specialty out of the veteran class. When judge Haworth Hoch selected Evil in 1979 in Detroit, it was without doubt on Evil's own considerable merits. In Evil's pedigree (Figure 14-5) note that he is of pure Chastel breeding, with the above-mentioned detour through Michigan.

Figure 14-5

```
                    Noceur de la Thudinie  B Ch
          Picolo de la Thudinie
                    Nolette de la Thudinie
Cambo's Thorton de la Thudinie  C Ch
                    Marc de la Thudinie  Ch; '63
          Oursonne de la Thudinie
                    Mabelie de la Thudinie
C/A Ch HOLLANDIA EVIL  '71
                    Olaf de la Thudinie  B Ch; '65
          Rino de la Thudinie  '68
                    Nala de la Thudinie
Sirka de la Thudinie  C Ch
                    Marc de la Thudinie  Ch; '63
          Oula de la Thudinie  B Ch; LOSH.237408
                    Nina de la Thudinie
```

Ch Zarco Iris v d Cerberushof was Best of Breed at the American Club Specialty in 1988. Bred in the Netherlands by Hank and Gerda Harmers, imported and owned by the Paquette family.
Sire: D Ch Falco Darwin van het Grendarcohof
Dam: Iris Babeth v d Cerberushof

Another major winner of these lines is Bill Miller's Alex (Figure 14-6), also a two-time American Specialty winner. (There was no Canadian Club, and thus no Canadian Specialty, at this time.)

Clearly, in the 1970s, first-rate Belgian-line Bouviers were being bred in Ontario. Much credit is due to David Westra, Carlo Vandermuren, Bill Miller, and others. However, Joseph McDonald made it all possible by bringing over the dogs on which the Canadian mini-dynasty was based.

In the pedigree of Alex (Figure 14-6), note that Thorton, who appears an incredible four times in three generations, was bred by McDonald. Quitte (who appears twice) and Sirka were imported by McDonald. The only other dog in the first three generations is Cindy, and she comes out of Andy Prinsen's lines, a daughter of Tarzan.

McDonald was not especially popular among previously established Bouvier breeders. I knew virtually nothing about him until his name kept appearing in

Figure 14-6

```
                    C Ch Cambo's Thorton de la Thudinie
          C Ch Euro's Gus
                    Marya's Cindy of Hollandia  '67
      C Ch Euro's Marco
                    Nic de la Thudinie
          Quitte de la Vallee du Lay
                    Orphee de la Vallee du Lay  '65
C/A Ch ADELE'S ALEXANDER '76
                    C Ch Cambo's Thorton de la Thudinie
          C/A Ch Hollandia Evil '71
                    C Ch Sirka de la Thudinie
      C Ch Denard's Evil's Jewel of Adele
                    C Ch Cambo's Thorton de la Thudinie
          A/C Ch Euro's Lucky Sonya Denard
                    Quitte de la Vallee du Lay
```

my research. I finally went through the stud books and highlighted his name whenever it appeared and then began to ask questions. From 1967 to about 1974, McDonald was incredibly active. In spite of his "rough edges," his Cambo Kennel had an immense influence on the breeding of the Bouvier des Flandres during a critical era.

Bouvier breeding in Canada and Michigan unfortunately became very tight. As a prime example, Alex's best-known son was Glenmiller's Beau Geste, who was out of yet another Evil daughter, Angel. Angel was out of yet another daughter of Thorton and Quitte. This dog did considerable winning but was second rate when compared to Alex or Evil. By failing to bring in outside blood early enough, this "Ontario initiative" burned itself out almost before it really got going.

My expectation is that the long-term influence on the breed is going to come largely from the Quiche program of Elaine, Louise, and Christine Paquette. Rather than breeeding a few winning dogs more and more tightly, they have over the years been innovative and aggressive in seeking outside stock and blending it into what is becoming an increasingly dominant line. A good example is Canadian Challenge (Figure 14-7), mother of Quiche's Fabulous Beau and thus a grandmother of Quiche's Geoffrey.

Figure 14-7

```
            Blandford's Raoel  '68
       Blandford's Toby
            Miss Boleyn  '69
  Jenbedon's Tuff Tully  '74
            Bica v d Rozenheerd  NHSB.512062 HD-
       Samantha v d Susannapolder
            Tosca v Dafzicht  NHSB.479406
A/C Ch QUICHE'S CANADIAN CHALLENGE '78
            Euro's Gus  C Ch
       Euro's Marco  C Ch
            Quitte de la Vallee du Lay
  Euro's Quiche Kim  C Ch
            Cambo's Thorton de la Thudinie   C Ch
       Euro's Lisa  Ch; '72
            Quitte de la Vallee du Lay
```

Ch Rombo Flaming Star, known as "Cricket." This beautiful bitch, shown her winning '85 Canadian Specialty, is perhaps the best known of the wonderful Rombo Bouviers of Rick and Diane Gschwender, which were dominant in the Detroit area in the early 1980s.

Sometimes a dog with an unpretentious name can nevertheless be of immense importance. Consider Bill Miller's "Angel", out of two-time Specialty winner Hollandia Evil and Euro's Lisa. In the 1980s, this female has had more influence on Canadian breeding than all but a handful of males.

```
                   Cambo's Thornton de la Thudinie C Ch
        Hollandia Evil C/A Ch; '71
                   Sirka de la Thudinie C Ch
C Ch Angel '78
                   Cambo's Thornton de la Thudinie C Ch
        Euro's Lisa Ch; '72
                   Quitte de la Vallee du Lay
```

By introducing Dutch blood relatively early in the game, the Paquettes opened up their lines and avoided the overly tight situations that, while producing winners in the short term, led other programs into oblivion. Tuff Tully was not of the then fashionable lines. The Paquettes nevertheless made good use of him, using their own judgment rather than relying on what everybody else said. The ability to look deeper than the surface, to have an intuitive sense of what an animal might produce, and to understand the significance of a pedigree have always been marks of the excellent breeder.

Perhaps the best known of the Quiche Bouviers is Gabriel (Figure 14-8), who, owner handled, has done considerable winning in both the United States and Canada. In Gabriel's pedigree, Euro's Gus, Euro's Lisa, Evil, and Euro's Lucky Sonya are all offspring of Joseph McDonald's Cambo's Thorton de la Thudinie. The chief outside line here is Victor, who was a nice tie back into the Thudinie line. (Because Victor was bred in Belgium by Justin Chastel, he should properly carry the Thudinie name.)

Other regions of Canada, apart from Ontario, evolved separately and were much more influenced

Figure 14-8

```
                   Ringo de la Thudinie  LOF.14296-256
        Tapin de la Thudinie  Ch Int; LOSH.279596 CQN
                   Nina de la Thudinie  LOSH.220997
Deewal Victor  Ch
                   Rico de la Thudinie B Ch; LOSH.256581
        Silette de la Thudinie  Ch; LOSH.274125 OFA
                   Quelly de la Thudinie  LOSH.252306
Quiche's Barrier  C/A Ch; '77
                   Euro's Gus  C Ch
        Euro's Marco  C Ch
                   Quitte de la Vallee du Lay
Euro's Quiche Kim  C Ch
                   Cambo's Thorton de la Thudinie  C Ch
        Euro's Lisa  Ch; '72
                   Quitte de la Vallee du Lay
A/C Ch QUICHE'S GABRIEL  '82
                   Hollandia Evil  C/A Ch; '71
        Denard's Davey  A/C Ch
                   Euro's Lucky Sonya Denard  A/C Ch
Quiche's Buffis  A/C Ch; '77
                   Denard's Canon
        Denard's Chickee Sonya
                   Euro's Lucky Sonya Denard  A/C Ch
Quiche's Extra Ruffles  C/A Ch; '80
                   Tapin de la Thudinie  Ch Int
        Deewal Victor   Ch
                   Silette de la Thudinie  Ch
Quiche's Brilliant Blossom  C Ch
                   Euro's Marco  C Ch
        Euro's Quiche Kim  C Ch
                   Euro's Lisa  Ch; '72
```

Quiche's Canadian Challenge, Canadian and American Champion whelped in 1978. Bred and owned by the Paquette family, number-one bitch in the Canadian ring in 1983. Shown here with Elaine Paquette, she makes a pretty picture that any breeder would be proud of.

Sire: Jenbedon's Tuff Tully '74
Dam: C Ch Euro's Quiche Kim

Quiche's Geoffrey, American and Canadian Champion, whelped in 1982. One of America's top producers by any standard, sire of many quality Champions. Bred, owned, and shown by the Paquette family.

Sire: A/C Ch Quiche's Fabulous
    Beau
Dam: Gerry Brena van Dafzicht

by United States and European lines. Bouvier activity began in western Canada about 1970. This was a decade later than in Ontario, with by far the most activity in Alberta. The best-known names are Diana Case and her Oomingmak Kennel, which became active in the early 1970s. The best known of Diana's dogs is Oomingmak's E'Ben, whelped in 1974. Ben obtained Canadian Championship, C.D. and was a well-known stud dog.

Another prominent name is that of Barrie and Bonnie Caskey, who produced the well-known Canadian Champion Sanche's Avanti. This dog, by Ch. Timlor Copain out of Ch. Maijeune's Buittoniere, was owned by Jim and Betty Vincent of Gloryhill's Kennel.

According to Diana Case, the first Champion in Alberta (early 1970s) was Borneo's Satchmo, out of imports King Noup van Dafzicht and Alberta Noup van Dafzicht.

A good example of western Canadian breeding is Grove's Grover, a very successful show winner. His sire, Highregard Onto Double Dart, is directly out of the Maijeune breeding of Carl and Gladys May and the Madrone Ledge stock of the Hubbards (that is, East Coast United States). The Highregard Kennel, owned by Martin and Lynne Kenney, is in Saskatchewan. On the lower half of this pedigree (Figure 14-9) are Dutch, Abady, and Blanford (Michigan) lines. This dog was bred by Jim Wheatley of Grove Farms in Alberta and owned by John and Sonja Tummers of the Kroankel Kennel.

Frisia's Black Prince, Canadian Champion, is typical of Andy Prinsen's breeding. Here he shares the spotlight with Miss Rebecca Allen. Owned by Judy Allen, JOY-A-LEN Kennels; bred by Andy Prinsen in 1973.

Sire: Frisia's Bello CKC.935955
Dam: Frisia's Geeske C Ch; CKC.839529

Figure 14-9

```
                        Tapin de la Thudinie  Ch Int; CQN
              Ulfio de la Thudinie  Ch
                        Sola de la Thudinie  '69
        Maijeune's d'Artagnan  Ch; '76
                        Prudhon des Preux Vuilbaards  Ch
              Maijeune's Alouette  Ch; '74
                        Madrone Ledge Venus  Ch
Highregard Onto Double Dart
                        Madrone Ledge Viking  Ch; '72
              Nomura Wave  Ch
                        Deewal Vlinder
        Madrone Ledge Highregard Zoe     C Ch
                        Madrone Ledge Viking  Ch; '72
              Madrone Ledge Winterset
                        Picolette du Posty Arlequin  Ch
A/C Ch GROVE'S GROVER OF KROANKEL
                        King Noup van Dafzicht
              Jubal Leo
                        Mac Donald's Zonia  '68
        C Ch Oomingmak's E'Ben C.D. '74
                        Task des Preux Vuilbaards  '70
              V'Dody des Preux Vuilbaards
                        Regine de la Thudinie  LOSH.266535
Grove's Bumper
                        Blandford's Toby
              Birdwing's Grizzly  '73
                        Blandford's Sheba  '72
        Silver Tips Grizzly
                        Blandford's Fionne of Norlock  '70
              Blandford's Sheba  '72
                        Blandford's Zarda  '70
```

The Bouvier people in Alberta have a lot on the ball; in fact, their Alberta Bouvier Club, formed in 1978, was recognized by the Canadian Kennel Club in 1980. They have had a couple of very successful specialties and in 1984 brought over Mrs. Van Gink-Van Es of the Netherlands as judge.

When a Canadian National Bouvier Club was organized in Ontario a couple of years later, apparently without any real discussion with anyone outside Ontario, much resentment was generated. The Canadian club has in general stumbled; in early 1987, the Alberta club had 143 members, while the Canadian club listed only 124. The real depth of the trouble was indicated by the fact that only twenty individuals were members of both clubs.

The Canadian club held its first Specialty at London, Ontario, in fall 1985 but was unable to organize one during the rest of the decade.

Ch Centauri's Irca demonstrates the Schutzhund hold and bark exercise. The helper in the photo is Ron Maloney.

Sire: Ch and W. Ch Centauri's Gambit
Dam: Centauri's Flandrienne
Owner: Pat Dowling and Centauri

CHAPTER FIFTEEN

The Working Bouvier Movement

The association of the Bouvier with police service goes back many years before the formal establishment of the breed, which occurred in 1913. The first serious, organized program in a metropolitan area began in Ghent, Belgium, in March 1899. Although the dogs were not specifically identified as Bouviers, the Bouvier was, after all, not formally established as a breed at that time. The photographs, however, clearly depict many instances of Bouvier progenitors. Although Germany is most prominently associated with the use of police dogs, its programs were initiated partially as a consequence of the success of the program in Ghent.

As the Bouvier breed began to take its modern form in the 1920s and 1930s, Europeans were emphasizing maintenance of the working character. At one time, Bouviers were prominent in the Belgian Ring Sport, with the "de l'Ile Monsin" Kennel of Edmond Moreaux in Liege being particularly well-respected. In Holland, the Bouvier has been important in the Dutch Police Trials and in actual police service. This European attitude is well-expressed by Justin Chastel, founder of the Thudinie line and a preeminent breeder for more than fifty years:

> You must keep in mind that character is of primary importance, more than type, more than gait. It is only after considering these things in order of their importance that you can turn your attention to lesser specific factors. It is here that the public and the inexperienced always go wrong, first by being anxious about details, such as color and length of coat. Would you have a Bouvier that does not act like one, who does not have all those moral characteristics for which the Bouvier has been chosen for centuries? Obviously the Bouvier no longer has to herd cattle, but does not the new owner want a dog that is courageous, bold, intelligent, and fond of work? It is up to the breeder to deliver such an animal.

In America, the Bouvier was not historically prominent in the public eye as a guard or protection dog until the late 1960s, when significant effort to promote the breed as such was made by New York breeder Bob Abady. Abady became the subject of an outrageous and much-talked-about article in *Sports Illustrated* magazine. While immense publicity was generated, apparently no dogs were demonstrated in a credible arena, and the people involved did not know much about the practical aspects of training and using such dogs. Basically, they were a little ahead of their time and did not make a long-term impact on the course of the breed.

The Bouviers were portrayed as attack and protection machines unlike anything ever seen in America. Unfortunately, this show of bravado did not stand up well to knowledgeable scrutiny and, in fact, left as a legacy a lack of credibility. Thus, it is essential for the working Bouvier community today to be sensitive to such issues and to be especially careful not to brag about what wonderful dogs they have. Rather, they need to go out on the sport field and let fellow working-dog enthusiasts draw their own conclusions from what they see.

Introducing the European heritage into America has not been easy, because many people did not want to understand. Even today, some kennels actively oppose the preservation of the Bouvier's protective heritage.

By the mid-1970s, a few isolated pioneers were Schutzhund-training Bouviers. They included Greg Filek in California, who, training with Jean-Claude Balu, put the Schutzhund II on a dog named Tanq of Pal-Mar, as well as the C.D. and the T.D. Mike Reppa in Detroit became the first American to reach Schutzhund III when his Ajax earned that title. Erik Houttuin put the Schutzhund I on a dog named Iwan out of the Dutch Champion Eros van de Zwikshoek. There was a working Bouvier organization in the Detroit/Windsor area under the leadership of Andy Prinsen and a few individuals here and there doing private

Left and Above: Ria Klep's Bram Pasja le Jardin du Moulin, 1988 North American Working Champion. Bred and trained by Ria Klep, Ulvenhout, The Netherlands.

Sire: Bonaparte Zierce v d Cerberushof
Dam: Pasja SchH I NHSB.1210045
Born: 1983

Ch Vacher's Alpha Centauri, known as "Tory", set many breed records in working competition, starting with the youngest to achieve the Tracking Dog title at the age of six months and four days. He was also the first to become both Champion of Record and Schutzhund III and the first to hold the FH, the advanced German tracking title. Bred by Janet Hudak, owned and trained by Kathy and Jim Engel.

Sire: Ch Lutteur du Val de Rol
Dam: Ch Yataghan du Clos des Cerberes

training. But overall the working Bouvier enthusiasts were few and far between and not communicating very well.

In October 1977, at the American Bouvier Club Specialty in Philadelphia, a breakthrough was made. Paul and Pauline DeRycke had been invited to come down from Canada and show what a well-trained Bouvier could do. Many of those present were astounded at what they saw.

The advent of the new era in working Bouviers came in October 1980 when Erik Houttuin founded the North American Working Bouvier Champion-

There was a tie for over all first place between Golf and the other German team of Hans Betzgen with Farko v. d. Stadt Homberg.

The Working Championships have always included AKC or CKC obedience competition, a Schutzhund trial, and carting. Agility and police competition were also included some years. At first, there was considerable experimentaion with the rules, which have since been standardized. Since 1984, the Championships have included conformation competition featuring a European judge and procedures.

In 1981, the California club picked up the torch

Left and Above: Mickey Hardin's "Devil", trained by Paul Theissen, became North America Working Champion in 1985 and 1986. Devil, whose formal name was Amman von Dreilanderech, was later trained and shown by Tom Rose.
Sire: Arco von Schloss Bruhl SchH III
Dam: Mira von der Stadt Homberg SchH III

ships. The first one was held in Labadie, Missouri. It was a bold move, but the time was right, and it forever transformed the American Bouvier scene. In some ways, this beginning was not overly auspicious, because publicity was virtually nonexistent, organization was sparse, and participation was not large. These were details, however, for Erik brought over two German working teams that put on a Schutzhund demonstration showing what real working Bouviers are all about.

The Schutzhund competition was won by Hans Brust and Golf v. d. Stadt Homberg of West Germany. The AKC obedience winner was Flandersfield Anka, owned by Dorothy Berger, and the Carting winner was Rosemary Lewis's Flandersfield Bilbo Baggins.

and held a tremendously successful Championship in Redlands in conjunction with a major conformation Specialty. The winner was Elaine Jeche with her Harlan's Little Bridget, C.D.X. Reserve Champion was Ch. Vacher's Alpha Centauri, Schutzhund I at the time. A number of good police Bouviers, mostly trained by Danny LaMaster, were entered. Police-style protection competition has been a popular event ever since.

While traveling in Europe early in 1982, Erik Houttuin heard tales of a big black dog in the village of Ulvenhout, just outside the Dutch city of Breda and within a few miles of the Belgian border. This dog, called Donar, had become both Schutzhund III and F.H. at the tender age of eighteen months and shortly

Left and Above: Mike Reppa and Ajax, first Schutzhund III Bouvier in North America (about 1978).

Working Championships, 1987, in Redlands, California. From the left: Martha Hochstein and Reserve Winner Ch Banjo von Schwartzen Barren; conformation judge Justin Chastel (president of the Belgian Club); unidentified woman; working judge Jean-Claude Balu; and Working Champion Centauri's Gambit with Jim Engel.

thereafter became the Bouvier Working Champion of Holland. Arriving at the the home of the owners, Jos and Ria Klep, Erik found only Donar and the Klep's two daughters home. Under the watchful eye of Donar, he left a note saying that they must come to America. There was, no doubt, much discussion of these strange Americans in the Klep household that evening.

Ria Klep was no novice trainer. She had previously reached Schutzhund III with a dog called Wodan le Jardin Etoile at a time when Schutzhund was new in the Netherlands. Wodan was apparently poisoned under mysterious circumstances, and for many

recognition — the dog knew that he was a winner! Reserve Champion was Centauri's Fleur de Lis, who became the first North American female to earn a Schutzhund title.

There was no doubting Donar's enthusiasm for tracking, for his style was akin to a freight train until he came to a corner, where he seemingly was able to suspend the laws of physics for a moment as he changed direction, full speed. This mode of operation is of course not without peril, and he did overrun one article. Ria could not believe that it was possible and went out with the track layer to inspect the missing article — it wasn't so much a question of doubting

Winners of the inaugural Bouvier Working Championships in Labadie, Missouri, 1980. From the left: Hans Betzgen with Farko v d Stadt Homberg; organizer Dr. Erik Houttuin; and Hans Brust with Golf v d Stadt Homberg. Both dogs were Schutzhund III, trained and residing in West Germany. American fanciers had never seen anything like it!

months Ria spent weekends traveling to evaluate Bouvier litters, looking for her next dog. The rest has become Bouvier history.

The Kleps accepted Erik's invitation and brought Donar to America. In October 1982, yet another innovative and successful trial was held at Niagara-on-the-Lake in Ontario, where the newly formed Canadian National Club sponsored the Working Championships as its first official function. There was never any question regarding who was star of this show, and Donar put on a working demonstration that opened the eyes of Canadians and Americans alike. When the placements were announced and the trophies awarded, Donar responded to applause by stretching out to a full alert posture and barking his

that the track was correct as it was having absolute faith in the dog. Watching this working team, both in Holland and in America, has always been an inspiring experience. The concentration and total dedication to excellence set an example for all of us.

In many ways, however, Donar's obedience was the most striking. This big dog executed with total enthusiasm at flank speed. When he went over the "A"-frame after the dumbbell, he hit it on the way back almost before the echo of his first strike had died away.

Donar and Ria went on to compete in the U.S. National Schutzhund Championships in Los Angeles, where they came in a strong third. Donar's tour of America was a huge success, and he is still remembered in Bouvier and Schutzhund circles alike, such was his presence on the working field.

In some ways, this big black dog was not a likely candidate for greatness. He had a simple, one-word name in a time of elaborate kennel names. He was a dog of pure Dutch breeding in an era when many of the Dutch were abandoning a fifty-year breeding tradition in a headlong rush to Belgian dogs. Many of his ancestors had great records in the Dutch Police Trials at a time when fewer and fewer Bouviers were competing in that arena. He was, above all else, a great

Jacobsohn and Miss Bowles at Belco Farm. She is thus a product of the fifty-year "du Clos des Cerberes" breeding program.

In the conformation competition under Annie Verheyen, both the Best of Breed male and female were "du Clos des Cerberes" Bouviers, demonstrating how faithfully the European concepts of Bouvier breeding were carried forward at Belco Farm over the years. Edmee Bowles survived the years of war and the struggle to begin again in America, and even in her sixth decade as a breeder of the Bouvier des Flandres, she

Ch Banjo von Schwarzen Baren, owned by Martha Hochstein, is among the world's most successful Bouvier working competitors. He holds the Schutzhund III and the IPO III and was the 1990 NAWBA Working Champion. He has twice placed highly in the American DVG National Championships and has been second in the German Bouvier Championships.

Sire: Marschel v d Stadt Homberg
Dam: Edel von Baronen Wald
Brd: Iris Haas

working dog when the eye of the fancy was being drawn increasingly to the show ring.

His pedigree is a litany of the Dutch heritage. It includes the great KNPV dogs such as Borisso, Dolfo, and Nerodan, and the founding kennels, represented in names such a Bica v d Rozenheerd, Rato v d Ouden Dijk, and Bianca Baakenstein. Only time will tell if he marks the end of an era.

In 1983, the Championships were held in the Detroit area in conjunction with a European-style conformation evaluation conducted by the respected Belgian judge Annie Verheyen of the van de Buildrager Kennel. Ch. Centauri's Fleur de Lis became Working Champion and the first North American bitch to hold Schutzhund III. "Leah" is out of April du Clos des Cerberes, who was leased to us in whelp by Bruce

set the standard for type and character.

The 1985 Championships were held in London, Ontario, in conjunction with the first Canadian Bouvier Club conformation Specialty. The winner was an exceptional German import, Amman vom Dreilaendereck SchH III, FH. "Devil" was owned by Mickie Hardin of Memphis, Tennessee, and professionally trained by Paul Theissen, a German Schutzhund judge. Devil repeated his Championship in Illinois in 1986.

In fall 1986, at the Working Championships in Illinois, the working Bouvier movement was formalized with the establishment of the North American Working Bouvier Association (NAWBA). In 1987, the Championships returned to California, where Justin Chastel served as conformation judge. This event

The 1986 North American Championships in Chicago. From the left: Dr. Erik Houttuin, NAWBA president; Robbie v d Plantage SchH I; Dagmar Wolf-Smith, Illinois Club president; judge Jean-Claude Balu; Jim Engel, NAWBA secretary, with Reserve Working Champion Ch Centauri's Gambit SchH III.

was the first under the auspices of the NAWBA and was most successful. Working Champion was Ch. Centauri's Gambit, and Reserve went to Martha Hochstein's Ch. Banjo vom Schwarzen Baren.

In 1988, the event was held near Manassas, Virginia. The winner was Ria Klep's Bram Pasja le Jardin du Moulin, son of Bonaparte Zierce v d Cerberushof and grandson of Donar. "Devil" was Reserve Champion. In 1989, the Championships returned to the Detroit area, where Gambit became the second dog after "Devil" to be a two-time winner. His son, Centauri's Ksar, owned and trained by Linda Schneider, was Reserve Champion.

One of the primary benefits of the Working Championships has been to bring significant numbers of Bouvier people into close contact with heavily protec-

tion-trained dogs. The 1981 competition in Redlands stands out, because a large group of spectators was congregated around the gate to the field. All of the dogs — the police dogs, the civil-guard dogs, and the Schutzhund dogs — came off the field after the most vigorous protection tests straight into the midst of the spectators. None of the handlers showed the least concern, none of the people had any fear, and no dog showed instability or the least confusion between what was to be done on the sport field and what was considered to be acceptable in a social situaiton, even when the two were separated by only a few moments in time.

Frank Krasinki's "Centauri's Irisia" has been one of America's most successful working females, holding both the SchH II and the CDX.
Sire: Ch and W Ch Centauri's Gambit
Dam: Fancy du Clos des Cerberes

The North American Working Bouvier Association

At the 1986 Working Championships near Chicago, a founding meeting for a working organization was held. Discussion centered around whether the association should be confined to the United States, encouraging a sister organization in Canada, or whether a North American entity should be formed. The Canadians present expressed the desire to be included, and as a result, the North American Working Bouvier Association (NAWBA) came into existence. Applications flowed in, and within five months, this new organization had become slightly larger than the American Bouvier des Flandres Club, making apparent the support for the working concept.

From the beginning, the working Bouvier leadership was equally committed to correct conformation and type as well as to the preservation and enhancement of the working character. NAWBA has succeeded in large measure because of two fundamental principles. First and foremost, it is, as a breed club, dedicated to the complete Bouvier, that is, to correct type and structure as well as to working character. Almost as important is the international outlook, the realization that unity with the nations of origin — Belgium, the Netherlands, and France — is essential for the association to realize its goals.

In 1987, at the first Championships subsequent to

its foundation, NAWBA was honored to have Justin Chastel serve as conformation judge. In 1988, the title "Working Champion" was formalized in connection with conformation as well as with working requirements. In order to qualify for this title, a Bouvier must:

1. Be an annual North American Working Championship winner.
2. Have been designated as "Very Good" or "Excellent" at a NAWBA conformation show (or a show designated by the NAWBA Board as a "Championship Level Show") or hold an AKC or CKC Champion of Record title.
3. Hold the I.P.O. III, Schutzhund III, or French Ring III title, earned in North America.
4. Have received a rating of "Fair" or better in hip-joint conformation by the Orthopedic Foundation for Animals.

The first three Bouviers to qualify as Working Champion were Centauri's Fleur de Lis, Amman vom Dreilaendereck, and Centauri's Gambit.

Although conflicts have occurred among individuals over the years, the relationship between the AKC-affiliated American Bouvier des Flandres Club and the NAWBA have not been overtly antagonistic. From the beginning, there have been two or three dual board members, and much of the membership is common.

In 1989, the American Working Dog Federation (AWDF) was formed as an alliance of the national breed organizations dedicated to the preservation and advancement of the protection-heritage working breeds. Founding member clubs were the United Schutzhund Clubs of America (for the German Shepherd dog), the Doberman Pinscher Club of American, the United States Rottweiler Club, and the North American Working Bouvier Association.

The primary short-term purpose is to move toward a common governing body for Schutzhund competition in the United States. Long-term, the intention is to become an umbrella organization for the protective-heritage breeds, ultimately with Federation de Cynologic International affiliation. To that end, the alliance is set up to allow other breed organizations (only one per breed) to seek membership. Activities are not restricted, and if the Ring Sport or European Police Trials become viable in America, their enthusiasts will be welcome under the umbrella.

The need to reaffirm the Bouvier as a working dog is not an isolated phenomenon, but rather the American manifestation of a worldwide movement. A number of years ago, Justin Chastel, president of the Belgian club and vice-president of St. Hubert, played a major role in establishing the "Certificate of Natural Qualities" (C.Q.N.) as a Championship prerequisite for the Bouvier and other working breeds in Belgium. The C.Q.N. is similar to the Schutzhund I, although no tracking test is involved and the full body suit is used for the protection exercise.

The introduction of the C.Q.N. as a Championship prerequisite imposed a significant obstacle for some Belgian breeders, who had previously not been active as trainers. Certain kennels substantially restructured their breeding programs in order to upgrade the character of their stock, while others became less active. The Dutch are considering the C.Q.N. as a Championship requirement, which would mean a common working prerequisite for the Championship in all the nations of origin. This is clearly a major step toward the unity necessary for the vigor of the breed.

Dutch Police Bouviers and their handlers. Photo taken at the Apeldoorn Police Department in 1987 by Jim Engel.

Filette Diana v d Overstort NHSB.1311021, Dutch Champion

Sire: D Ch Picard Generique v h Lampegat
Dam: Bette Diana v a Overstort
Brd: Joop Pater

I first saw Filette in the Open class at the World Show in Vienna in 1986. Although she was obviously the best bitch, and arguably the best Bouvier, the judge ignored her. This was corrected when she quickly went on to obtain the Dutch Championship. Breeders should examine this photo with great care: this is your goal!

CHAPTER SIXTEEN

Pedigrees: Portals to the Past

On the surface, a pedigree is simply a record of the direct ancestors of a particular dog. Between the lines, however, is carried the history of a breed — a record of the decisions of our predecessors upon which we must build for the future. Properly understood, a pedigree is a road map of history. It ties together facts that are of themselves relatively unimportant and helps you to know something about the forest rather than just the location of a few of the trees.

There is a universal format to pedigree listings that enables them to express much information in a very compact form. This is best explained by an example, illustrated in Figure 16-1.

In this pedigree of Gambit, it can be seen that his father was Donar and his mother was Centauri's Fleur de Lis, known as Leah. In a similar manner, the father of any dog is listed on the line above him extending the most to the left, and the dam is on a similar line below. Thus, Gambit's grand sire and Donar's sire was Barrie, and Donar's mother was Tusor van de Overheide. Similarly, Leah's sire was Bavard du Posty Arlequin and her mother was April du Clos des Cerberes.

Many dogs' names incorporate a kennel name that indicates who bred the dog and where he was born.

Bica v d Rozenheerd was, for instance, bred in Holland by J. S. Flikkema, who for many years has been a major influence on the breed through his Rozenheerd line. Similarly, just by seeing his name, it can be seen that Bavard du Posty Arlequin was bred in Belgium by Felix Grulois. You can quickly become familiar with the various kennels and thus know where the dog was bred and his general background simply by glancing at the name.

Many abbreviations are used within names to conserve space. "v d," for instance, stands for "van de" in Dutch and the equivalent "von der" in German.

Following the dog's name are listed various working titles, conformation designations, and similar relevant achievements. Some of these, as they appear on pedigrees of American dogs, are:

Ch.	Champion, granted by the AKC or CKC
CD.	Companion Dog, an obedience title granted by both the AKC and the Canadian Kennel Club (CKC)
C.D.X.	Companion Dog Excellent
U.D.	Utility Dog
T.D.	Tracking Dog, again with both AKC and CKC versions

Figure 16-1

Wodan NHSB.501692
Barrie NHSB.616808 '72
Roza NHSB.476964
Donar SchH III,FH,Dutch Ch. of Work, NAWC '82 '79
Bica v d Rozenheerd NHSB.512062 HD-
Tusor v d Overheide NHSB.964040 '77
Anouschka NHSB.729886
Ch & Work Ch. Centauri's Gambit SchH III, CD,OFA/Ex
Zadi du Posty Arlequin B.Sel
Bavard du Posty Arlequin OFA
Yole du Posty Arlequin
Centauri's Fleur de Lis Ch; SchH III,CD,TD,OFA,NAWC'84
Dax du Clos des Cerberes Ch; '70
April du Clos des Cerberes OFA,TT '76
Ishtar du Clos des Cerberes Ch; '73

Ch Galbraith's Iron Eyes, bred by Dave and Joan Galbraith and owned by Nat and Gloria Reese, has achieved more than seventy Best in Show wins as a relatively young dog. He is a grandson of the Dutch Working Champion Donar.

T.T.   Temperament Test given by the American Temperament Test Society (ATTS) successfully passed

Work Ch.   Working Champion, granted by NAWBA

OFA   Orthopedic Foundation for Animals, which indicates that the dog has been radiographically examined for dysplastic hips and been graded as "Excellent," "Good," or perhaps only "Fair"

Thus, referring to the pedigree in Figure 16-1, Gambit carries my kennel name (Centauri), and he is an American Champion. He is certified by the OFA as having excellent hips, by the American Kennel Club as a Companion Dog, and holds the Schutzhund III, the most advanced German-style police- or protection-dog title. Finally, he is listed as a Working Champion, under the auspices of the North American Working Bouvier Association.

Only titles actually granted by the AKC appear on the "official" pedigrees issued by that organization. These are their Championship; the obedience titles C.D., C.D.X., and U.D.; and the tracking titles T.D. and T.D.X. Pedigrees generateed by others carry whatever information they think relevant or helpful, and you rely on their integrity for the accuracy of the information.

In the Netherlands, when a dog is to be radiographically examined for an official evaluation of his hips, the owner takes the animal to a designated veterinarian, who examines the tattoo and sends in the X-rays and the tattoo number without the owner ever actually having them in his possession. The results of the hip dysplasia evaluation appear on the Dutch pedigrees. These designations are:

HD —   Negative evaluation, that is, free of dysplasia

HD/Tc   Intermediate between negative and light positive
HD + −   Light positive
HD +   Positive evaluation for hip dysplasia

In Belgian pedigrees, the birth year of virtually every Belgian dog is indicated by the first letter of the individual name. Thus, each Bouvier whelped in 1944 and registered in Belgium has an "S" name, such as Soprano de la Thudinie. Those born in 1951 became "A" dogs, such as Argus de la Thudinie, and so on. Cendrillo de l'Ile Monsin was born in 1953, Marc de la Thudinie in 1963, and Tania du Posty-Arlequin in 1970. In recent years, many American kennels have adopted this custom.

This convention was optional before 1940, and many breeders of the prewar era did not observe it. After 1940, the convention was imposed by the Societe Royale Saint-Hubert, and in all subsequent years, only one exception appears, the French bitch Wandru des Coudreaux, registered so that she could be imported by Edmee Bowles. This was necessary, because the AKC would not recognize the French Bouviers at that time (early 1950s).

The letter cycle is repeated every twenty-five years (the "W" not being used), thus eliminating confusion. Names are sometimes reused. For example, there are two females named Silane de la Thudinie, whelped twenty-five years apart.

French kennels in the 1940s and 1950s for the most part observed a similar custom, although they used the "W" and apparently ommitted a "Z" year. For example, Wanda and Wandru des Coudreaux were whelped in 1948, and Carol du Maine Giraud was born in 1953. The system worked well through 1972, when, for instance, Vulcain du Clos des Cytises followed the traditional formula. The next year, apparently at the whim of a government bureaucrat, a two-decade-old tradition was abandoned, and the French jumped from "V" in 1972 to "I" in 1973. They more or less were correct in 1974, because that was a "J" year, but then they skipped "K" and went to "L" for 1975. (Lutteur du Val de Rol was an example of a dog born in 1975.) They seem to have gone forward from there but ever since have been completely out of synchronization with the Belgians.

It is difficult to attempt genealogical research in France, because the numbering system and name-letter code more or less change at random, and it is difficult to obtain breeding records. However, this problem is surmountable, for virtually all modern French Bouviers are derived almost directly from Belgian breeding.

In the Netherlands, many dogs take their mother's first name as a second name. For example, Claudia van de Maceeliers is the dam of Dayan Claudia van Hagenbeek.

In Europe, the same document serves as a dog's registration certificate and his official pedigree. The listing for each dog includes the registration number and Championship designations or working titles. If the dog is registered in the nation whose club is issuing the document, it is generally simply printed as is, while those for dogs in another nation always have some sort of designation. "LOSH" is Belgian, "NHSB" is Dutch, and "LOF" is French. As usual, Championships and working titles in other nations are not normally recognized.

"LOSH" is an abbreviation for Livre de Origines Saint-Hubert, or the official registration number assigned by the Societe Royale Saint-Hubert (the Belgian equivalent of the AKC). "ALSH" (Annexe au livre de Saint-Hubert) sometimes appears on a Belgian pedigree rather than "LOSH." This translates as "supplementary studbook of Saint-Hubert" and indicates that the dog with such a registration number has a foreign ancestor in the first three generations. The official pedigree of such dogs was often colored pink, such as the pedigrees of a number of Chastel's dogs in the early 1950s, when they went to France for stud services.

This situation is a bit mysterious, for although Canaille de la Thudinie, out of the French male Ygor des Coudreaux, was denied a LOSH number, Argus de la Thudinie, also out of a French male but born two years previously (in 1951), carried a LOSH registration. It seems that there were problems in France at the time, because a number of French dogs of this era were imported but their owners were never able to register them with the AKC.

In Belgium, it is still possible to register a dog with an ALSH number and eventually have the progeny recognized. The process is complex and demanding in that certain show evaluations must be achieved, but the mechanism is still there.

Although they are not likely to be seen on a modern pedigree, there are also Belgian numbers with "R.S.H." (Registre de St. Hubert) that are given to dogs appearing in exhibitions or sport competitions. "Bouviers" exhibited before the first Belgian standard was approved in 1912 had such numbers. Note carefully that an R.S.H. number does not constitute proof that a dog is purebred or even a member of any recognized breed.

All continental European pedigrees incorporate the symbol of the Federation Cynologique Internationale (FCI), which translates as the International Canine Federation. This is the predominant international organization throughout the world, with the exception of England, Canada, and the United States.

Centauri's Gambit, owned by the author, was North American Working Champion in 1987 and 1989 as well as Reserve twice. Gambit is also AKC Champion of Record.

C.Q.N. is the Certificate of Natural Qualities, which is a working test required of the Bouvier and some (or perhaps all) of the working breeds in Belgium as a prerequisite for the Championship. Currently, it is not as difficult as the Schutzhund I, but even so, it is apparently more difficult than it was previously. This is a vigorously debated subject in Belgium.

Belgian Select is the breeding recommendation for young dogs. Again, the rules seem to be changing, and there is a "Select" for "beauty" and for "work," which adds to the confusion. On the Select dog's pedigree, there is an oval stamp with the word "Selection" on the top and "Selectie" on the bottom (the designation in French and in Dutch). In the center is the year and a "B" for beauty. On the progeny, the designation appears under the dog's name; for example, "(S.82 B)" indicates that a dog was designated Select for beauty in 1982. The "Select" for work is not a rigorous test. It is apparently controlled byconformation-oriented breeders and adjusted to the lowest common denominator.

The Dutch numbers are designated as "N.H.S.B.," which is the abbreviation for Nederlands Hondenstamboek, or Netherlands Dog Registration. The Dutch canine organization is the Raad van Beheer, which has its headquarters in a quaint old building in Amsterdam. The original Dutch stud book, all handwritten, is on display under glass.

The Belgian pedigrees are even more confusing than normal in that most everything is in both Dutch and

French. The following may be helpful:

ENGLISH	DUTCH	FRENCH
Pedigree of	Stamboom van	Pedigree de
Breed	Ras	Race
Father	Vader	Pere
Mother	Moeder	Mere
Sex	Geslacht	Sexe
Date of birth	Datum van geboorte	Date de naissance
Breeder	Fokker	Producteur
Male	Reuen	Male
Bitch	Teven	Femelle
Litter	Nest	Portee
Color	Kleur	Couleur

The abbreviation of Champion in French is "Ch.," just as it is in English, but in Dutch the abbreviation is "Kamp."

On Dutch pedigrees can be seen "KNPV," which is an abbreviation for Koninklijke Nederlandse Politiehond Vereniging, or Royal Dutch Police Dog Association. It is often seen behind the names of dogs in Dutch pedigrees, which indicates that the dog holds the Dutch Police Trial Certificate. "Met lof" means "with honors," and the point total is often printed. This is perhaps the most respected working title in the world.

As an example, the entry "Dolfo KNPV m.lof'61 NHSB.225069 '59" indicates that the dog named Dolfo was born in 1959 and was assigned the number 226069 by the Dutch Kennel Club. In 1961, he achieved the Royal Dutch Police Certificate by pasing the examination and did so well that he won the designation "with honors." (Dolfo is a famous working dog and sire. A long and fancy name is not a prerequisite for canine greatness!)

"SchH" is the abbreviation for the German "Schutzhund," which means "protection dog" and indicates that the dog holds that title. "FH" indicates the advanced Schutzhund tracking title. On the Dutch pedigrees, the Schutzhund title appears as "VH," with Schutzhund III being designated as "VH III." The elementary title is "Schutzhund I" and the most advanced title is "Schutzhund III."

In Holland, starting about 1985, the Schutzhund program was to a large extent replaced by the almost identical FCI-preferred "International" (IPO) program, and Schutzhund titles were no longer placed on the official pedigrees. (In German, "IPO" is Internatinale Prufungsordnung.) Although the Dutch Kennel Club (Raad van Beheer) no longer recognizes or authorizes Schutzhund trials, some competitions are still going on in Holland under German auspices. This German interference in Dutch affairs seems to be escalating into a fairly serious dispute with important

long-term international consequences. The IPO program is also becoming prominent in Belgium and, perhaps to a lesser or more delayed extent, in France. For practical purposes, Schutzhund I through III and IPO I through III are equivalent.

Pedigree Computer Software and Data Base

Over the years, the author has gathered an extensive collection of breeding records. These include the complete Belgian records beginning in 1913 and the Dutch records from 1921. A comprehensive computer program, for the IBM Personal Computer and compatibles, has been created for maintaining an extensive data base and printing out the actual pedigree charts. This program and a Bouvier data base with over three thousand dogs are available from the author.

Breeders of the Bouvier des Flandres

Figure 16-2 lists the founding kennels, grouped according to nation, and provides a convenient guide, especially when reading pedigrees. In each group, the kennels are listed in approximate order of origination, with the most senior appearing first.

In the early days, the founders of the Bouvier breed often did not feel the need for a pretentious kennel name, and they simply called a dog Nic, Filou, or Cora. Clearly, when a man such as Moerman bred a Bouvier and called it Pic or Bella, that was enough — no further pretense was necessary to establish the importance of the animal. Thus, men such as Scharlaken, Jules Boone, and Berteloot were active breeders and founders over many years, yet never associated with a kennel name. Even after the Second World War, Madame deBlander was a breeder for a number of years before "ten Roobos" was appended to the name of a Bouvier des Flandres.

Very often names are spelled differently, especially geographical names, in Dutch and French. Wherever possible, the local spelling is used.

The following city names are often confusing:

Dutch	French
Kortrijk	Courtrai
Antwerpen	Anvers
Veurne	Furnes
Roeselare	Roulers
Leper	Ypres

Figure 16-2

Belgium

Important early breeders, not associated with a kennel name:
Joseph Moerman of Roulers
Louis Scharlaken in Roulers (Veterinarian)
Jules Boone in Turnhout (near Holland)
A. Berteloot in Beythem
N. Debruyne in Courtrai

KENNEL	FOUNDER	LOCATION
de la Lys	Philemon Gryson	Saint-Denis Westrem
de Ramillies	Joseph Mottoulle	Mont-Saint-Andre
de Sottegem	Norbert Barby	Sottegem
de la Surete	J. Bogaerts	Herzele (Near Liege)
des Farfadets	Mme A.deSpirlet	Angleur (Near Liege)
de la Mandel	Ed.Deryckere	Roulers
de Turnhout	Alphonse Faes	Turnhout
de la Loutre	J. Pittomvils	Turnhout
du Viel-Escaut	H.VanCauwenberghe	Oudenaarde (Audenarde)
de Pont-a-Rieu	H.Delwart	Tournai
de la Barriere	P.Geudens	Hoboken (Near Antwerp)
du Pandore	O.Vincke	Jumet (Near Charleroi)
de Royghem	F.Verbanck	Ghent
du Sellier	Mme.A.Cambien	Kortrijk (Courtrai)
de Belgique	Auguste Franshet	Zwynaerde (Near Ghent)
de Groeninghe	Ed. van den Broucke	Kortrijk (Courtrai)
van het Molentje	J.Vercruijsse	Roeselare (Roulers)
de Maeter	R.Beghin	Maeter
du Bungalow	G.Geerung	Vivegnis (Near Liege)
de la Gendarmerie	Ferdinand Nijs	Deinze (Near Ghent)
de Sang-Froid	A.Draye	Charleroi
de l'Ile Monsin	Edmond Moreaux	Liege
du Beryl	Albert Depry	Marchienne-au-Pont (Near Charleroi)
des Champs Clos	G. Plennevaux	Montignies-sur-Sambre (Near Charleroi)
de Biercee	Ernest Ruol	Biercee (Near Thuin)
du Vi-Blanc	Houyoux	Roux (Near Charleroi)
du Gabari	E.Piette	Tongres (Near Liege)
du Pont d'Adinkerke	A. Vantielcke	Adinkerke (Near Veurne)
van het Kantienje	A. Vanoutryve	Kortrijk (Courtrai)
l'Ideal de Charleroi	A. Lebon	Montignies (Near Charleroi)
de la Ville de Doges	Victor Martinage	Ath
de la Thudinie	Justin Chastel	Thuin
de Gratte-Saule	R. Guerriat	Thuin
du Ble d'Or	Ad. Meeus	Thuin
du Posty-Arlequin	Felix Grulois	Thuin
de Bronchain	J. Demierbe	Courcelles (Near Charleroi)
van Leie en Schelde	G. Sellier	Ghent
Remado	Maurice Dauwe	Lochristi (Near Ghent)
ten Roobos	E. de Blander	Buggenhout
van de Buildrager	Alfons & Annie Verheyen	St. Job in't Goor (Near Antwerp)
de la Chaussee Romaine	R.Hancq	Ophain (Braine-L'Alleud)
van de Macecliers	Omar Bastelier	Benrzel
van het Lampegat	Rex Keeman	Leopoldsburg

Figure 16-2 (Continued)

Holland

KENNEL	FOUNDER	LOCATION
van Eindhoven	F. Verbeek	Eindhoven
van Maarland	J.L.H. Wolfs	Oss
van Sappemeer	J.W. Koeneman	Hoogezand
van Arnwald	Hub. Arnold	Rozendaal
Hibernia	Otto Dicke	Dordrecht
uit het Zuiderlicht	J.H. Klinkers	Beek
van de Zaanhoeve	Mevrouw Ooms-Tiemeyer	Zaandam
van de Rakkers	B. Nachenius-de Jongh	Den Haag
van het Zuiderland	W.J. Bell	Eindhoven
van Baakenstein	H. Habraken	Eerde bij Veghel
van Domburg	J. van Vught	St. Michiels Gestel
van de Ouden Dijk	J. v.d. Vorst	Oud Gastel
van de Niervaert	H. Schoone	Geleen
van de Veenhoeve	J. Hoiting	Groningen
van de Horzeldijk	W.J. van Kuyk	Utrecht
van de Banishoek	Ina en Ab Dennekamp	Rijssen
van de Ponyhoeve	Th. Munster	Obdam
van de Zwikshoek	Gerrit Kiuper	Enschede
van Dafzicht	Coen Semler	Eindhoven
van het Klumpke	A.J. Klomp	Mierlo
van de Rozenheerd	J.C. Flikkema	Rutten
van de Sylverhof	E.M. Ducker	Veldhoven
van Pleinzicht	Bart en Riet Krist	Drempt
van het Vonderke	Jan en Fransier Klerks	Eindhoven
van der Cerberushof	Henk en Gerda harmers	Hoofddorp
van Rovika	Rombout/Vingerhoets	Tilburg
vom Uleaborgh	Arnie & Hanni Bergsma	Dokkum
van de Boevers Garden	Th. de Wagenaar	Hilversum
van het Witteveeseven	Sien en Harry Lescher	Geesteren
van het Grendarcohof	H. Boomsma	Noordbergum
van Hagenbeek	D.H. Postma	Zwaagwesteinde
van de Vanenblik Hoeve	H. Bruintjes-Schaap	Enschede
van de Overstort	Joop en Annie Pater	Kampen

Photo of kennel de la Lys, circa 1925.

Figure 16-2 (Continued)

France

KENNEL	FOUNDER	LOCATION
de la Boheme	Jean Cotte	Amiens
de la Vallee de l'Ecaillon	Fernand Malaquin	Monchaux par Thiant
des Coudreaux	Corbier	Montfermeil
de Maine Giraud	Dr. Bernard Bourinet	Montauban (Lot & Garonne)
du Chateau Marocain	M. Delsipee	
des Hauts Chesneaux	Mme. Nadine Hecquet	Saint-Astier
de Faubourg Rouge	Jacques Bleusee	Fresnoy-le-Grand
de la Vallee du Lay	M. Ardouin	
de Clos du Petit Neuf Pres	M. Dissaux	Avre-sur-la-Lys
des Casseaux	Etienne Cibot	Limoges
de l'Epee	Laurette Lepage	Darnieulles
des Herbages Normands	Pierre Poiret	Saint Gauburge
de Lann Breiz	Dr. Andre Le Lann	Lanester
de Firmvert	M. Claude Beraud	Firminy
du Clos des Cytises	Simone Jousse	Villiers-sur-Marne
du Val de Rol	Marie-Claude Niquet	Le Vaudreuil
de la Buthiere	Gaston Desfarges	La Chapelle-la-Reine
du Clos des Jeunes Plantes	Gerard Gelineau	Le Blanc
du Bas Berry	Robert Langlois	Gagny
de la Chatrene	Jean-Claude Masson	Dragey
d'An Naoned	Yann Bouriaud	Suce

Germany

KENNEL	FOUNDER	LOCATION
von der Stadt Homberg	Willy Reisloh	Duisburg

Canada

KENNEL	FOUNDER	LOCATION
Frisia	Andy Prinsen	Windsor, Ontario
Hollandia	David Westra	Woodstock, Ontario
Bronville	Hank Hagen	Ontario
Bolshoy	Paul DeRycke	Oxford Station, Ontario
Oomingmak	Diana Case	Edmonton, Alberta
High Sierra	Marjory Fraser	Caledonia, Ontario
Quiche	Paquette Family	Maidstone, Ontario
Glenmiller	Bill Miller	Milverton, Ontario

United States

KENNEL	FOUNDER	LOCATION
du Clos des Cerberes	Edmee Bowles	Collegeville, Pennsylvania
van de Mainliner	Evert van de Pol	San Francisco, California
Madrone Ledge	Ray and Marion Hubbard	California
Deewal	Fred and Dorthy Walsh	New Jersey
Maijeune	Carl and Gladys May	Pennsylvania
des Preux Vuilbaards	Bob Abady	New York
Flandersfield	Erik Houttuin	Missouri

Ch Nack du Clos des Cytises, imported from France in 1982
by Marion Hubbard and Judy Higgins, became a very
influencial stud.

C/A Ch Glenmiller's Bandit

For many years, the Dorothy Walsh Trophy went to the Winners Dog or Bitch at the American Specialty, with the provision that permanent possession would require one person to win it three times. Finally, in 1982, Dr. Erik Houttuin succeeded when Glenmiller's Bandit became Winners Dog in Detroit and took permanent possession of the trophy. In the photo, from the left: judge Ralph Goldman; handler Jimmy Campbell; and American Club president Wenzel Dvornik with Dorothy Walsh Trophy.

Brd: Bill Miller
Owners: Dr. and Mrs. E. Houttuin and Y. Savard and D. Elb
Whelped: November 20, 1979

Euro's Marco C Ch; CKC.EL7355
Adele's Alexander C/A Ch; '76
Denard's Evil's Jewel C Ch
C/A Ch Glenmiller's Bandit
Hollandia Evil C/A Ch; '71
Angel C Ch; '78
Euro's Lisa Ch; '72

The Passing of the Torch

The Price of Progress

The industrialization of Europe and America has caused farm populations to dwindle from an overwhelming majority to a minute fraction, irrevocably transforming the human social order. Many of us share a sense that much has been lost in the process, lamenting the passing of the "family farm" with its closeness to the earth, its self-sufficiency, and the proverbial American rugged individualism. No doubt our perception of the pastoral existence of our forefathers is overly romanticized, and few of us would willingly give up the material comforts that we have come to take for granted.

Changes in the nature of the relationship between people and their dogs are but a part of this, and the ultimate consequences are only now beginning to emerge. Our ability to maintain the working breeds, such as the Bouvier, when the majority do not work is very much at issue. Prospects in many ways seem better in Europe because the canine organizations there to some extent are conscious of the problems and are seeking, with varying degrees of determination and success, to devise solutions. However, today's reality is that the world in which the Bouvier evolved is gone forever, and the breed will either lose its working ability or a revised ethic, a new mode of existence, will evolve. There simply can be no turning back.

That the herding function is obsolete must be accepted. The modern working roles must be drawn from the remainder of the primitive functions and from the new tasks that have developed as people have sought to cope with the new technological society — tasks such as family proteciton, drug detection, and police building searches. Nostalgia for a passing mode of life must not stand in the way of perceiving that the work function is the essence of the Bouvier, and that the tasks undertaken must be of use to the people with which he lives.

The same changes that technology has produced in human society have created new work for the Bouvier and new need for his special capabilities and qualities. Just as the work that we do is much different from that of our forefathers, the work of our dogs must also be adapted to new needs in order for the working integrity to be maintained. It is a simple but significant fact that the lack of a purpose causes the same degeneration in the soul of a working dog as it does in that of a human being.

To preserve the Bouvier breed, emphasis must be placed on attributes that have practical modern application, such as protection, tracking, and searching. The diverse qualities that suit the Bouvier to his modern functions are generally those that enabled him to serve the stockman. Character traits such as loyalty, courage, intelligence, and tenacity render the Bouvier des Flandres a useful working dog for our era.

Our Fragile Gift

Prior to the advent of breeders, kennel clubs, and conformation shows, the farmer was the custodian of his working dogs. Breeding was a simple business: dogs that did not earn their keep were not kept. The dogs were expected to work, and in the long term that was enough. The process, imperfect and informal though it no doubt was, worked.

The shift in the custodial responsibility from farmer to breeder — the passing of the torch — negated the natural selectivity for working character. This was the crucial point in the evolution of each utility breed. Some breeds disappeared or saw the original working ability dissipate. To preserve and protect the working dogs, various breed organizations created working trials to identify animals with functional capability and willingness. Success in the trial was intended to be a universal prerequisite for a place in the breeding program.

Ch Galbraith's Faire la Roue CDX, bred and owned by Dave and Joan Galbraith.
Among the most notable show winners and stud dogs in California in the early 1980s.

The effectiveness of this venture has been varied. Custodians of some breeds have been able to maintain good overall working stock, while others have allowed it to dissipate. For example, the predominance (in the homeland) of the German Shepherd as a working dog and the requirement of satisfactory performance of all breeding stock is not coincidence but cause and effect. The dramatic and rapid decline of the general working potential of the German Shepherd of long-term American breeding graphically illustrates the consequences of breeding without regard for working character.

The Bouvier is in jeopardy because the ancestral homeland has, by the accident of politics and war, fallen into several modern states. No individual nation seems dominant enough to serve as the national homeland of the Bouvier or appears able to provide the leadership for long-term, worldwide vitality. In the United States, a working culture did not even begin to emerge until the 1970s. Generally, the canine establishment has been opposed to protective dogs.

And so what will become of the Bouvier? Will someone finding this book in a dusty attic thirty years hence know the Bouvier as a fine breed of working dog in his rightful place among the others? Or will he or she wonder how the guardians of a once great canine race could have allowed it to fade into oblivion? The answers to these questions are to be found in the hearts of the men and women who love the Bouvier des Flandres, for the fate of our breed will ultimately be determined by their dedication and devotion.

Our theme has been the unique and noble Bouvier soul. However, this is not a momument of stone predestined to endure; rather, it is the fragile gift of our forefathers, a precious heritage to be preserved and protected with the utmost vigilance. Each generation must pass on the torch, fulfill the obligation imposed with the gift, and pay its debt to the breeders of the past. The ultimate burden, therefore, must be on the breeder.

A and C Ch Centauri's Hercule ("Tigger")
Sire: Ch Abbas v d Boevers Garden
Dam: Fancy du Clos des Cerberes
Owner: Jerry and Joyce Osicek
Brd: Jim and Kathy Engel

Suggestions for Further Reading

Unfortunately, many of the really useful and interesting Bouvier books, such as the one by Justin Chastel, are in French or Dutch. Even for those not fluent in these languages, many of the European books are most useful for the photographs, for one can usually get the gist of the caption.

The following books represent my selection as the best available in their individual areas:

1. "Training the Competitive Working Dog," Tom Rose & Gary Patterson, Giblaut Publishing Company, 1985 — An excellent book, primarily for the Schutzhund enthusist, but of great interest to all serious trainers.
2. "The Koehler Method of Dog Training," William R. Koehler, Howell, Book House, N.Y. 1976 — Fundamentally sound, but read with care and make sure you understand what Mr. Koehler is telling you before you apply it to your beast. Perhaps the companion dog owner's best friend, and some serious insight for the competitive trainer.
3. "Tracking Dog Theory & Method," Glen Johnson, Arner Pub., 1975 — Solid, good book. Pay close attention to comments on motivation and read section on food carefully.
4. "Scent and the Scenting Dog," William G. Syrotuck, Arner Publications, 1972 — This little paper back is a really useful and interesting reference.
5. "How to Be Your Dog's Best Friend," The Monks of New Skete, Little, Brown and Company, 1978 — The monks tend toward ambivalence on the protection work, but overall some useful insights for the novice.
6. "Bouvier Belge des Flandres," G. F. van Gink-Van Es, Uitgeverij El Perro, 1979 — It's in Dutch of course, but it's surprising how much you can dig out of it.
7. "The Bouvier des Flandres Today and Yesterday," Justin Chastel, 1976 — In French, but worth some serious effort.
8. "The Natural History of Dogs," Richard and Alice Fiennes, Natural History Press, 1968 — Fascinating. A most readable account of the evolution of the dog from the wolf, will greatly enhance your understanding of both.
9. "Genetics for Dog Breeders," Frederick B. Hutt, Freeman and Co., 1979 — Readable, reliable, useful.

About The Author

Jim Engel is a professional engineer, with a bachelor's degree in Electrical Engineering from the University of Detroit and a Master's degree in the same discipline from Purdue University.

In the canine world he has become well known as a writer, trainer, breeder, and commentator as well as an office holder in national canine organizations. His work has appeared in *Dog World* and *Dog Sports Magazine* as well as numerous national publications for the working breeds.

Although his commitment to the dog sports began earlier, his love for the Bouvier des Flandres began in the seventies when his wife Kathy purchased a male pup destined to become Ch. Vacher's Alpha Centauri, known as Tory. This dog became the second Bouvier in American to earn a Schutzhund III (the first Champion to earn that title) and the first to receive the FH, the coveted German advanced tracking title. The Engel family established a breeding program under the Centauri banner during the eighties.

For a decade Jim Engel's *Dog Sports* magazine column has strongly influenced the evolution of the American working dog movement. Justin Chastel, Belgian club President, has requested permission to run his articles in the Belgian journal and a number of his commentaries have appeared in the Dutch club magazine.

Jim has shown dogs in Europe and served as conformation judge for the California Club and will judge at the 1991 Michigan club Specialty. For a number of years he served as a Certified DVG Schutzhund Trial Agitator. He is well acquainted with Bouvier leaders worldwide and counts many among his close personal associates.

Jim Engel is President and a founder of the North American Working Bouvier Association. He was also a key player in the establishment of the American Working Dog Federation, under which the working organizations for the German Shepherds, Rottweilers and Dobermans have been unified. He presently serves as Secretary of this umbrella organization.

Author Jim Engel (left) and Belgian breeder and judge Annie Verheyen. The dog is Ch Centauri's Lyon van de Jajte, SchH I.

Index

Looking for more information to help you with your dog?

The following titles may be purchased at your local bookstore or pet supply outlet, or ordered direct.

How to Raise a Puppy You Can Live With
2nd edition
Rutherford and Neil

Skin and Haircoat Problems in Dogs
Ackerman

Owner's Guide to Better Behavior in Dogs
2nd edition
William Campbell

Beyond Basic Dog Training Workbook
Bauman, Santo, Zurburg

All Breed Dictionary of Unusual Names
Jarrett

Canine Reproduction, A Breeder's Guide
Holst

Positively Obedient
Handler

The Art and Business of Professional Grooming
Walin

For a Free Catalog
or information on other Alpine Dog Books, please write or call
our Customer Service Department.
Alpine Publications, P.O. Box 7027, Loveland, CO 80537
1-800-777-7257